Santa Clara County Free Library

CALIFORNIA - WESTERN AMERICANA

REFERENCE

 5816

First Mail West

First Mail West

STAGECOACH LINES ON THE
SANTA FE TRAIL

BY

Morris F. Taylor

Albuquerque

UNIVERSITY OF NEW MEXICO PRESS

FOR MY DAUGHTERS

MARY AND REBECCA

Acknowledgments

STARTING FROM A DESIRE to know more about Barlow, Sanderson and Company, owner of the stage line that served Trinidad, Colorado, my investigation led me into a research area of greater breadth, complexity, and time span than I had expected. As the project expanded, I needed assistance, and that I received in full measure from numerous sources. It is impossible, of course, to mention every word of encouragement, every bit of guidance, and every generosity in making data available.

Some of the assistance was so important, however, that those individuals and institutions giving it deserve public words of thanks. Without their help my work would have been more difficult and incomplete. I wish to express my sincere appreciation to the following: Dr. Maxine Benson, Colorado state historian; Mrs. Enid Thompson and her staff of the State Historical Society of Colorado Library; Mrs. Alys Freeze and the personnel of the Western History Department, Denver Public Library; Mrs. Alma Vaughan, newspaper librarian, State Historical Society of Missouri; Mr. Nyle H. Miller, secretary, and members of the staff of the Kansas State Historical Society; Miss Jane F. Smith and the staff of the Social and Economic Records Division, National Archives and Records Service; Mrs. Samuel McCleery, librarian of the St. Albans Free Library, St. Albans, Vermont; Dr. Myra Ellen Jenkins, deputy for archives, New Mexico State Records Center and Archives; Dr. Jacob R. Marcus, director of the American Jewish Archives, Cincinnati, Ohio; Mr. David L. Jarrett, New York City; Mr. A. R. Mitchell, curator of the Old Baca House and Pioneer Museum, Trinidad, Colorado; and Mr. N. L. Persson, Northbrook, Illinois. My wife's assistance and patience are gratefully acknowledged.

Morris F. Taylor

Trinidad, Colorado

Contents

Illustrations

Following page 54

Introduction

WHEN WALDO, HALL AND COMPANY'S mule-drawn mail wagon left Independence, Missouri on July 1, 1850 for the more than 800-mile journey to Santa Fe, capital of the imminent Territory of New Mexico, it started a pioneer venture that was given some mention in the regional press but which hardly caused a national stir. The first vehicular transportation of United States mail across the Great Plains under a congressionally authorized, four-year contract was an event of national significance. But, like that of many similar developments, its importance was realized mainly in retrospection. This stage line was first the progenitor of, then a significant contemporary with, and finally the successor to famous mail enterprises bearing the names of John Butterfield, William H. Russell, Ben Holladay, and Wells, Fargo and Company.

The Santa Fe Trail—the route of the mail wagon—was, in a sense, an extension of the National Road (or Pike) that had been started by congressional appropriation at Cumberland, Maryland in 1811, and which was still in its final phase of construction into the terminus town of Vandalia, Illinois. Use of the word "national" was misleading because Congress had turned over maintenance of the road to the states through which it passed. Congress had also provided money in 1825 for a survey of the Santa Fe road from western Missouri to the international boundary of the Arkansas River. Other than that, however, the federal legislature showed slight interest in building a graded, macadamized road with masonry bridges out into the Unorganized Territory that was then Kansas.[1] The presence or immediate prospect of more people might have encouraged Congress. The Arkansas River, of course, was the frontier of a foreign country, an alien culture, from 1819 until 1848, and extension of American sovereignty over the Mexican Cession was for a long time little more than an exchange of political control. For most Americans the new Southwest had neither the attraction of the wilderness sanctuary of Utah nor the exciting lure of gold in California. New Mexico looked harshly different without compensatory features.

Nearly thirty years of trade along the Santa Fe Trail had developed valuable commercial relations, but they were not a sufficient foundation for quickly binding a conquered land to the United States. Congressional approval of a postal route to Santa Fe may simply have been a reflexive response to demand by American officials and traders for better communication than that afforded by military and private expresses. In any event, Congress did provide for such a route, which formed the nucleus of much that followed. Certain circumstances of the region south of the Arkansas require more extensive delineation. They furnish the special context of this study.

In 1819 negotiation of a treaty by President James Monroe's secretary of state, John Quincy Adams, and the Spanish minister in Washington, Don Luís de Onís, set a definite boundary between the United States, enlarged by the Louisiana Purchase of 1803, and the declining Spanish Empire. Part of the agreement was Spain's abandonment of her claim to the Oregon country and relinquishment by the United States of any claim on Texas. The boundary angled northwestward from the Gulf of Mexico to the Pacific coast, following natural features (the Sabine, Red, and Arkansas rivers) and imaginary lines including the 100th meridian and the 42nd parallel. There were strong protests against recognition of Texas as part of the lands of the Spanish crown. American settlement had long before reached the Mississippi River, and the Union had admitted Kentucky (1792), Tennessee (1796), Mississippi (1817), and Illinois (1818). The first state west of the Mississippi was Louisiana (1812), and Missouri and Arkansas became territories in 1812 and 1819, respectively. Missouri Territory was originally known as Louisiana Territory before Louisiana's admission as a state.[2]

Brevet Major Stephen H. Long, Topographical Engineers, led an exploratory and scientific expedition in the summer of 1820 from the Missouri River along the Platte and South Platte Rivers to the Rocky Mountains, and from there south to the Arkansas, the international line.

At a point on the north bank not far from the later site of Bent's (Old) Fort, the expedition was divided. Major Long took some of the men southward into Spanish Territory to seek the source of the Red River. While accumulating information about the plains country between the Platte and Canadian rivers (he thought the latter was the Red), Major Long applied the term "Great American Desert" to what he had seen, an appellation that caught the popular mind.[3]

Admission of Missouri as a state, Senate ratification of the Adams-Onís treaty, and the successful Mexican revolution against imperial Spain all occurred in 1821. The Republic of Mexico lay south of the treaty line. That meant that the commercial restrictions imposed by Spain would be relaxed, and trade with the provincial capital of Santa Fe and beyond was practically invited.

Captain William Becknell, out from Missouri to trade with the Comanche in the summer of 1821, learned of the new republic through a chance meeting with some Mexican soldiers. Forgetting the Indians, he and his party went on to Santa Fe, where he disposed of his small stock of merchandise at a good profit. The route that he followed over the Raton Pass later came to be known as the Mountain Branch of the Santa Fe Trail.

The next year Becknell took the first wagons to Santa Fe. The vehicles were three farm wagons drawn by horses. On that second trip Becknell cut south from the Arkansas River through plains and mesa country east of the Raton Pass, opening what soon was known as the Cimarron Cutoff of the Santa Fe Trail.[4] Then larger wagons—"road wagons" with a thousand-pound capacity and the smaller "Dearborns" with bows and cloth covers—were used. Mules were used increasingly to draw the wagons and became a principal export from New Mexico to Missouri.[5]

When Becknell went out to trade with the Comanche in 1821, a significant change was taking place in the pattern of Plains Indian occupation of the country along the Arkansas in present-day eastern Colorado and western Kansas. In the last phase of their long southwestward migration, the Arapaho and Cheyenne were seen in growing numbers along the Arkansas and for considerable distances south of it, bringing the Indian population of the region—already including Comanche, Kiowa, and Kiowa (or Plains) Apache—to its composition of the late historical period.[6] Farther east were the Pawnee, Osage, and Kansas, and to the south on the approaches to Santa Fe were the Jicarilla Apache, who had

3

been displaced from the plains in the eighteenth century by southward-moving Comanche and Kiowa.[7] Bands of Ute (usually Mohuache) were frequently seen on the Mountain Branch, especially in the Raton Mountains.[8]

The new commercial connection with New Mexico aroused much interest, and by 1824 organized wagon caravans plied between Franklin, Missouri, and Santa Fe. The public became interested in the growing trade, and soon Congress was asked to assist with a road and its protection. Congress responded in the spring of 1825 with a total of $30,000—$20,000 to obtain rights of transit from the Indians and $10,000 to survey a road to the international boundary.[9]

On August 10 in a hickory grove beside the Neosho River, a place known from that time on as Council Grove, the assembled Osage promised safe passage to citizens of the United States and the Mexican Republic. Six days later the Kansas Indians gave similar assurances. By September the road survey was completed to the Arkansas River, and the next year the Mexican government allowed the survey to be extended to the town of Don Fernando de Taos in the mountains about seventy miles north of Santa Fe. Taos already had an association with Americans through the mountain men and the fur trade.[10] In practice, many American traders bypassed Taos and went by the Cimarron Cutoff to Santa Fe. But others—Dr. David Waldo and Charles Bent, for example—established themselves in Taos.[11]

Unfortunately, similar agreements were not reached with the Plains tribes farther west along the Arkansas River and south of it. Attacks on trader caravans increased in scale and frequency, but pleas to Congress brought no results. It was only after the inauguration of President Andrew Jackson, veteran of direct action against Indians, that military protection was provided as far as the Arkansas. Similar action was taken by the Mexican government south of the river. Neither country, however, provided regular escorts.[12]

Major Bennett Riley, in command of the first American military escort in 1829, introduced oxen to pull wagons on the Trail, and the next year Charles Bent employed oxen for his wagon train to Santa Fe.[13] By 1832 Santa Fe traders had learned to rely on themselves, using larger caravans and paramilitary organization to ward off the raiders, a method that was generally successful.[14]

The commerce with Santa Fe was mainly an outgrowth of American fur trade, and pelts were an important part of nearly every cargo shipped to Missouri during the first fifteen years.[15] Mexican independence in 1821 stimulated and expanded the fur trade so that trapping and trading were extensive on the southern plains as well as in the mountains of southern Colorado, New Mexico, and Arizona. Fort Smith, on the lower Arkansas, became a center for it, and trading posts appeared on the Arkansas, the Canadian, and the Red rivers. In the mountains and on the plains, the business in furs was part of a broader trade with the Indian tribes. It is worth noting that Captain William Becknell was a trapper and Indian trader before he became a leading figure on the Trail.[16]

Over-trapping and a craving for silk hats in the world of fashion lowered the commerce in beaver pelts. By that time, some of the renowned names among the free trappers had become associated with companies trading with the tribes. The fortified adobe trading post of Bent, St. Vrain and Company (Charles and William Bent, and Ceran St. Vrain), built about 1833 on the north bank of the Arkansas, is one of the best examples. Transition was made from beaver pelts to buffalo robes, a change that was aided by development of bigger wagons capable of transporting the bulkier buffalo hides.[17]

Other exports from New Mexico in the early years were livestock and specie. Missouri's traditional specialty in mules derived from the Santa Fe trade, and jacks, jennets, and horses were sent to New Mexico in exchange. Important to the economy of Missouri was the influx of Spanish gold and silver coins which helped to offset wildcat banking, an influence pleasing to the state's hard money advocate, Senator Thomas Hart Benton.[18] A variety of dry goods and hardware was sent out to New Mexico, but a major demand was for bleached and unbleached American cottons, or, as Josiah Gregg put it, "both bleached and brown."[19] From the inception of the commerce to about 1850, the flow of commodities to Santa Fe and Taos was greater in volume than the amount exported from New Mexico.[20]

Growth of trade over the international road required more formal contact between the two governments. An American consulate was established at Santa Fe in 1825, in charge of Augustus Storrs. Business interests in Santa Fe were impressed by the trade potential with the United States, and some official support was given to them. That same year the governor of New Mexico sent Don Manuel Escudero, the first Mexican citizen to take wagons over the Trail, to St. Louis and Washington in the interest of promotion, and a Mexican consulate was set up in St. Louis.[21] The main activity of the Mexican government, however, seems to have been the collection of customs duties, which were burdensome, inefficient, and often corrupt and discriminatory.[22]

The Santa Fe Trail was predominantly a commercial route, distinguishing it from the mainly emigrant route of the Oregon Trail.[23] Settlers were attracted to parts of the Oregon country because of its similarity to the humid forested region east of the Mississippi, and there was no clear boundary between British and American claims to deter them. Oregon travelers reached a kind of haven after crossing the Great American Desert, but along the Santa Fe road the forbidding aridity did not end.[24] The environmental hardship was strengthened by the international line right in the middle of the desert. The Mexican government was not attracted enough by Americans along the Arkansas to allow them to come in and settle as it was doing through a series of *empresario* grants in Coahuila-Texas.[25] Americans were simply not that numerous on the central plains.

Commercial penetration of Mexico by way of the Santa Fe Trail was at best limited and seasonal, even though some American traders spent most of their time in Santa Fe or Taos, some married Mexican women, and a few went so far as to become naturalized Mexican citizens—for example, Ceran St. Vrain and David Waldo.[26] There was no U.S. postal service west of Council Grove. South of the Arkansas the Mexican government maintained no service to Santa Fe, and the semimonthly mail that operated between Santa Fe and Chihuahua, where American interests reached, had become an irregular express service because of Indian hostility.[27] Reliance on wagon trains for transportation of letters and newspapers between Missouri and New Mexico meant a two- to three-month lag, depending on such variable factors as weather, grass, and the moods of the Plains tribes. That plodding communication remained unchanged until the outbreak of the war with Mexico in 1846.

By 1831 westward extension of population in Missouri, especially in the valley of the Missouri River, brought new towns and a westward shift of the Trail's end from Franklin to Independence (established in 1827),[28] from which most of the freight wagons departed on the arduous 800 miles to Santa Fe. Council Grove, however, continued to be the place where most of the caravans were organized. There, the hardwood timber along the bottoms of the Neosho River provided the last wood that would be seen for much of the trip. As Josiah Gregg observed, Council Grove seemed to be on "the western boundary of the truly rich and beautiful country of the border. . . . All the country that lies beyond is of far more barren character."[29] The change was gradual, of course, but Council Grove was only a little over a degree east of the 98th meridian, which is sometimes roughly cited as the eastern boundary of the Great Plains.[30]

From there to the adobe town of Las Vegas at the edge of the Sangre de Cristo Mountains, the trader and traveler encountered such a harsh changeable environment—so different from that of Missouri and east— that they tried to get through it as quickly as possible. The semiaridity —not a true desert condition—and the treelessness of the plains were forbidding to many people. Drought, heat, flash floods, high winds, blizzards, and extreme cold would have turned away settlement-minded men and women of that day even if Indian harassment had been lacking. It was a land of sharp and frightening contrasts to the uninitiated.

Between the Arkansas and the (Dry) Cimarron was a fifty- to sixty-mile dry stretch that was worrisome to people who traversed the Santa Fe Trail. Traders from the States called it a water scrape, and the Mexicans referred to it as the *jornada,* a word meaning journey or day's travel[31] but particularly connoting difficulty and danger. Even that feature of the landscape sometimes offered brief but startling variations. Gregg recorded that while crossing the Cimarron *jornada* "we fortunately had a heavy shower, which afforded us abundance of water." On the same trip his caravan was uncertain of its position and direction for some time, mistaking Sand Creek for the Cimarron. In retracing their steps in search of the "lost river," they watched for the "dry ravine" which they had crossed, not realizing it was the Cimarron. A couple of Indians directed the caravan to the Cimarron. The traders were astonished that the river, "with its delightful green-grass glades and flowing torrent (very different in appearance from where we had crossed it below), had all the aspect of an 'elysian vale,' compared with what we had seen for some time past."[32]

The high plains also offered baffling eccentricities, which men tried to explain. For example, the California-bound gold seekers in 1849 thought that the Mormons had planted sunflowers on their route west, so great was the profusion of those flowers along the Platte River. Actually, 1849 was a very wet year, and the moisture had germinated the seeds exposed by the wheels and hooves of the Mormon caravans.[33]

Some of the country through which the Santa Fe Trail passed was comprised of land grants made by the Mexican government. Those tracts differed from land available in the American public domain in their greater size and how they were awarded. A grant to induce land occupation as a deterrent to Indian attacks on villages along the Pecos River resulted in the little settlement of Las Vegas (1835) on the Rio Gallinas, a northern tributary of the Pecos.[34] North of it was the Tecolote town grant, and beyond that was the Mora Grant (1835) on the Mountain Branch of the Trail. The Fort Union military reservation was located on the Mora Grant in 1851.[35]

Farther north two major grants were approved during 1841 to 1843 by Manuel Armijo, the Mexican governor in Santa Fe, in response to the need for defense along the unprotected northern frontier.[36] In 1841 Charles Beaubien and Guadalupe Miranda received land (later known as the Maxwell Grant) south of the Raton Mountains and north of the Mora Grant. Two years later Cornelio Vigil and Ceran St. Vrain obtained a grant north of the Ratons in the wide angle between the Arkansas and Purgatoire (Las Animas) rivers.[37] Just across the Arkansas, on the north bank or American side about 140 miles upstream from the Cimarron Crossing, was Bent, St. Vrain and Company's trading post. Its location and activities had brought renewed interest in the Mountain Branch of the Santa Fe Trail, which was first used by wagons when George and Robert Bent, younger brothers of Charles and William, traveled northward over the Raton Pass in 1832, the year before the adobe post was established.[38]

A common sight on the Cimarron Cutoff (because it was buffalo and Plains Indian country) were men who played an important part in provincial Mexican economic life—the *ciboleros*, or buffalo hunters, and the *comancheros*, or traders with the Plains Indians, primarily the Comanche. Both types used pack mules and ox-drawn, two-wheel *carretas* (Chihuahua carts), which were gradually supplanted by American wagons with spoked wheels and iron tires.[39] Only the most perceptive Americans recognized the interdependence of the Comanche and some of the Indian Pueblos, particularly Pecos and Taos, through the *comanchero* trade. But the differences between the nomadic life of the Plains Indians and the community life of the Pueblos were obvious to the less observant, although they might have difficulty seeing the distinctive features of Jicarilla Apache and Mohuache Ute existence in the foothills and mountains.

Protestant Americans realized the predominance of the Catholic Church, although New Mexico was on the periphery of an immense bishopric centered in distant Durango, in the central Mexican state of the same name. Santa Fe had a *custodio*, which was a kind of administrative center for the missions of New Mexico,[40] and for many Americans the Catholic churches and priests signified an alien culture.

American expansion absorbed the Oregon country in 1846, the same year in which war broke out between the United States and Mexico. Conflict between the two republics sharply increased the need for American communications with the region south of the Arkansas River. Colonel Stephen Watts Kearny's Army of the West invaded Mexican territory from Bent's Fort and reached Santa Fe after crossing the Raton Pass, favoring the Mountain Branch of the Trail as a military road. While Kearny was at Las Vegas, an officer from Fort Leavenworth rode in with his promotion to brigadier general.[41] Dispatches, mostly military, were carried by military express riders on horseback or by private persons, usually experienced plainsmen who often preferred mules to horses. When the Army of the West later split, Brigadier General Kearny took part of the force to California while Colonel Alexander W. Doniphan marched other units southward to Chihuahua and Monterrey. The demands on express communications were greatly extended. Kit Carson has been credited with carrying the first U.S. mail from the Pacific coast to Washington, D.C., under military sponsorship in the spring of 1848, about two months after ratification of the Treaty of Guadalupe Hidalgo ended the war with Mexico.[42]

The boundary line of 1819 was obliterated, and an area about two and half times the size of France[43] (the entire Southwest except for the Gadsden Purchase of 1853) came under American sovereignty. That political fact did not alter the ethnic and cultural differences, even though the Treaty of Guadalupe Hidalgo made United States citizenship available to Mexican nationals. In the long run, however, annexation was bound to alter the cultural patterns, just as American attitudes would be modified south of the Arkansas.

Achievement of any fusion depended in considerable measure on the state of communications. American institutions, both public and private, could hardly be established and accepted without improved contacts, especially since there was little likelihood of massive American migration over the Santa Fe Trail to impose them by weight of numbers if nothing else. In contrast with the growing American presence in the Pacific Northwest and California, the small number of Americans going out to New Mexico ensured only a slight dilution of the indigenous culture for some time to come.[44]

The Catholic Church in the United States, for example, reached out to embrace the strongly Catholic acquisitions. From a plenary council in Baltimore went a petition for a new vicariate apostolic with headquarters at Santa Fe, which was approved by Pope Pius IX in the summer of 1850. The Right Reverend J. B. Lamy, recently consecrated titular Bishop of Agathonica, arrived in Santa Fe about a year later. His vicariate was still a part of the Diocese of Durango, but in 1853 the new Bishopric of Santa Fe was created for Lamy, thus canonically binding the Southwest to the American hierarchy.[45]

Compromise was used in dealing with the language problem. Both Spanish and English were official languages during the entire territorial period in New Mexico,[46] and during much of the time newspapers carried columns in both languages.[47] Many American newcomers showed a sensitivity to the beauty of the Spanish language and some of the customs and other features of the Indo-Hispanic culture. The second American governor, William Carr Lane (1852-1853) was one of them.[48] But all too often, the American view was disdainful and at best patronizing.[49]

Official Washington viewed the immense reaches of territory acquired in a two-year-period from Great Britain and Mexico as requiring immediate effort to effectively secure them to the United States. That meant more than simply providing the constitutional framework of government for the new territories. It demanded reliable commercial, communications, and military contacts and, in the case of the Mexican Cession, adjustments and accommodations with skill and imagination. One of Congress's practical approaches was locating mail routes across those great distances.

Postal policies and methods also improved during the time of the huge territorial enlargements of 1846-1848. In response to recommendations of the United States Postal Commission (created in 1844), Congress passed the act of March 3, 1845, which greatly reduced postage rates, setting 5 cents as the rate for a letter of less than half an ounce going less that 300 miles. For more than that distance the rate was 10 cents.[50] The Postal Commission urged lower rates to stimulate greater use of the postal system by the public, for whom the network was developed in the first place. The act of March 3, 1845, was a long-sought victory over those people who argued that a postal system should be judged by its revenue rather than its service. The new direction was more than justified when departmental revenues showed the greatest increase in 1848 in the history of the service. Another innovation was the official adoption of the adhesive postage stamp in 1847; as a result, prepaid postage gradually replaced collection of postage from the addressee, a trend that made letter delivery simpler and more efficient.[51]

When Congress authorized a postal route from Independence, Missouri, to Santa Fe, New Mexico, via Bent's Fort on the Arkansas, and from Independence to Astoria in the Oregon country,[52] the decision undoubtedly reflected the enthusiasm of Missouri's Senator Thomas Hart Benton and a young Mexican War veteran and Independence booster, William Gilpin (later first governor of Colorado Territory). Both men were encouraging the idea that the Ohio, Mississippi, and Missouri rivers should form part of a trans-North American route to the Orient, which would strike cross-country at the point where the river route of the Missouri turned northward.

In 1846, Gilpin advocated a transcontinental mail line that would cross the Rocky Mountains by the South Pass, and a route to Santa Fe was secondary in his mind. Promotion of Independence governed his ideas and plans, which incidentally would greatly benefit real estate he had purchased along the Missouri north of Independence and known as Gilpintown. His schemes were so grandiose that he prepared a map of "Centropolis," a huge city plat complete with national capitol and observatory located on his property of Gilpintown.[53] In the meantime, U.S. mail to and from Santa Fe was carried from Fort Leavenworth under individual trip contracts let by the Quartermaster's Department at that post.[54]

Reports of the discovery of gold in California hit the States in the summer of 1848 and turned attention to that part of the distant new lands. Consequently, the public viewed the road to Santa Fe as a segment of the new route to the Pacific coast—a relatively minor one, because most of the overland traffic to the gold fields went over the Oregon and California Trail. Some of it went through Santa Fe, either all the way over the Trail or on the route from Fort Smith, Arkansas, and from there to

11

California by a more southerly route.[55]

While the glamor of gold in California seized public attention and brought such rapid Americanization that the local society was swamped, change and adjustment remained slow in New Mexico. War bitterness, expressed by the quick violence of the Taos uprising and the rapid decline of trade with Chihuahua, slowed down any significant transition, but military occupation and plans for permanent military posts in the Mexican Cession aroused a need for freighting supplies. In the spring of 1848 the practice of the Quartermaster's Department contracting government business with private carriers was begun,[56] becoming a feature of traffic on the Santa Fe Trail in the 1850s and 1860s along with the expanding volume of civilian commerce.

Conducting the Santa Fe trade was difficult because of the remoteness of the market and the lack of dependable information about its fluctuations. In 1848, for example, most Santa Fe merchants were overstocked, and a number of them failed.[57] Faster communication with Independence might have helped to prevent that, and a regular mail service would have helped the American editor of the Santa Fe *Republican* (started in 1847),[58] since exchanges from other parts of the country were important to success. Establishment of a U.S. post office in the town on October 1, 1849, with William S. McKnight as postmaster,[59] was a hopeful sign of things to come and a reflection of the new departmental emphasis on service.

The first territorial census, taken in 1851, gave New Mexico's population as 56,984, of course including the later Arizona, which was formed in 1863.[60] In 1860, the first federal census in New Mexico put the population at about 86,000, around 90 percent of whom lived north of Fort Craig mainly along the Rio Grande.[61] The comparative figures indicate that New Mexico offered few attractions to Anglo-Americans[62]—nothing like those of California or the Pacific Northwest. In any event, the population was small, spread over a huge area (granting concentration along the Rio Grande), and predominantly Spanish-speaking, which, coupled with a growing Anglo-American ethnocentrism, helped to delay statehood for New Mexico and Arizona until 1912.[63]

In the period between the militarily imposed Kearny Code (1846) and the territorial status granted by the Compromise of 1850, there was a hotly contested question of whether New Mexico should go through the territorial stage or have immediate statehood. The controversy was not simply over the best solution to a general political problem. Individual support for territorial status or statehood was often based on opinions as to which form would better protect the big land grant interests, would allow for greater local autonomy, would ward off Texas claims east of the Rio Grande, or would increase the profits of the powerful Missouri merchants, to say nothing of which would provide greater political preferment.[64]

In addition, New Mexico was enmeshed in the mounting sectional rivalry in which slavery was such a strong issue. There was a genuine fear that slavery in New Mexico would bind it closely to Texas so that native New Mexicans would be subjected to unfriendly Texans, and Missouri mercantile interests would lose out to businessmen from the former Lone Star Republic. The territorial proponents were victorious after an extraordinarily complicated sequence of events in which the final determinant seemed to be the sudden death of President Zachary Taylor, who favored statehood and who was succeeded in July of 1850 by his vice-president, Millard Fillmore, a supporter of Henry Clay's compromise proposals which included territorial government for New Mexico.[65]

It so happened that on July 1, eight days before President Taylor's death, the first regular four-year contract for carrying mail from Independence to and from Santa Fe went into effect. Originally planned as a monthly schedule from Fort Leavenworth to Santa Fe and back, the eastern terminal was shifted to Independence before the contract became operative.[66] The change indicated the changeover from military to civilian primacy south of the Arkansas. The selection of an old Santa Fe hand from Independence, Dr. David Waldo, as winner of the contract showed the continuing preeminence of the Missouri merchants.

Although the contract was in Waldo's name, Waldo, Hall and Company, a partnership of Independence men engaged in the New Mexico trade undertook transportation of mail over the Santa Fe Trail (via the Cimarron Cutoff). The mail run was inaugurated with some publicity, particularly in the Independence-based *Missouri Commonwealth*. Specifically mentioned were the new, water-tight, beautifully painted stages acquired for the service and specified in the contract as six-mule carriages with elliptical springs and iron axles.[67]

Business records of the operation are not available, but other contemporary sources indicate that during Waldo's contract and the subsequent two contracts held by Jacob Hall (one of the partners), vehicles of differing descriptions were used and that the contractual specification of "elliptical springs" was not strictly observed. It seems most likely that the types known as the Dearborn wagon (sometimes called a carriage) and the Jersey wagon, both with bows and canvas tops, were usually employed. Their use was natural under the circumstances; Dearborns and Jerseys were well known to Santa Fe traders as light, carryall wagons often found at the head of caravans of heavier vehicles. But it is certain that occasionally, at least, ambulance wagons were utilized for passengers.[68] Certainly not during the twelve years of the Waldo and Hall contracts (1850-1862) were Concord coaches used on the Independence-Santa Fe run.

With few exceptions, mules pulled the mail stages to Santa Fe and back until after the Civil War. Even though six-mule teams were called for in the contracts, it appears that four-mule teams were commonly hitched to mail wagons.[69] Mules were a feature of the Southwest, and their export to Missouri soon made them popular at that end of the Trail. Their qualities as draft animals had long been appreciated in New Mexico, and their hardiness and speed in the Santa Fe trade quickly inflated their prices. As early as 1832 David Waldo's brother, Lawrence, said that only the government and the more successful freighters could afford to use them.[70] General acceptance of mules undoubtedly accounted for Colonel Samuel Woodson's choice of them as pack animals for carrying the first official mail to Salt Lake City from Independence and back under a contract of the same date as the one awarded to Dr. Waldo.[71] Utilization of mules with mail wagons south of Santa Fe to both San Antonio and El Paso was almost inevitable.[72]

In the gold camps of California, however, early stage lines used four, six, and sometimes eight horses to pull mail and passenger vehicles, except for first and short-lived dependence on pack mules. By 1850 Concord mud wagons and coaches were fairly common on California roads.[73] Those differences in Pacific coast transportation can probably be explained by the great influx of men from east of the Mississippi, where horses and Concords had long been in everyday use, and by the prodigal wealth and heavy demand that made concern for investment and operation costs less important.

Old and alien methods survived in New Mexico and impressed newcomers in countless ways, as was evident in the method of hitching animals to the mail stages. Below the border, Mexican stagecoaches often had an unusual hitch—six mules, two at the pole and four abreast in the lead.[74] Occasionally the mail stages on the Santa Fe Trail used a modification of that hitch—two on the pole and three in the lead. The arrangement was adopted mainly for mountain roads, such as the Mountain Branch of the Santa Fe Trail, which was followed as a mail route after 1861.[75] The Mexican-style hitch may have held on there until well into the post-Civil War period, when horses were being introduced on the line.

Mexican influence, however, did not normally penetrate the highest ranks of mail stage personnel. Spanish surnames were not among those of owners, drivers, or conductors on the Santa Fe-Independence run, but they were frequent among the freighting outfits on the Trail. South of Santa Fe a few stage drivers had Spanish names.[76]

A very important part of the mercantile influence in New Mexico was exercised by the Jewish community in Santa Fe. Probably the earliest, Solomon Jacob Spiegelberg came out from Leavenworth during the war with Mexico. Mostly from Germany, Jewish merchants were soon established in the principal towns along the Trail, especially from Trinidad, Colorado, south, and they were regular patrons of the stage line on their way to and from eastern markets. Some of them were prominent in the mail contracting business in New Mexico south of the territorial capital during the 1860s. Among them were Jacob Amberg of the firm of Elsberg and Amberg, Levi Spiegelberg (Solomon Jacob's brother), Aaron Zeckendorf, and the firm of A. and L. Zeckendorf. Jewish names did not appear, however, among those of mail contractors from Missouri and Kansas to Santa Fe. They were also absent from the roster of contractors on the Platte and Smoky Hill routes, but in 1867 Abraham Jacobs, a Jewish merchant in Denver, developed the Denver and Santa Fe Stage Line, which really ran only to Trinidad where connections were made with Kansas-New Mexico coaches.[77]

Accommodations en route for passengers and employees of the lines serving Santa Fe were neither numerous nor, with few exceptions, very comfortable. At no time were stage stations distributed somewhat equidistantly over the entire system, although some portions had stops every ten to fifteen miles, especially in the late period. During the earliest days the mail stages traveled about 550 miles from Council Grove to the Mora (Barclay's) Fort (the distance was shortened by about six miles in 1851 when Fort Union was established) without a stage station in between except for Fort Mann-Fort Atkinson on the Arkansas, abandoned in 1853. Over the years that the mail route used the Cimarron Cutoff of the Santa Fe Trail (1850-1861), there was never an unrelieved gap of less than about 375 miles, which was the stretch separating Camp on Pawnee Fort (established in 1859 and later renamed Fort Larned) and Fort Union. Such great distances required that the mail stages be equipped for making night camps, which meant provision of food, fuel, fodder, arms, and ammunition. An available supply of buffalo or antelope meat, buffalo chips, and grass could not be counted on in any season. Extra mules needed outriders, and in that category there is one mention of a black man employed by the stage company. Occasionally, three or four wagons were needed to carry passengers, mail, baggage, and supplies on one trip; then the number of company men might be ten or a dozen. Similar practices were followed by the mail stages south of Santa Fe.[78]

In response to demand, mail and passenger service increased in frequency and decreased in running time over the years. Performance was dependent to a great degree on weather and Indians, but the evidence—mainly newspapers—indicates that, much more often than not, trips were made in less than the contractual running time. That was true even in the 1860s when military escorts tended to slow them down. From once a month to and from Santa Fe under the contract of 1850, the schedule became semimonthly in 1857, weekly in 1858, and triweekly in 1866. After that, of course, the distances were progressively reduced as the eastern terminus retreated westward from railhead town to railhead town.[79]

Fares were remarkably stable during the years from 1850 to 1866. In 1850 Waldo, Hall and Company charged a fare of $100 in the summer and $120 in the winter from Independence to Santa Fe. In 1857 Hockaday and Hall received $125 per person from May to November and $150 for the winter rate. Slemmons, Roberts and Company levied a single rate of $125 to Santa Fe in 1862, while a passenger could go to the Colorado mining camp of Buckskin Joe for $85. Two years later M. Cottrill and Company obtained $75 per person for the trip from Denver to Kansas City.[80] There were, of course, fares to and from stations along the way and express rates over the same routes. Beginning in 1866, fares, like running time, went down in relation to shortened lines as railroads were built from east to west and from north to south. Lack of company records, except for a way bill covering about a four-year span (1858-1862) for the route south of Santa Fe, makes it difficult to say much about volume of business. Available contemporary sources, however, give the impression of generally good and sometimes heavy business.

David Waldo's 1850 contract to transport the mail to and from Santa Fe for $18,000 was the first government subsidy of mail stages across the Great American Desert (Woodson used packmules on the Salt Lake route). It projected a longstanding practice into a different and difficult locale—the first contract for carrying mail by stagecoach was let by Postmaster General Ebenezer Hazard in 1785. But in the intervening sixty-five years other modes of transportation had come on the scene and had driven mail stages from some roads, mainly east of the Mississippi River. In 1813 Congress declared that all waters used for steam navigation would be post routes, and in 1838 railroad lines were given the same status.[81]

Shortly before Congress authorized mail routes from Independence to Santa Fe and the Oregon country, the railroad age had its significant beginnings in Missouri with the charter of the Hannibal and St. Joseph Railroad. Railroad service between the Mississippi and Missouri rivers began on February 16, 1847. Two years later the Pacific Railroad of Missouri was planned westward from St. Louis, but its construction was extremely slow. Both lines were thought of as future links in transcontinental ones. Railroad mail delivery was more costly than by stagecoach, but Congress was attracted by the greater speed.[82] Here was another example of emphasis on public service rather than revenue, a guideline that was further extended by Congress by the act of March 3, 1851, which lowered letter postage rates to 3 cents up to 3,000 miles and 6 cents over that distance. Other rates also were lowered, and a fund was authorized to cover deficits, along with a provision that no postal route would be discontinued because of loss of revenue.[83]

Steam locomotives and railroad cars cast long shadows over the Great American Desert. Congress authorized Pacific railroad surveys in 1853, resulting in four proposed transcontinental routes. The routes were soon immersed in the sectional rivalries with Secretary of War Jefferson Davis and Illinois Senator Stephen Douglas as proponents of the South and North, respectively.[84] Only the so-called central route, marked by Captain John W. Gunnison and his men along the upper Arkansas and over mountain passes between the 39th and 41st parallels,[85] could seriously affect the future of the mail and stage line to Santa Fe from Independence.

Waldo, Hall and Company, succeeded first by Hockaday and Hall and then by Hall and Porter, ran the mail stages on the Santa Fe line creditably and with reasonable regularity during the decade of the 1850s. It was never a spectacular operation, and public attention was quickly drawn away in 1858 when the big Butterfield Overland Mail Line began service from Memphis and St. Louis to Los Angeles and San Francisco by way of the southern, or ox-bow, route through Fort Smith, El Paso, and Tucson—a triumph for the South. Less than two years later, public fancy was more dramatically caught by the experiment of the pony express along a central route between St. Joseph, Missouri, and San Francisco. This countervictory for Northern interests also helped to strengthen the Platte River valley as the main emigrant route to the gold diggings of the Pike's Peak region.

In 1859 the Pike's Peak gold rush drew many people from the eastern rim of the Great American Desert to the front range of the Rocky Mountains. Although the Platte River road carried the bulk of the traffic, the new emigrant surge was felt on the Smoky Hill Trail through central Kansas, between the Overland Trail on the Platte and the Santa Fe Trail on the Arkansas. As part of the three-way competition for the new business, promoters of the Arkansas River route soon dubbed it "the greatest natural road in the world."[86]

Evidence of the urban frontier quickly appeared in and along the mountains in the form of mining camps and towns to supply them. Among their demands was mail and passenger service, and one of the first to supply the need was the Leavenworth and Pike's Peak Express—not under government contract—generally following the Republican River between the Smoky Hill Trail and the Platte River.[87] Partly as a result of the gold rush, Fort Wise was located at the upper end of Big Timbers on the Arkansas near Bent's New Fort in 1860.[88] The government's decision to send the Santa Fe mail over the Raton Pass meant abandonment of the Cimarron Cutoff as a mail route in 1861. Soon the Missouri Stage Company, successor to Hall and Porter, was permitted to carry the U.S. mail on a branch line up the Arkansas to the mining towns of Canon City, California Gulch, Fairplay, and other points.[89]

Santa Fe itself was affected very little by the gold fever that impelled thousands of people into the mountains several hundred miles to the north. Compared with the burgeoning and bustling Rocky Mountain mining towns, so dominantly American, Santa Fe remained a small, easy-going, provincial capital with a population of 4,635, while Las Vegas and Albuquerque each had a little over a thousand people. There had been some increase in the territorial population during the 1850s—from 60,000 to 90,000—but this came not so much from immigration as from an increased birth rate among the Spanish-speaking residents. The economy was prosperous, and the territorial assembly was largely controlled by perhaps 500 to 700, well-to-do, native families. On the eve of the Civil War the Anglo inhabitants still numbered only a few thousand, mainly merchants (quite a few of them Jewish), government officials, professional men, and a few miners.[90]

One of the most notable effects of the gold rush was the dangerous reaction of the Plains Indian tribes through whose hunting grounds the routes to the Pike's Peak region passed. The surge of immigration coincided with mail contractor Jacob Hall's attempt to locate a mail station on the Pawnee Fork of the Arkansas. The Comanche and Kiowa were strongly opposed to the station, and it was set up only with the help of the military from Fort Riley. The most serious attack was the destruction by Kiowa of a mail party near there in September 1859. Numerous mail stages were molested during the entire era, but most of their experiences fell short of tragedy, as was the case around 1866 when Cheyenne were warded off by Barlow, Sanderson and Company employees and their passengers until the coach reached the security of a passing wagon train.[91] And there were occasional attempts at robbery by white men, but they were generally minor affairs because mail stages on the Santa Fe road infrequently carried much cash or treasure.

At the eastern end of the mail line, the population of Kansas Territory (created in 1854) increased from about 8,500 inhabitants to more than 100,000 in 1860. Concentrated in the eastern counties, the growing number of inhabitants helped to qualify "Bleeding Kansas" as a free state in 1861, after the bitter conflict of the forces for and against slavery. At the same time, part of western Kansas Territory was detached and included in the new Colorado Territory, which showed a population of about 25,000 centered in the mining camps north and south of Pike's Peak.[92] The vast central plains—the Great American Desert to most—were still chiefly the domain of the Plains Indians.

19

In 1863, a little more than two years after the nation exploded into civil conflict, the eastern terminus of the mail route to Santa Fe was officially moved from Independence to Kansas City, Missouri. In the meantime, the stage line's control had passed from the Missouri Stage Company to Slemmons, Roberts and Company, to Cottrill, Vickroy and Company, and then to M. Cottrill and Company.[93] The Missouri River town, also known as the City of Kansas, was fast becoming a major commercial center despite the formidable rivalries of St. Joseph, Missouri, and Leavenworth, Kansas, as well as the uncertainties of Confederate guerrilla and other Civil War actions in the vicinity.

A combination of geographical advantage, political maneuvering, ardent promotion, and vagueness of the Pacific Railroad Act of 1862 resulted in the start of construction of the Union Pacific Eastern Division Railroad (later the Kansas Pacific) westward from Kansas City in September 1863, while the Pacific Railroad of Missouri was still crawling slowly across the state toward Kansas City. Work on the Union Pacific Eastern Division, however, was far from speedy; service over the first forty miles from Kansas City, Missouri, to Lawrence, Kansas, was not opened until mid-December 1864.[94]

Those railroad tracks were the first west of Missouri and were intended to traverse the plains, antedating the start of the Union Pacific itself from Omaha by a little over two months. Gradually the old notion of the Great American Desert was discarded after the Civil War, a change stimulated in part by the attractive terms of the Homestead Act of 1862 and a coincidental wet weather cycle on the Great Plains.[95] More and more people were looking upon the plains as an area to be exploited rather than to be crossed or avoided. Occupation of the Great Plains—the last phase of the frontier—was at hand.

The Union Pacific Eastern Division maintained its faltering construction from Lawrence to Junction City and Salina, generally following the Smoky Hill Trail. When the railhead was at Junction City in 1866 the stage line to Santa Fe withdrew its eastern terminus from Kansas City to Junction City. At the time the line was owned by Barlow, Sanderson and Company.[96] From then on, contraction of service in the face of expanding railroad construction was an accepted business calculation.

A succession of railhead towns in western Kansas and eastern Colorado provided terminals for the mail stage line to and from Santa Fe and up the Arkansas to some of the Colorado gold camps. In utilizing connections with the westward-building railroad, Barlow, Sanderson and Company abandoned segments of the Arkansas Valley-Santa Fe Trail route. By 1869 the easternmost point on the Trail served by their coaches was Fort Lyon on the Arkansas in eastern Colorado.

When the Central Pacific and the Union Pacific tracks were joined near Promontory Point, Utah, in 1869 to complete the first transcontinental railroad, Barlow, Sanderson and Company's operational subsidiary, the Southern Overland Mail and Express Company, offered the only other booking to California, however tenuous it may have been through Arizona at times.[97] The service south and west of Santa Fe was accomplished mainly through subcontractors and associated companies, and railroad development destroyed that connection just as it ended the stagecoach service north and east of Santa Fe.

The Union Pacific Eastern Division Railroad was renamed the Kansas Pacific in 1869, and the next year it was completed across the plains of eastern Colorado into Denver. Also in 1870, Barlow, Sanderson and Company acquired the mail route and stage line south from Denver to Pueblo and Trinidad, thus giving it control of the remaining staging enterprises between the railroad and Santa Fe.[98] The monopoly was short-lived. In October 1871 the narrow-gauge Denver and Rio Grande Railway extended as far south as Colorado City, and in the spring of 1876 it reached a point on the Purgatoire River about four miles below Trinidad.[99] Stagecoaches no longer rolled up the valley of the Arkansas from Bent's Old Fort to Pueblo, nor did they run any longer between Denver and Trinidad via the old Denver and Fort Union Road. Both standard and narrow-gauge railroad tracks took care of that.

The destroyer of the truncated main stage line to Santa Fe was the Atchison, Topeka and Santa Fe Railroad, which reached the little town of West Las Animas on the Arkansas River by September 13, 1875. Continuing up the Arkansas about twenty miles, passing the ruins of Bent's Old Fort, the tracks reached the new railroad town of La Junta in mid-February, 1876. The fate of Barlow and Sanderson's Southern Overland Mail and Express Company was determined when Santa Fe Railroad officials decided to follow the Mountain Branch of the Santa Fe Trail to Trinidad and over the Raton Pass to Santa Fe. After a nip-and-tuck struggle with the Denver and Rio Grande for control of the Pass, victory for the Santa Fe brought on the final withering of the stage line when the first train came into Las Vegas, New Mexico, in July 1879. Technically, the *coup de grace* was administered by the first train into Santa Fe on February 16, 1880, which was about the same time that the Southern

Pacific Railroad, building east from California, put its first train into Tucson.[100] In effect, the Southern Overland Mail and Express Company was squeezed to death between two railroads—the Atchison, Topeka and Santa Fe and the Southern Pacific—both of which ultimately became transcontinental lines.

Barlow and Sanderson, of course, had been phasing out their operations in view of such irresistible forces, and when the time came that the Santa Fe Trail was no longer a mail or freight route, they were already doing business in the mountains of central and western Colorado and north-central New Mexico,[101] and on the Pacific coast between California and Oregon.[102] But those enterprises were, whatever their need and importance, on the periphery of things—feeder lines and service to remote hinterlands where railroads had not yet reached. How different the new circumstances were from the extensive system of communication and commerce which had been provided by a succession of mail contractors and stage companies from Missouri and Kansas to New Mexico and Colorado, with extensions to Texas, Arizona, and California.

By 1880, of course, other fundamental changes had come about along the old Santa Fe stage road and its branches. The Indians were on reservations, and the remaining military posts—Forts Lyon and Union— were expiring relics of the past. The buffalo had been supplanted by longhorns and foreign breeds of cattle on the open range. Control of waterholes, within the letter but hardly within the spirit of the Homestead Act, allowed great cattle companies to dominate thousands of acres on the public domain, and governmental decisions affecting some of the big Mexican land grants bequeathed resistance, resentment, and clouded land titles. Coal mining was beginning to take its place beside that of gold.

Colorado had become the Centennial State and New Mexico, though still a territory, had experienced a shift in political and economic control that greatly augmented the power of the Anglo community. In spite of the railroad and other developments New Mexico was by no means absorbed by dynamic, late nineteenth-century America. Perhaps New Mexico "was still dramatically behind the rest of the country in income, education, population, economic opportunity, and political standards,"[103] but certainly part of the explanation was in the persistence of ancient ways of life that stood in the path of the earliest Americans south of the Arkansas.

1

The Preterritorial Years

1846-1850

ON THE LAST DAY of its official existence, March 3, 1847, the Twenty-ninth Congress of the United States authorized the transportation of mail by two routes—one from Independence, Missouri, via Bent's Fort to Santa Fe, capital of the recently occupied Mexican territory south of the Arkansas River, and the other from Independence to Astoria in Oregon Territory.[1] The proposed route to Santa Fe followed the Bent's Fort (or Mountain) Branch of the Santa Fe Trail, used by Colonel Stephen Watts Kearny's Army of the West the previous summer.

War with Mexico was still in progress, although the main theaters of conflict were by then far to the south and west. But the region surrounding Santa Fe was under severe military control because of the Taos uprising in which Governor Charles Bent and others had been killed less than two months before. Despite the congressional action the post road over the Santa Fe Trail was delayed for some time. The state of war with Mexico and the less formal hostilities with the Plains Indians placed the responsibility for the mail primarily with the military.

Communications between Santa Fe (Fort Marcy) and Fort Leavenworth were kept open by expresses, which often were nonmilitary. The latter post was on the right bank of the Missouri River near the eastern edge of the vast plains—the Great American Desert, as the plains were called by many people. As early as 1828 there was a post office at Leavenworth (then only designated as a cantonment).[2] Santa Fe had no post office until 1849.[3] A variety of expresses were operating, sometimes with official sponsorship, but frequently in an almost casual and empirical manner, which perhaps was more effective under the circumstances.

Nearly nine hundred challenging miles confronted them.

One of the earliest expresses left Santa Fe on October 17, 1846, using the Cimarron Cutoff of the Santa Fe Trail and, as might be expected, meeting much military traffic.[4] Widely known frontiersmen occasionally carried dispatches and mail. Thomas O. Boggs and seven other men left Santa Fe on muleback about December 15, traveling by the Bent's Fort route in severely cold weather. On the Purgatoire River, they met a similar westbound party, among whom was young Lewis H. Garrard, later the author (1850) of the well-known *Wah-To-Yah and the Taos Trail*. More than 200 miles farther east at Coon Creek, Boggs's party lost nine mules to marauding Pawnee Indians and had to walk the remaining 300 miles to Fort Leavenworth. Boggs was under a round-trip contract, probably with the Quartermaster's Department of the Army, and apparently he returned in March 1847 with ten men, two wagons, and a heavy mail. The men were a military escort led by Second Lieutenant Joseph O. Simpson, Missouri Volunteers.[5]

Mountain man Solomon P. Sublette and three others left Fort Leavenworth on muleback January 8, 1847 with Washington dispatches for Colonel Sterling Price in Santa Fe. Sublette, with two men and six mules, returned to Fort Leavenworth in April with government dispatches and mail.[6] He may have been under contract. On February 3, trader Thomas J. Caldwell left Santa Fe with twelve men, several wagons, and a heavy mail. They followed the Cimarron Cutoff but had to leave the mail snow-stalled about twenty-five miles east of the Cimarron crossing of the Arkansas.[7]

Two important installations appeared beside the Santa Fe Trail in April 1847. About midway between Fort Leavenworth and Santa Fe, the government established a small fortification on the Arkansas River's north bank, below the crossings, near a places called the Caches, where a party of winterbound traders had buried their goods in 1822.[8] The fort consisted of four log houses connected by timber framework and was named for Daniel P. Mann, the government wagonmaster in charge of construction. It was not a post with a regular garrison, but was to be a place for rest and wagon repair.[9] The other development was the opening of a store at Council Grove by Albert G. Boone and James G. Hamilton, who held a Kansas Indian trading license.[10]

Francis X. Aubry carried the mail into Santa Fe in late April. Apparently mail was also taken into Independence beginning in the spring of 1847. On May 23, for example, a group of homeward-bound Missouri Volunteers, discharged for ill health, came into Independence with the mail. Later in the summer Aubry brought a heavy mail into the same town. And military units continued to carry the mail to both Leavenworth and Independence.[11]

Another familiar frontier figure, Jim Beckwourth, took a mule express to Fort Leavenworth, leaving Santa Fe on November 21 and stopping at Fort Mann for fresh mules. He did not always stay on the Santa Fe Trace but sometimes struck cross-country when it seemed advisable.[12] Nor did he travel with military units. A government express had left for the States a few days before,[13] but Beckwourth believed that the military presence assured clashes with Indians and that association with soldiers would make him a certain target later. He placed no confidence in troops, particularly against the Comanche.[14] Beckwourth and two other men left Fort Leavenworth for the return trip on January 2, 1848; two days later at the point known as Hundred and Ten[15] they met Francis X. Aubry, who was thirteen days out on one of his many trips across the plains. Farther along, between the Pawnee Fork of the Arkansas and Fort Mann, Beckwourth and his party met an eastbound express in charge of an "old and celebrated mountaineer" named Fisher[16]—undoubtedly Robert Fisher.

The Senate's ratification of the Treaty of Guadalupe Hidalgo on March 10, 1848, ending the war with Mexico, brought no immediate changes in the handling of mail to and from New Mexico. At the time, B. F. Chouteau had a quartermaster's contract to carry mail from Santa Fe to California and back for $1,000,[17] and a June mail left Santa Fe for the States with G. R. Gibson and party and a Major Singer.[18]

But there was dissatisfaction with the irregular service. The editor of the *Santa Fe Republican* expressed particularly strong disapproval of the failure to receive any news from the States for two months. He hoped that Congress would move quickly to provide a dependable line of communication,[19] but response in faraway Washington was not quick.

In November, a man named Newman took letters in his private packages from Santa Fe to Fort Leavenworth,[20] and late in December J. W. Folger contracted with the army to carry the U.S. mail from Santa Fe to Fort Leavenworth and back for $600.[21] At least two contracts, one of them for $800, were obtained in the winter and spring of 1849 by that prominent trail figure Ceran St. Vrain.[22]

A man named Haygood left Santa Fe on June 6, 1849 with a mail party for Independence, accompanied by some Chihuahua merchants and a military escort commanded by Brevet Captain Abraham Buford, First Dragoons.[23] When they reached the Trail's crossing of Running Turkey Creek, about twenty-five miles east of the Little Arkansas River in present central Kansas, they came upon a large stone which bore the fresh inscription: "To Fayettville, Ark., 300 miles—Capt Evans' Com'y, May 12, 1849."[24] That information referred to the Cherokee Trail which came in from the southeast. From there Captain Buford, with eight troopers, headed down it to Fort Gibson, Indian Territory, sending the rest of his men to Independence with the mail party and merchants.[25] In midsummer James C. Bean contracted to carry the mail one way to Fort Leavenworth for $100.[26] His mail was an unusually heavy one, including more than 400 letters that had come from California into Santa Fe, as well as a heavy mail from Santa Fe.[27]

William Bent abandoned his fort on the north bank of the Arkansas River in August 1849, removing a principal reason for using the Mountain Branch of the Santa Fe Trail.[28] And a tragic incident occurred on the Cimarron Cutoff in late October. Santa Fe merchant J. M. White and several others were killed by Jicarilla Apache, who also abducted White's wife and daughter and a female Negro servant.[29] That attack doubtless prompted a twenty-man escort from the First Dragoons to accompany an eastbound mail in charge of John Phillips and James Clay. On November 3 the express left Las Vegas, where a small force had been stationed since 1846.[30]

Mail expresses made it back and forth about once a month in the early part of 1850. Daniel P. Mann, builder of Fort Mann on the Arkansas, carried the one in January.[31] The expresses appear to have been unescorted; the military alert was probably relaxed during the height of the winter, when Indians were not usually very active. James Clay and Frank Hendrickson took the mail in a single wagon to Fort Leavenworth about the middle of March,[32] and, with a man named Branton, they set out on the return trip on April 18. On the way they overtook a wagon train led by Thomas W. Flournoy, who was going out to relieve James Brown's twenty wagons, stranded by weather on the *Jornada*[33] about thirty miles south of the Arkansas. The mail carriers and Flournoy reached Brown around the end of April. Then Clay, Hendrickson, and Branton resumed their trip with the mail. Flournoy accompanied them, as did Moses Goldstein, a Santa Fe trader who had wintered with Brown's train on the *Jornada*. En route they were joined by five men, apparently from an eastbound train. About May 7, the ten-man party was attacked by Jicarilla Apache and Mohuache Ute near the well-known landmark of Wagon Mound; all ten were killed. The arrow-studded bodies of the men and mules and the scattered mail were discovered on May 19 by a party of twenty or more men who had set out northward that day from Barclay's Fort,[34] a trading post built in 1848 between the Mora and Sapello rivers near the present Watrous, New Mexico.[35]

Toward the end of May 1850 a mail party headed by Elliott Lee, together with wagon trains belonging to the firm of Hickman and Adams and a Mr. Harley, left Las Vegas for the States. With them went Second Lieutenants Ambrose E. Burnside and Peter W. L. Plympton and an escort of twenty-two men, past the "massacre" site and as far as the crossing of the Cimarron.[36] This large group was not molested.

While the uncertain communications between the States and Santa Fe were being kept open, along with the even more tenuous connection to California, the amorphous state of affairs in the huge Mexican Cession was coming to an end. Wartime President James K. Polk had given way to war-hero President Zachary Taylor, and the Thirty-first Congress, in a great turmoil of sectional debate, was working toward a territorial agreement based on Henry Clay's set of resolutions.

2

Waldo, Hall and Company

1850-1854

THERE WERE OTHER SIGNS of closer official ties between New Mexico and the States, one of them being a post office for Santa Fe on October 1, 1849. That link may have introduced prepaid postage to the region (adhesive postage stamps were approved and issued in 1847), but the old method of sending mail postage-collect continued for some time.[1] As Congress inched toward a compromise which, among other things, would give territorial government to New Mexico and Utah and statehood to California, the Post Office Department called for proposals in the spring of 1850 for carrying the U.S. mail from Fort Leavenworth via Bent's Fort to Santa Fe. Nine bidders submitted twenty-six proposals. The winner of the four-year contract was David Waldo, a former Independence medical doctor who had become a Santa Fe trader.[2] His bid of $18,000 per annum was accepted by the department on May 11.

Scheduling departures from alternate ends of the line at 8 A.M. on the first day of the month, Waldo agreed to transport the mail in a maximum of twenty-nine days aboard six-mule carriages with elliptical springs and iron axles. Some of his competitors—one was Thomas W. Flournoy, who was killed with the Clay-Hendrickson mail party in May—proposed to use four-mule carriages, four- and six-horse carriages, covered wagons, or pack animals if road conditions and Indian depredations made them advisable.[3]

Inauguration of the Fort Leavenworth-Santa Fe mail route—perhaps the first of its kind across the plain—was scheduled for July 1, 1850.[4] In the meantime, the eastern terminus was changed from Fort Leavenworth to the Trail town of Independence, reducing the total distance of what was officially known as Route No. 4888 from 885 miles to 840 miles.[5]

Although David Waldo was the mail contractor, the mail stages belonged to the Independence firm of Waldo, Hall and Company (David Waldo, Jacob Hall, and William McCoy), all of whom were prominent businessmen experienced in the Santa Fe trade and government freighting. McCoy was the first mayor of Independence (1849-1850), and it appears that his brother John, also a leading citizen, was associated with the company.[6]

Just after his mail contract went into effect, David Waldo, as a contractor for government freight, was helping to supply posts on both the Oregon and the Santa Fe Trails. Nineteen of his wagons set out for Fort Laramie (the old trading post had recently become a military one), carrying 97,592 pounds of government freight.[7] On July 26, forty-five of Waldo's wagons left Fort Leavenworth for Santa Fe with 236,669 pounds of army supplies.[8] And for the fiscal year 1850-1851, Waldo sent the greatest number of wagons to Santa Fe by a single contractor—154.[9] Although such listings are in Waldo's name, the firm of Waldo, Hall and Company was probably involved.[10]

As matter of terminology, a "mail stage" did not necessarily refer to a stagecoach in the popular sense of a Concord coach by Abbott-Downing Company. A stage was any coach, wagon, or sleigh used for staging purposes.[11] Waldo's contractual specification of carriages with elliptical springs ruled out the Concord coach with its body slung on leather thoroughbraces.

Wagons were used in the early years of the Independence-Santa Fe mail run, although the original, eight-passenger ones had bodies "beautifully painted and made water-tight, with a view to using them as boats in ferrying streams." Power was furnished not by spirited, matched teams of four or six horses as specified in the contract, but by six sturdy unglamorous mules. As protection against Indians, a mail stage was guarded by eight men, each armed with a Colt rifle, a Colt revolver, and hunting knife. The men could fire 136 shots without reloading, a rather formidable firepower in case of attack.[12] Apparently, however, the first arrangements for equipment, animals, and men did not remain constant for long. Less than two years later, an eyewitness said the mail was transported in a Jersey wagon[13] drawn by four mules. The mail party consisted of four employees and several passengers, who paid from $100 (in the summer) to $120 for the trip. The guards could shoot fifty times without reloading.[14]

Bertram Spratt was in charge of the first mail stage that left Independence for Santa Fe, arriving about July 28, 1850. After two or three days in the former provincial capital, Spratt and his party headed back on August 1, reaching Independence on August 28 after a round trip of seven weeks and three days.[15] The first venture in staging by Waldo, Hall and Company was completed within contract time, but a St. Louis publication implied that the trip would have been faster if the company's teams had not failed (probably from exhaustion).[16]

At Council Grove, about 150 miles from Independence, the government established a blacksmith shop in 1847 for the convenience of wagons on the road from Fort Leavenworth to Santa Fe; it was maintained by the U.S. Army Quartermaster's Department. That same year, William Mitchell, blacksmith for the Kansas Indians, also put up a shop in Council Grove. In 1850, however, he sold his shop, house, corral, and cultivated field. The buyers quickly accepted $400 for the property from Jacob Hall, of Waldo, Hall and Company, who purchased it for use as a mail station.[17]

But along the wearisome and dangerous miles west of Council Grove, there was no relief or help (except for the little station of Fort Mann on the Arkansas) until one reached the Mora River (Barclay's Fort) about a hundred miles east of Santa Fe.[18] On the return trip, Spratt and his men probably stopped at the new Camp Mackay on the Arkansas. The camp was established by order of Lieutenant Colonel Edwin Vose Sumner, First Dragoons, on August 8, 1850, to replace Fort Mann, and was a short distance east of the former post.[19] Waldo, Hall and Company may have already set up their repair and relay station there.[20] Soon they took out a license to keep an Indian trading house at Council Grove, to comply with the law and maintain a mail station on the reservation.[21] For the next season the firm planned a stopping place at Walnut Creek, near the Big Bend of the Arkansas.[22]

A heavy September mail went out in charge of Jacob Hall, who arrived in Santa Fe on September 24, well ahead of schedule. The Independence *Missouri Commonwealth* commented: "This is already an important branch of the U.S. mail service. . . . The Mail to Salt Lake is as yet a small one, though it is much needed."[23] The latter reference was to a mail line from Independence to Salt Lake City recently contracted for by Colonel Samuel H. Woodson.[24] Waldo, Hall and Company's first run to Santa Fe in July had missed the big news of President Zachary Taylor's death on the 9th, as well as President Millard Fillmore's appointment of Nathan K. Hall as Postmaster General on July 23. And the September mail was on the way when word came through to Independence that Congress had passed that part of the Compromise of 1850 that gave territorial status to New Mexico.

The alternating departure schedule was dispensed with, and mail stages then left from each end of the line on the first day of the month.[25] In October 1850, they passed each other at the new military post on the Arkansas.[26] In November the mail stages began service to the new United States Post Office in the adobe town of Las Vegas.[27] Death took a Waldo, Hall and Company mail carrier by the name of Borland, so the December mail from Santa Fe to the States was carried by trader John E. Sabine.[28]

In February 1851, Griffith H. Williams was in charge of the westbound mail stage, comprised of two "carriages" and outriders. The stage met a military express at Diamond Spring about fifteen miles west of Council Grove, and they traveled together as far as the New Post—Camp Mackay renamed and relocated.[29] Near Walnut Creek they saw a band of mounted Pawnee warriors but had no trouble; the Indians apparently decided that the party was too large and too well armed to molest.[30]

Weather was often a severe problem. In summer, the heat and rain plagued mail stages, express riders, and the numerous wagon trains. The shutdown of wagon traffic during the winter left the mails and expresses to take the brunt of the snows alone. The mail bound for Santa Fe in June 1851 was delayed five days because of heavy rain and swollen streams.[31] Six months later, the one headed for Independence, in charge of William Allison, bucked through twelve to fourteen inches of snow on the Dry Cimarron, south of the Arkansas. Three bad storms were encountered on that trip: one at McNees' Creek[32] below the Dry Cimarron, another at Fort Atkinson—the New Post renamed—and the third one near Lost Spring, west of Diamond Spring.[33]

Nature appeared in another guise along the Santa Fe Trail during the summer of 1851. In July the mail carriers found that two soldiers had died of cholera at Fort Atkinson. The mail party preceding theirs had skirmished with Indians at the Narrows and had fallen back to one of

Preston Beck's wagon trains for protection along the Trail.[34]

Complaints about the mail service were heard before David Waldo's contract had been in operation a year, although the criticism was directed not at him but at Jacob Hall. One Santa Fe resident, disgruntled when the March mail left a few days late, remarked that "blame must be laid to mail agent Hall a most unaccomodating man to the public generally."[35] The statement implies that Hall was the most active of the three partners in managing the mail transportation.

The fastest time ever run under Waldo's contract was seventeen days from Santa Fe to Independence in March 1852.[36] But however satisfactorily the contract was fulfilled, there was strong pressure as early as February 1851 for at least a semimonthly mail. A petition dated February 5 was sent by citizens of New Mexico to Postmaster General Hall. They acknowledged that the service had been performed "with a punctuality not excelled, if equalled, by that of any other Contractors in the United States," but argued that the best interests of contractors and patrons, as well as the exigencies of Indian threats and the increase in the number of troops in the Territory, demanded more frequent mail delivery.[37]

South of Santa Fe, men and mules transporting the mail had their problems with Indians on the famed *Jornada del Muerto*. Anticipating trouble on one occasion in February 1852, U.S. soldiers (probably from Fort Fillmore) were hidden in the mail wagon. When the Indians attacked, they were permitted to come in close before the soldiers jumped out and beat off the raid. One of the military men was killed, and another was wounded, along with a traveler (probably a passenger). The critical factor, however, was the killing of one mule and the crippling of another, which caused the mail party to return to Doña Ana. That mail finally reached Santa Fe on March 17.[38]

Across the nation were growing demands for a reduction in postal rates. Responding to those demands, Congress passed a measure on March 3, 1851 which set a letter rate of 3 cents (per half ounce or less) for any distance within the country not exceeding 3,000 miles. It also provided lower rates for newspapers, that were so important to distant places like Santa Fe which had not yet been reached by telegraph. In effect, Congress abandoned the concept of a profit-making postal service and subscribed to the idea that a good service network was vital to the nation.[39]

The Independence-Santa Fe contract was not scheduled to change until 1854, so Waldo, Hall and Company maintained and strengthened its monthly liaison between the States and Santa Fe. A mule relay station was set up in August 1851 at the new Fort Union, another post established by Lieutenant Colonel Sumner, near "the Holes" or clear ponds that were close to the juncture of the Cimarron Cutoff and the Mountain Branch of the Trail. That made three places—with Council Grove and Fort Atkinson—where fresh animals and corn were available. But there were still 300 miles between the forts with no set places for aid or protection.

Fort Union received a post office on September 26, 1851.[40] After that date, the mail stages probably no longer used that portion of the Cimarron Cutoff from the crossing of the Canadian to the vicinity of Barclay's Fort. Instead they traversed a military road from the crossing to the fort, passing north of the Turkey Mountains, then back to the Cimarron Cutoff at Barclay's Fort.[41]

Mail stage mules usually trotted briskly over the relatively level terrain. Night camps were made off the road to avoid attracting Indians, and the journey was resumed after the mules were hitched up about one-half to three-quarters of an hour before daylight. William Carr Lane, the second governor of New Mexico Territory and successor to James S. Calhoun, traveled to the Territory by Waldo, Hall and Company stage in August 1852. In his diary he recorded that the stage was drawn by six mules and the baggage wagon by four, and that William Allison and two assistants rode on horseback.[42]

The eastbound mail for that same month was accompanied from Santa Fe by a man traveling in his own two-mule vehicle. A man named Rupe was in charge of the mail party. On that trip they followed Aubry's Trail from Cold Spring to the Arkansas River instead of the usual portion of the Cimarron Cutoff.[43]

A little over a year later, after a brief gubernatorial administration—beset with Indian troubles and personal difficulty with Lieutenant Colonel Sumner, commander of the Ninth Military Department[44]—Lane journeyed east with the October mail, which was in charge of Francis Booth. Among the notations in Lane's diary is one that Little Coon Creek, on the Dry Route, had been drained by the immense herds of buffalo in the area.[45] The Dry Route, which was used by the mail stages, was a cutoff from the southward bend of the Arkansas, roughly between

Pawnee Fork and a point on the Arkansas about ten miles east of Fort Atkinson.

When former Governor Lane made his return trip, Fort Atkinson had been recently abandoned. The post was too remote and poorly constructed—it was made of sod and was commonly known as Fort Sod or Fort Sodom—for soldiers to occupy another winter. The small garrison marched east about ninety miles to Walnut Creek, and with them went the property of the Post Office Department in the care of Postmaster Samuel G. Mason, who opened a new office at Walnut Creek on August 23, 1853. Apparently, business had never been brisk at Fort Atkinson; for the year ending July 30, the postage collected amounted to $21.78. Waldo, Hall and Company's station was also abandoned. The troops stayed at Walnut Creek only a short time before retiring to Fort Riley,[46] and the post office and station did not remain much longer.

A man from Columbus, Ohio, on his way to New Mexico to purchase mineral lands, was evidently afraid he might be slightly delayed in getting into Independence in time for the September mail stage. Somehow he sent ahead the following attempt at poetry for publication:

> Running fast and living well,
> Greiner's on the Isabel,
> Bound to meet the mail, so he
> Can passage take to Santa Fé[47]

Conductor Booth had the westbound run in November. One of his passengers was William W. H. Davis, appointed U.S. District Attorney for New Mexico,[48] whose account of the journey is the most detailed record of the first contractual period of the Independence-Santa Fe mail. Davis and G. Rodman bought seats for $150 each, which included board and forty pounds of baggage. There were two other passengers. The stage was made up of a mail wagon, a wagon for baggage and provisions, and an ambulance for the passengers. The mail and baggage wagons were each drawn by six mules, and four were hitched to the ambulance. Of course, each vehicle had a driver, and there were two outriders to hurry the extra mules. Six company employees, including the conductor, and four passengers made a party of ten. The capacity of the ambulance must have been four people, because another wagon with a six-mule team was added when two more passengers wanted to get on a short distance out of Independence. About twenty miles along, at New Santa Fe,

Missouri, the company's agent found some accommodations for the passengers on the first night.

After an early start next morning they drove about fifteen miles to
Lone Elm, where Booth and his men prepared breakfast. The site was one
of the first stopping points west of the Missouri border in unorganized
territory; there was nothing left of the landmark except a stump.[49]
Eleven miles farther, they crossed Bull Creek and passed its nearby trading post. They made their night camp at Hickory Point. A before-break-
fast drive of about eighteen miles brought them to Rock Creek, some
ninety-five miles from Independence, where they saw discharged soldiers
on their way home from Fort Massachusetts beyond the Sangre de Cristo
Mountains in distant New Mexico. They made camp beside Switzer's
(Switzler's) Creek that night and rolled into Council Grove the following
day.

The call at Council Grove was a brief one, mainly to hitch up the
fresh mules provided by the company's representative, a man named
Withington. The team that brought them out from Independence would
rest and wait for the next westbound mail. Davis logged Council Grove
as 150 miles out. Fifteen miles beyond was Diamond Spring, one of the
Trail's earliest and best-known spots. There, although Davis does not
mention it, Waldo, Hall and Company had a station.[50] Diamond Spring
was really the jumping-off place, and that night the mail party camped
some twenty-nine miles west of it at Cottonwood Creek, a popular
campground.

On December 9 they reached the Little Arkansas, a tributary of the
main Arkansas River, and the next night they were at (Big) Cow Creek.
Two days later they saw the Arkansas itself at Great (Big) Bend. They
made camp eight miles farther at the Pawnee Fork of the Arkansas.

By this time the mail party was well into the high plains country—
the range of buffalo and antelope. Moving on to Coon Creek, Davis and
his companions prepared for the thirty waterless miles of the Dry Route.
Somewhere along that stretch they met the eastbound mail from Santa
Fe in a single wagon with four men. The westbound party came again
to the Arkansas that night, and on the next segment of their journey
they saw the remnants of Fort Atkinson. After another overnight stop,
they forded the Arkansas at the Middle (Cimarron) Crossing.

From there, the Waldo, Hall and Company vehicles headed southwestward across the fifty-mile, dry expanse of buffalo grass country—

the *Jornada,* with its haven of the Lower Spring of the Dry Cimarron at its southern edge, about 445 miles from Independence.[51] They had a meal at a spot beside the Cimarron bearing the doleful name of Stranger's Grave, and in a short time they reached a place called Mule Head, where there were piled the bones of 120 mules that had perished during one bitterly cold night a few years before.[52]

When they stopped briefly at Cedar Spring, they could see the Mesa Mayor (Mesa de Maya) to the west. Between Rock Creek and the Whetstone branch of the Canadian, Davis observed the place where the White family had been attacked by Jicarilla Apache in 1849.[53] The mail stage travelers had breakfast at Point of Rocks on December 20. That night, with some twenty more miles traversed, they camped on the Canadian (or Red River or Rio Colorado), which Davis designated as the Canadian Fork of the Arkansas, an early but little-used name.[54] Snow was falling when they resumed their journey. They ate breakfast at Ocate Creek, where they used the last of their rations. That was no problem because they could make Fort Union by nightfall. After crossing the Canadian, they were on the road that passed north of the Turkey Mountains to the military post with its sutler's store and post office. Fort Union then was a group of quadrangles edged by unconnected log structures that were used by the cavalry-infantry-artillery garrison.[55]

For a few miles south of the fort, the Waldo, Hall and Company mail stage took the Mountain Branch of the Santa Fe Trail until it merged with the Cimarron Cutoff near Barclay's Fort. They had breakfast at Las Vegas, a "mud town" of some 700 people. A short distance out of Las Vegas, the Trail led through the foothills of the Sangre de Cristo Mountains via Tecolote[56] and San Jose, passing its southernmost point before turning northwest to Santa Fe, the territorial capital.

Like many journals, Davis's account is selective and leaves some readers wishing that he had been more detailed in his descriptions and observations.[57] His lack of references to wagon trains and Indians doubtless had a seasonal explanation; activity along the Trail was greatly reduced during the winter months. And the absence of military escorts for the mail was due to the policy of providing them only when requested by the Post Office Department or the mail contractor,[58] who evidently saw no need for them in November 1853.

Unescorted mail placed great responsibility on the conductor, and his success depended more or less on personal traits and fortuitous circumstances. One of Waldo, Hall and Company's conductors was a man with the commonplace name of John Jones, but a couple of his experiences suggest that he was a man of unusual courage. In December of 1853, Jones was in charge of the Santa Fe-bound mail party which was suddenly jumped by fifteen or twenty Osage Indians near the Arkansas River at Pawnee Rock. During the chase, some of the Indians managed to cut through the canvas at the back of one of the wagons and took some clothing. As they rode off, he pursued them alone on horseback, caught up, drew his revolver, and forced them to return the stolen items.

In May 1854 Jones was headed for Independence with the mail, accompanied by W. F. Dever and a man named Kelly (probably Matthew or Peter). They had made a noon halt near Cedar Spring when they were encircled by about forty Cheyenne, who were armed with bows and arrows. While some of the Indians were asking for various articles of food, others ran off the mail party's grazing mules. After being informed of the deception, resourceful John Jones pointed a gun at the chief's head. The mules were returned, and the Cheyenne were given some provisions.[59]

Encounters of this kind, along with the February memorial to Congress from the territorial legislature to reestablish Fort Atkinson and its mail station,[60] brought a decision to send Major Albemarle Cady and Companies H and F of the Sixth Infantry from Fort Riley to occupy a summer camp near the deteriorated post; they reached there on June 13 and withdrew on October 13.[61] The presence of troops close to the former fortifications on the Arkansas was reassuring to people involved in summer traffic on the Trail. The first westbound wagons of the season were met by the east-bound June mail stage at the Lower Cimarron Spring.[62]

The June mail run to Santa Fe encountered a minor difficulty only incidentally related to Indian dangers. New Mexico's Governor David Meriwether—appointed in 1853—had been in the States for some weeks and was hastening back to Santa Fe because widespread Indian disturbances seemed certain. Upon reaching Independence, Meriwether and his son, Raymond, obtained the three-seated, mule-drawn carriage they had left there on their way to Washington. They decided to accompany the westbound mail stage, at least on the dangerous midsection of the trip. The Governor was to ride in the carriage with his driver, Louie, and Raymond was to ride horseback.

Waiting for the stage in Independence was Dr. Michael Steck, agent for the Mescalero Apache, who was persuaded to give up his seat in the stage to ride in Meriwether's conveyance instead. Apparently the stage line's Jacob Hall did not object to losing a passenger. He even offered to have a sack of corn, which Meriwether would purchase at Council Grove, carried in the baggage wagon.

But conductor Francis Booth, according to Meriwether, did not take kindly to the loss of a fare. The governor's party left three days ahead of the stage and stopped at Council Grove to purchase the corn. They were nearing the crossing of the Arkansas when they decided to wait for the stage, because Meriwether was not sure whether Booth would take the Dry or the Wet Route from Pawnee Fork. The next morning Booth and his wagons passed the governor's camp "driving like Jehu" and then camped eight or ten miles farther on, where Meriwether and his party overtook them. When asked if he had the sack of corn in his baggage wagon, Booth said he had been unable to find it in Council Grove. Nor would Booth share his own corn supply, saying he did not have enough, which may have been true.

At the crossing of the Dry Cimarron, the governor met a sergeant and ten soldiers, who had been sent out from Fort Union on orders from the department commander, Brevet Brigadier General John Garland, to escort the governor and the others over the Cimarron Cutoff. At that night's camp, Louie, Meriwether's driver, obtained about a half-sack of corn from the sergeant, who asked him not to tell Booth. When asked why the secrecy, the sergeant said that Booth was angry because he had lost a passenger and was hoping that Meriwether's team would break down and the Indians scalp him. At least, so Meriwether would have us believe.

The following morning, Booth and the troopers left before the governor was ready to travel, but they all camped together that night. The next morning Meriwether made the sergeant divide his force, and the governor's group departed first. This rather ridiculous seesawing continued the rest of the way to Santa Fe, with Meriwether beating Booth into the capital by about half a day. Not a single hostile Jicarilla Apache or Mohuache Ute bothered the rival parties.[63]

The June mail parties, Governor Meriwether's group, and all the other travelers on the Trail between the Missouri River and the 38th parallel were within the boundaries of a new political subdivision. Kansas Territory was created by the controversial Kansas-Nebraska Act, signed into law by President Franklin Pierce on May 30, 1854.

3

Hockaday and Hall

1854-1858

DAVID WALDO AND JACOB HALL bid separately on the new four-year contract to carry the Independence-Santa Fe mail that began July 1, 1854. A total of six bidders presented thirty-eight proposals to the Post Office Department. Approval was given to Jacob Hall's offer to provide a maximum twenty-five day service in six-mule coaches for $10,990 per annum, with the privilege of increasing the departures from monthly to fortnightly for an annual compensation of $22,000.[1]

The firm of Waldo, Hall and Company was dissolved, with Jacob Hall buying out the other partners' interests in the mail line. As part of the transaction, the Council Grove stage station became Hall's property as, presumably, did the Fort Atkinson relay station and other mail facilities along the route.

Although not such an old hand as his predecessor and recent associate, David Waldo, mail contractor Hall was familiar with the problems and hazards of the Santa Fe Trail. An Independence resident since about 1842,[2] Hall may have been the otherwise unidentified "Mr. Hall" who served as wagonmaster of the train which left Independence in June 1846, accompanied by Susan Shelby Magoffin.[3] His first commercial experience as an entrepreneur on that route was in the fall of 1846. To take advantage of the promising market with the Army of the West at Santa Fe and beyond, Hall and A. P. Kean took nine wagons with goods and provisions to Santa Fe in October; Hall returned to Independence in the spring.[4]

Route No. 4888 was changed to No. 8912.[5] The postal rates provided in the act of March 3, 1851, remained in force. Jacob Hall was joined in the enterprise by John M. Hockaday; their authorized agents were W. H. Davis, in Santa Fe, and John S. Harris, in Westport, Missouri.[6] Westport was included in a Post Office Department order of August 16 to be served under Hall's contract without any change in pay, because it was on the road from Independence to Fort Union. The first of the month was still the departure date from each end of the line,[7] and passengers could make the trip for $150 from November to May and $120 from May to November.[8]

When a Hockaday and Hall mail wagon rolled into the plaza at Santa Fe and the conductor deposited the leather bags at the door of the post office, dates from the Atlantic seaboard were about six weeks old. Letters sent to St. Louis were answered about three months later.[9]

There was also a mail connection between Santa Fe and San Antonio, Texas, which was carried by George H. Giddings.[10] Fairly direct connection between the two provincial capitals had been opened as early as 1787,[11] but the speed of communication had not been improved very much by 1855 according to local wags in Santa Fe, who dubbed Giddings' vehicles "The Lightning Express train." That service brought newspapers from New Orleans, Louisiana, and Charleston, South Carolina, that carried old dates even by the schedule standards of that day.[12]

The Post Office Department wanted faster service on the Independence-Santa Fe run and asked for proposals for weekly departures all the way or at least between Fort Union and Santa Fe. If a prospective contractor thought he could make it in less time, the Department was ready to consider his suggested schedule. At the beginning of Jacob Hall's contract term, the only established post offices were at Independence and Westport, Missouri, and at Fort Union, Las Vegas, and Santa Fe, New Mexico Territory,[13] but Hockaday and Hall provided passenger, mail, and express service to several other places in Kansas and New Mexico Territories. In 1855, nine additional post offices were provided on the Independence-Santa Fe route. Eight of them were in Kansas Territory (Hibbard, Davis, Richardson, Council City, Allen, Miller, Council Grove, and Fort Atkinson), and the ninth was a revived one at Tecolote, New Mexico Territory, between Las Vegas and Santa Fe.[14]

As the mail contractor and more active partner in the firm, Jacob Hall asked Congress for additional compensation, alleging increased costs because of Indian hostilities.[15] In the act of March 3, 1855, Congress allowed him an extra $11,010, increasing his total compensation to $22,-

000 for one year, beginning August 18, 1854.[16] The exact nature of Hall's losses is not known, but it may be surmised that Indians ran off livestock and stole supplies.

The summer of 1855 was also a difficult one. Indian Agent John W. Whitfield reported from the Upper Arkansas Agency at Bent's New Fort —established in 1853 on the north bank of the Arkansas at the upper end of the Big Timbers—that "all the tribes from Council Grove to the headwaters of the Arkansas have been and still are behaving badly. They have regular stands on the road, where they exact and enforce the payment of toll in the way of sugar, coffee &c. No train has been permitted to cross without having to submit to this imposition, whilst a large number of horses, mules and oxen have been stolen during the present season."[17]

Apparently unable to recoup his losses, Hall petitioned Postmaster General James Campbell in the fall of 1855 to be released from his contract. Campbell, acting within his authority, refused, tempering his decision by indicating that sufficient compensation would probably be provided in the next contract. Hall felt that he could not carry on without more funds before that, so he turned again to Congress. There the House Post Office Committee, satisfied that Hall spared no expense in trying to fulfill his contract, recommended allowing him $25,500 per annum, but the departmental appropriations act of August 18, 1856 simply continued the $22,000 until the end of the contract term in 1858.[18] Contractor Hall had to be content with Congress's action on his operational losses, and Hockaday and Hall employees had to cope with further skirmishes with Indians, such as the unsuccessful Cheyenne attack on the run to Santa Fe in September of 1856.[19]

Early in 1857, natural obstacles confronting Hockaday and Hall vehicles were about as serious as the Indian raids. By February, the weather had so disrupted the service that there was no regular conductor in Santa Fe to take charge of the mail stage. So, the Santa Fe postmaster made a special contract for $1,200 with Major Thomas F. Bowler to carry the mail to Independence, which he did between February 3 and 27, 1857. Forty men from the Third Infantry accompanied the mail as far as Walnut Creek, Kansas Territory, and it was claimed that the escorted mail party encountered the worst road conditions ever known. Wagons had to be taken apart so that their beds and planks could be used as scows for getting mail and passengers across swollen streams. Water had even cut arches through the drifted snow that filled the creeks. Twelve days were required to get from Santa Fe to the Arkansas River crossing, but even at that the overall trip was managed within the twenty-five days allowed.[20]

On the Trail in Kansas Territory was a new trading post known as Allison and Booth's Walnut Creek Station (also commonly known as Allison's Ranche). The proprietors advertised groceries, provisions, and forage at reasonable prices.[21] Bill Allison has been described as a one-armed plainsman,[22] and the partners may have been the former Waldo, Hall and Company mail stage drivers, William Allison and Francis Booth.[23] Their place was given a post office in December of 1856, but, for some reason, it was discontinued in November of the next year.[24] Growing settlement of eastern Kansas was reflected in May and June 1857 in the establishment of two new post offices east of Council Grove—Palmyra and Wilmington. Also in June the Fort Atkinson office was discontinued for the third and last time after it had been restored to service in August of 1855.[25] The pullback was again to Walnut Creek, lengthening the unrelieved stretch from the last Kansas post office to Fort Union in New Mexico by about ninety miles. When the Walnut Creek office was withdrawn in November, the gap was about 140 miles greater, because Council Grove became the westernmost post office in Kansas Territory for awhile. Discontinuing a post office did not necessarily mean abandoning a trading post or a settlement, however. Walnut Creek Station, or Allison's Ranche, continued to be a welcome place on the Trail.

Growing volume of business and good prospects for the future brought a renegotiation of Hall's contract, effective July 1, 1857, which stepped up Hockaday and Hall's service to a semimonthly one. The new terms specified an additional $11,000 per annum, bringing the yearly compensation to $33,000, and called for transportation in six-mule stages as usual.[26] The only change in passenger fares was a $5 increase to $125 from May to November; the winter rate remained at $150. Passages were paid in advance, and conductors were empowered to accept money and give receipts. Each passenger was allowed forty pounds of baggage in addition to his own bedding. Provisions, arms, and ammunition were furnished by the proprietors. In Santa Fe the line's agent was Levi Spiegelberg; J. and W. R. Bernard and Company, of Westport, Missouri, served at the other end.[27]

When the Independence-Santa Fe mail and passenger service was expanded, military forces were chastising some of the Plains tribes, especially the Cheyenne. The commander, Colonel Sumner, First Cavalry, was primarily concerned with Cheyenne hostilities on the emigrant road along the Platte River. But he sent four cavalry companies under Major John Sedgwick to sweep along the Arkansas River from the Big Bend to above Bent's Old Fort. The two commands joined on the South Platte near present Fort Morgan, Colorado, and marched into northwestern, present-day Kansas, where they found a battle-ready force of about 300 Cheyenne on Solomon's Fork of the Kansas River. After defeating the Cheyenne and destroying their village of more than 300 lodges, Sumner and Sedgwick pursued the remnants of the Indian force as far as the vicinity of Fort Atkinson's site on the Arkansas.[28]

On August 11, at the crossing of the Arkansas, Colonel Sumner met the "inward-bound" mail to Independence and was told of a minor incident with a small band of Kiowa on the Dry Cimarron.[29] Farther up the Arkansas at Bent's New Fort, Indian Agent Robert C. Miller was extremely uneasy. The Cheyenne annuity goods were stored at the fort, but William Bent had taken his family and his private stock of goods to Independence in anticipation of a major Cheyenne attack.[30] Agent Miller was greatly relieved when an express from Colonel Sumner rode in on August 15 to tell him that the colonel planned to reach the fort on the 18th.[31] Upon his arrival, the colonel ordered Miller to abandon the fort and return to the States with him.[32] Miller turned over food items to Sumner's quartermaster, distributed all but two wagonloads of goods to some Arapaho at the fort, and threw powder, lead, and flints into the Arkansas before leaving with Sumner and his men on August 20.[33]

Evidently the Independence-Santa Fe mail was not seriously disrupted during the summer of 1857. The same Hockaday and Hall mail party that Colonel Sumner met at the Arkansas River crossing had a scare, however, when several young Cheyenne warriors relieved them of their sugar and coffee after shaking hands.[34] Perhaps the mail parties were lucky; there was no firm indication that the Kiowa, Cheyenne, and others were about to become docile and agreeable. And it is probable that some Hockaday and Hall employees were less cautious than others. On September 9, surveyors working on the southern boundary line of Kansas met a five-man mail party, conducted by a man named Field, traveling alone on the Cimarron Cutoff a few miles below the Middle Cimarron Spring. Colonel Joseph E. Johnston, commanding the survey group, advised Field that it was dangerous for so small a party to travel alone and suggested that they wait and join a wagon train led by Mr. Wells (John M.?).[35] It is not known whether Field followed the colonel's recommendation.

At any rate, the army felt the danger was grave enough in the fall of 1857 to warrant ordering escorts for the mails. Brevet Brigadier General Garland, from his headquarters in Santa Fe, issued instructions that most escorts were to ride in mule-drawn wagons, although mounted escorts were not forbidden. Easier defense and scarcity of grass explained the change.[36] The commandant at Fort Union, Colonel William W. Loring, instructed a lieutenant in charge of an escort that "your marches will not be farther than 30 miles a day or as far as in your judgment your horses can possible [sic] go.[37]

Restraint on running time was unpopular with mail contractors, and they ignored it as much as possible. Colonel Loring probably realized that army animals would be unable to take the full 600 miles from Fort Union to the Arkansas and back. In March 1858, General Garland asked the adjutant general of the army to require the mail company to slow down their wagons to the pace of the escorts, and he proudly reported that no mail had been lost to Indian attacks during the more than four years he had commanded the department. The absence of interference with the mail, despite earlier predictions, prompted General Garland to discontinue escort service on the western half of the Santa Fe Trail in May.[38]

A traveler on the Trail in June of 1858 wrote a descriptive account of transportation of the U.S. mail on the Kansas plains. He was a German by the name of Heinrich Balduin Möllhausen, who was with an eastbound government wagon train temporarily detained on the west bank of Cow Creek by high water. Here are his observations.

In the course of the forenoon the United States mail arrived at Cow Creek. It had left the Missouri river only eight days before; its carriers were unpleasantly surprised that they were held up in their flying trip by the flooded little river. The carriers are obliged by contract to make the trip through the prairies within a certain time and only truly insurmountable obstacles are accepted as an excuse for lost time; in other cases they have to expect a reduction of pay. The post-office business in the United States is almost exclusively in the hands of private persons; they receive considerable sums from the government for the fast and safe transportation of letters and persons. They also have the right to requisition escorts, where the roads are very unsafe at times, from one military post to the next on the routes between the Missouri river and the Pacific. These escorts are then forced to keep up with the little caravan.

The mail caravan normally consists of one to six light-traveling wagons, depending upon the number of passengers that have registered for the trip; each wagon is provided with four or six of the best mules, but takes along a double number so that the mules can be exchanged every four to six hours; since the larger part of the freight consists of heavy nutritious fodder, and the animals are therefore not dependent on grass, they are given at the most six or eight hours of the 24 for rest. Besides the driver there are two riders with each wagon, one of whom has to supervise the unharnessed animals while the other one rides at times on the other side of the wagon and keeps the draft animals in fast motion with the help of a long whip. Thus the mail hurries across the endless plains at an average speed of four miles per hour. Provided with the best animals, it is not difficult for the mail coach to cover 50-70 miles per day and to get to Santa Fe from the Missouri or back in the incredibly short time of 18 days.

Several times at a nocturnal hour when I walked around the camp and no other sound disturbed the stillness except the deep breathing of resting men and animals, I could hear the sound of the mail in the distance like the uncanny rumbling of a ghostly hunt. More and more distinctly I could hear the encouraging calls, the cracking of whips, the tramping of hoofs and the rattling of wagons. I would try peering through the darkness but could see nothing but the sparks emanating either from iron-clad hoofs striking the pebbles on the road, or from the wind blowing into glowing pipe-bowls. The indistinct silhouettes of wagons, riders and animals would gradually become clearer as the flying caravan came closer and closer.

Suddenly at shooting distance it would stop. I would hear the cocking of pistols and at the same time the call: "Who is camping there?" "A government expedition" would be the answer. "The mail" it would come back, the whips would crack, the chains and rings on the harnesses would ring, and with a loud "Hallo!" the United States mail would trot past. A rider would leave the caravan, address a few questions to me concerning the road or the natives, answer my questions briefly, urge his horse on, and gallop after the wagons and the riders who had already disappeared in the darkness but whose sounds were still audible far in the distance when I crept back into the tent to wake up my replacement.

Such a caravan had arrived at Cow Creek at an early morning hour, and had camped almost opposite us. We greeted the riders that accompanied it but the rushing stream disturbed our conversation although we would have preferred to keep it up for a long time. The shade of the tents and the wagons was more welcome to everyone than the sunny river banks sheltered from every current of air.[39]

Aside from his misapprehension about the degree of private control of postal matters in the United States and his implication that mail contracts covered the transportation of passengers also, Möllhausen's narrative is a good delineation of mail transportation. Its special significance is in the proof that night travel had become a part of the procedure, probably in response to the semimonthly, twenty-five-day schedule and the curtailment of military escorts.

4

Expansion and Competition

1857-1859

WHILE HOCKADAY AND HALL mail wagons regularly traversed the more than 800 miles of the Independence-Santa Fe route, a serious threat to their existence loomed briefly and then died away. On March 4, 1857 Franklin Pierce was succeeded in the presidency of the United States by James Buchanan. The new chief executive's appointee for postmaster general was Aaron V. Brown, a proslavery Tennesseean, who was given virtually a free hand by the Post Office Department Appropriations Act of 1857 in choosing a contractor to carry the mail from some point on the Mississippi River to San Francisco, California.[1]

If Brown had not been such an ardent southerner he might have accepted the first plan proffered by John Butterfield, President Buchanan's close friend, who proposed traveling along the Santa Fe Trail, then south to Albuquerque and westward along the 35th parallel to California.[2] But when the Postmaster General successfully pushed his preference for the extreme southern route from Missouri through Arkansas and Texas to El Paso, the danger of probable absorption of the Independence-Santa Fe line passed. The attention of the promoters of the Overland Mail Company, most of them heavy investors in the big express companies, particularly Wells Fargo,[3] was shunted to the south. And Congress allowed a year's time to put the line into operation.[4]

When contract-letting time for the Independence-Santa Fe line came around again in the spring of 1858, twelve bidders sought to secure the job of carrying the mail over the route, which had been renumbered 10532. The one-trip, special contract awarded to Thomas F. Bowler in February, 1857, must have whetted his appetite for more, because in

47

1858 he submitted twenty-seven proposals out of a total of fifty-one. Quite a few of Bowler's propositions, however, were designed for a 1,097-mile route from Council Grove via Santa Fe to El Paso. Also among the contenders was a William McCoy, presumably the former Waldo, Hall and Company partner.

But it was one of Jacob Hall's four bids that was accepted on April 24; his offer of $39,999 was to carry the Independence-Santa Fe mail weekly in six-mule coaches with iron axles and elliptical springs—still not Concord coaches.[5] The innovation in the 1858 contract was conversion of the line to a weekly one, with departures every Monday at 8 A.M. from each end. Maximum running time was set at twenty days instead of the twenty-five stipulated in the previous contract.[6]

And so, on July 1, 1858, Jacob Hall started his second term as sole mail contractor operating between Missouri and New Mexico. Operation of the Butterfield Overland Mail did not begin until September 15.[7]

John Hockaday terminated his association with Jacob Hall to test his business acumen on the central route to California. That same spring a two-and-a-half-year contract to carry the mail to Salt Lake City was awarded to Hockaday and Company, and soon he and George Chorpenning were transporting mail to California on a revamped route from St. Joseph, Missouri, to Placerville. Chorpenning held the Utah-California contract, and his joint venture with Hockaday put the central route in competition with Butterfield's southern line.[8] The growing rivalry was a reflection of the burgeoning sectional frictions that were besetting the nation.

When the Post Office Department rejected Bowler's proposal for carrying the mail from Council Grove through Santa Fe to El Paso, Jacob Hall was left alone to develop the potential of his new contract; the problems were internal ones, free from competition or absorption, at least for the time being. Service was expanded to include the new post offices at Olathe, Gardner, McCarnish, Black Jack, McKinney, Walton, Marion, Waushara, and Agnes City, all between Independence and Council Grove in Kansas Territory; in the same part of the line the name of Council City was changed to Burlingame. West of Council Grove the post office at Walnut Creek had been discontinued in November of 1857, and soon after the new contract went into effect the little adobe towns of San Jose and San Miguel, below Fort Union, were given post offices.[9]

In the fall of 1858, along the Trail as far west as the crossing of the

Arkansas River, the mail wagons of Jacob Hall and his new partner, Judge James Porter, more and more frequently met gold seekers headed west to try their luck in the most distant part of Kansas Territory on Cherry Creek. Emigrant traffic was a new and disruptive element along the Arkansas River. Of course, there had been emigrant trains on the upper Arkansas where the Cherokee Trail followed it to the Platte and on to California, but the newcomers foretold settlements on the headwaters · of the Arkansas and other streams flowing eastward from the mountains.

At the Upper Arkansas Indian Agency, William Bent predicted, from his wide experience and knowledge, that the gold discoveries on Cherry Creek would be dangerous to the region of the upper Arkansas. A letter from him at Bent's (New) Fort to A. M. Robinson, Superintendent of Indian Affairs, and dated December 17, 1858, put it this way:

Cheyenne, Arapaho, and other Indians of this river are now very uneasy and restless about their country, the whites coming into it, making large and extensive settlements and laying off and building towns all over the best part of their country on this river, also on the South Fork of the Platte & Cherry Creek, this is their principal hunting ground. . . .

The emigration to the Gold Diggings this fall has been very large and they still continue to come, they have all passed unmolested by the Indians, although they have stolen several horses . . . losing their favorite hunting ground & their only place to get their summer's and fall provisions, that goes rather hard with them. . . .[10]

Reasons for the aggravated restiveness among Kiowa and Comanche are less readily discernible, but they were related to the increased commercial traffic on the Santa Fe Trail toward the end of the decade. The wool trade, for example, was increasing greatly.[11] About the time that General Garland dispensed with regular military escorts of the mails, Indian Agent Robert C. Miller, nearing the close of his stint at the Upper Arkansas Agency, warned against any attempted discipline of the Kiowa, such as withholding their presents; he feared for those traveling the unprotected route from the Missouri border to Santa Fe and the inability of the War Department to send in a force large enough "to occupy the road." Miller believed that "the immense commerce of the plains recommend[s] that the usual presents be sent to them [the Kiowa] also."[12] In summary, the trigger for Indian hostilities north of the Arkansas was white emigration and settlement; south of the river it was mainly the increase in commerce and the temptation of loot. And underlying it all was the mounting destruction of the buffalo herds, the basis of Indian life on the Plains.[13]

On his first trip for Hall and Porter in the fall of 1858, James Brice braved the uncertainties of man and nature on the long road to Santa Fe. His conveyance was a six-mule ambulance marked on each side in large letters: *U.S.M.* Starting on a Monday morning from Jacob Hall's residence in Independence, the mail party, in charge of Conductor Michael Smith, called first at the Westport post office for an exchange of mail and then headed out through Olathe, Gardner, Baldwin City, and Burlingame to Big John Spring and Council Grove.[14] There was a sack for Santa Fe mail and one for way mail at points along the route; Brice made no mention of passengers.

At Council Grove the mail was transferred to a covered wagon drawn by six large mules, with a bell-pony attached to the offside team. A man rode alongside on a saddle-mule to guide the teams in response to the conductor's directions. Two extra mules were taken along. Also, an assistant helper was taken on for the difficult journey to Fort Union. The wagon had a boot for provisions and cooking utensils. Two-bushel sacks of corn for the mules were loaded into the vehicle, and wooden rails were fastened to the axles, to be used for cooking fires when buffalo chips could not be found.[15] Brice's description points out the diversity of conveyances and methods employed in transporting the Independence-Santa Fe mail.

West of Council Grove the mail party made a few more stops before reaching Cow Creek, the last mail station—not an official post office—before the big jump to Fort Union. In the roughly 425 miles between the two points, the weekly mail wagon was used as a distributing post office by freighters, emigrants, and all other travelers. Letters addressed to persons along the Trail were delivered, and those picked up were mailed at the next post office.

After crossing the Pawnee Fork of the Arkansas and Coon Creek, Conductor Smith directed the mail party as usual over the Dry Route to the Caches on the Arkansas and from there to the Cimarron, or Middle, Crossing. All along the way from Missouri they had passed numerous gold-seekers headed for the Pike's Peak region, but no more were seen after the mail party turned south along the Cimarron Cutoff into Kiowa-Comanche country.

The first place south of the Arkansas mentioned by Brice was Battle Ground Bone Yard; he gave no explanation, but evidently it was between the river and Sand Creek. He told of only one Indian threat on the entire trip. They had made a noon stop at a place he called Dead Man's Hollow, about 150 miles from Fort Union. Some of the men were greasing the wagon when a Kiowa party made a menacing appearance and then rode off. For most of the trip from Missouri, the progression was three drives a day, starting with one before breakfast. Always included was a midday stop of half an hour to allow the mules to water and browse. A man was left at Fort Union to get things ready for the eastbound mail. From there into Santa Fe, the closing miles were made in easy and uneventful laps.[16]

In northwestern Missouri the commercial importance of towns was shifting. Independence had yielded to Westport as the starting point for the Santa Fe Trail, but by the mid-1850's, wagon freighters were beginning to operate out of what Westporters referred to simply as "the landing." The ledge of rock, a natural levee on the Missouri River between the Kansas and Big Blue rivers, had already been favored by the military. The name of Westport Landing was in fairly common use for the little settlement there, but the town was rightly known as Kansas. By 1855, the single word Kansas was supplanted by City of Kansas or Kansas City,[17] the designation that will be used here for the booming river town.

Although the eastern terminus of the Santa Fe mail remained at Independence, thriving Kansas City was a base for other stage lines in 1858. A. B. Squires operated daily, four-horse, post coaches from Kansas City to Fort Scott, Kansas Territory. Similar coaches of the Kansas Stage Company left every morning at four o'clock for the Kansas towns of Monticello, De Soto, Lexington, Udora, Franklin, Lawrence, Lecompton, Big Springs, Tecumseh, Topeka, Osawkee, Silver Lake, St. Mary's Mission, Louisville, Manhattan, Ogden, Fort Riley, Junction City, and Kansas Falls. L. G. Terry was general superintendent and James Roberts was Kansas City agent for that line and the Kansas City-Fort Scott line.[18]

Kansas City merchants and other business interests were alert to new opportunities and competition along other routes besides the Santa Fe Trail. They were aware that trade was booming in St. Joseph, the Missouri town in the northwestern corner of the state, about seventy-five miles upriver from Kansas City. St. Joseph had been designated the eastern terminus of Hockaday and Chorpenning's line to California via Fort Laramie and Salt Lake City.[19]

But during the late summer of 1858, Kansas City businessmen were especially aroused by reports of William Green Russell's discovery of gold on Cherry Creek in the farthest reaches of Kansas Territory. That and other finds set off the Pike's Peak gold rush, and Kansas City competed with other towns to be the chief point of departure. Plans were made for a regular connection from Kansas City, Missouri, and the Kansas towns of Wyandot (now Kansas City, Kansas) and Leavenworth. Scheduled runs of the Pike's Peak Express were advertised to begin on January 15, 1859,[20] but it was not until April that the Leavenworth and Pike's Peak Express Company—heavily invested in by William Russell of the freighting firm of Russell, Majors and Waddell—began to function from Leavenworth under the management of John S. Jones.[21]

Kansas City's best bet for cutting into the promising trade with the gold camps was to encourage the use of the Santa Fe Trail to the point where the Mountain Branch turned south from the Arkansas River above Bent's (Old) Fort, and continuing westward along the river. From the upper reaches of that stream, wagons could fan out to various mountain camps and Denver City, making the route competitive with the Smoky Hill Trail to the north.

Promoters began to advertise the Santa Fe road as the best way to the Cherry Creek mines, preferable in every way to the Smoky Hill route. An editorial, probably based more on hope than fact, appeared in the *Kansas City Daily Western Journal of Commerce* in January 1859, noting that emigrants were shifting from Leavenworth and the Smoky Hill route to Kansas City and the Santa Fe road.[22] For those who did not want to provide their own transportation and gear for the trip, a man named Smith organized a Pike's Peak Express from Kansas City. Letters and small express packages were carried, and for a one-way fare of $80.00 passengers were accommodated in mule-drawn, covered wagons equipped with stoves.[23] Travel time to the gold mines was about fourteen days.[24]

An elaborate table of distances from Kansas City to Pike's Peak was published in the *Kansas City Daily Western Journal of Commerce*, giving the availability of wood, water, grass, and wild game, but, like many such itineraries, it never mentioned the presence of Indians along the way.

The distance from Kansas City to Pawnee Fork (281 miles) was surveyed in the summer of 1858 for Jacob Hall and "the great Santa Fe Mail Company" by Captain L. J. Berry, former deputy U.S. surveyor.[25] Berry also set up suitably marked stones every twenty miles, and within each twenty-mile section Hall located a mail station. Maps of the route were filed in the General Land Office and the land offices in Lecompton and Ogden, Kansas Territory. They were also placed in each mail station, as well as in the line's main office and the hotels of Independence. Hall's activity conformed with the Post Office Department Appropriations Act of March 1, 1855 and subsequent statutory and Interior Department modifications (1857) which allowed mail contractors west of the Mississippi to hold 320-acre, preemptive claims to their mail stations when the land came on the market.[26]

The route along the Arkansas was frequently described as "the best natural road in the world." Pawnee Fork of the Arkansas was listed as the last mail station.[27] Five miles beyond, travelers reached the forks of the Santa Fe road. There, they could bear left and follow the Arkansas around its South Bend or bear right over the shorter Dry Route via the headwaters of Big Coon Creek, although that shortcut was not recommended after July 1 for emigrant or freight wagons, because of heat and drouth. The mail wagons used it in all seasons.

The intermediate distances from Pawnee Fork 271 miles to the mouth of the Huerfano, a southern tributary of the Arkansas, were compiled in 1853 by Captain John W. Gunnison, Topographical Engineers, in his quest for a central railroad route to the Pacific. The prospectus described the route from the crossing of the Arkansas (apparently meaning the Middle, or Cimarron, Crossing) to the Huerfano as that followed by emigrants bound for California and by mountain traders. Twenty-four miles up the Arkansas, people headed for the gold mines reached the little settlement of Pueblo. From there to Pike's Peak was forty-eight miles, making a total of 624 miles from Kansas City.[28]

John S. Jones, already associated with the Leavenworth and Pike's Peak Express line, made plans to carry freight, passengers, and baggage over the Santa Fe road and up to the mines, saying that he would send fifty trains of twenty-six wagons each during the coming summer if necessary.[29] In March 1859, Irwin, Porter and Company organized the Kansas City Gold Hunter's Express Transportation Company for the same purpose. The possibilities of the Pike's Peak traffic encouraged officials of the Kansas Stage Company to try for a share of it. That firm announced in the spring that it would make connections at Junction City, Kansas Territory, to the gold mines with Jones, Russell and Company's Passenger and Express Line (better known as the Leavenworth and Pike's Express Company).[30]

As early as 1855, proponents of the central route to the Pacific wrote a provision into a post roads act for such a route from Independence, Missouri, to Stockton, California, via the settlement at the mouth of the Huerfano on the Upper Arkansas and the Little Salt Lake settlements on the headwaters of the Nicolet River.[31] But when the Post Office Department called for bids in the spring of 1858, the eastern terminus had been changed to Kansas (City), omitting Independence, and the settlements on the Arkansas and the Nicolet had been eliminated as points on the line "so as to convey the mails in the shortest time possible, by a proposed schedule, [which] will be considered."[32] Jacob Hall was the successful bidder in a field of six; his offer was to carry the mail in six-mule coaches (wagons) within a maximum of sixty days, beginning October 1, 1858. The official points of call on his route were Kansas City, Council Grove, Fort Union, Albuquerque, and Stockton, and his proposal was accepted on May 28 with the marginal notation *A. V. B.*[33] The initials undoubtedly were those of Aaron V. Brown, the postmaster general.

On the previous day, the same initials indicated approval of a proposal by Thomas F. Bowler, of Santa Fe, to carry the mail from Neosho, Missouri, to Albuquerque, New Mexico.[34] Congress, in 1854, had generally authorized such a post road,[35] and in 1856 provided more specifically for a route from Neosho via Spartansville and Gilstrap's Ferry to the Grand Sabine River in the Cherokee Nation, Indian Territory.[36] There is considerable obscurity about the exact location of the Neosho-Albuquerque route, which was designated as No. 10615. It may have followed the proposed post road into the Cherokee Nation, and then somewhere apparently joined the road from Fort Smith, Arkansas, to Santa Fe, which had been laid out by Captain R. B. Marcy in 1849.[37]

Bowler was one of six bidders who turned in eleven proposals. He indicated that he would carry the mail over the 850-mile course twice a month in six-mule spring coaches for $17,000 a year; the mail was to

Jared L. Sanderson
(Cragin Collection, Pioneers' Museum, Colorado Springs, Colorado)

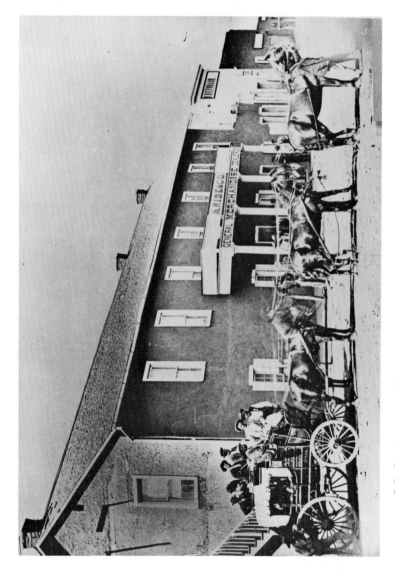

J. L. Sanderson and Co. Coach, on Main Street in Trinidad, Colorado, c. 1878
(Collection of Mr. A. R. Mitchell, Trinidad)

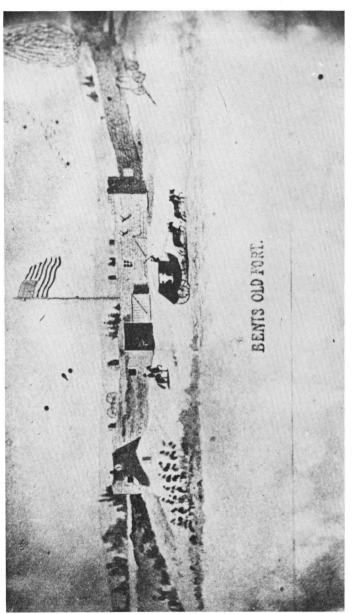

BENTS OLD FORT.

Bent's Fort. A contemporary sketch given by J. L. Sanderson
to Professor Cragin, Colorado College
(Cragin Collection, Pioneers' Museum, Colorado Springs, Colorado)

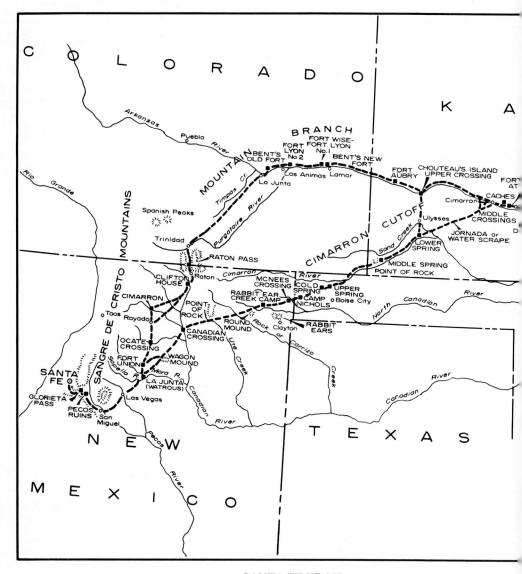

SANTA FE TRAIL

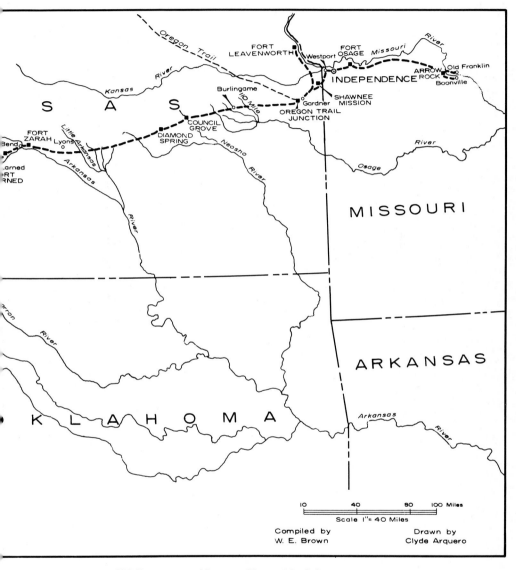

Oregon Trail

FORT
LEAVENWORTH

Kansas River

FORT
OSAGE

Missouri River

Old Franklin

Westport

ARROW
ROCK

Boonville

INDEPENDENCE

Burlingame

SHAWNEE
MISSION

Gardner

S A S

10 Mile

OREGON TRAIL
JUNCTION

COUNCIL
GROVE

DIAMOND
SPRING

FORT
ZARAH

Little Arkansas

Lyons

Neosho River

River

Bend

Larned
RT
RNED

Arkansas River

Osage

MISSOURI

arron River

ARKANSAS

K L A H O M A

Arkansas River

| 10 | 40 | 80 | 100 Miles |

Scale 1"= 40 Miles

Compiled by
W. E. Brown

Drawn by
Clyde Arquero

U.S. Department of Interior; National Park Service

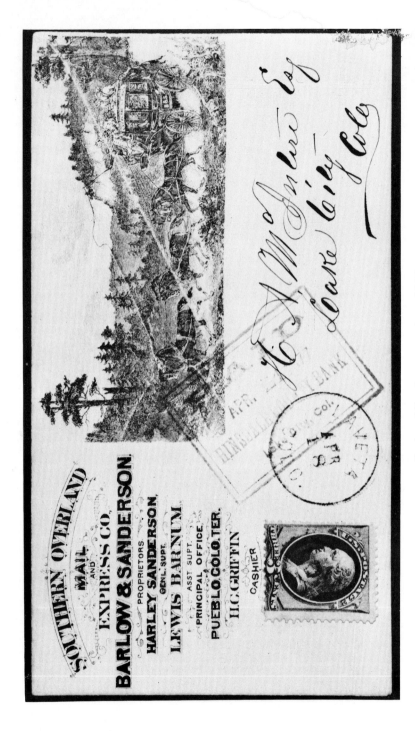

Barlow & Sanderson envelope, 1877

(Collection of William J. Little; photograph by David L. Jarrett)

Stage line postal cancellation

(Collection of N. L. Persson; photograph by David L. Jarrett)

PROSCECTUS

OF

Butterfield's Overland

DESPATCH.

MARCH, 1865.

New York:

WM. L. S. HARRISON, STEAM BOOK AND JOB PRINTER,

Nos. 80 and 82 Duane Street, near Broadway.

1865.

Prospectus of Butterfield's Overland Despatch

leave each end of the line on the 15th of the month and arrive at its destination on the 10th of the following month. October 1 was set as the starting date for the service,[38] and any mail to California brought into Albuquerque over the route would be forwarded on the Kansas City-Stockton line.[39]

Both lines were short-lived, but the one from Kansas City to Stockton had the longer span. Since Jacob Hall already held the Independence-Santa Fe contract, extension of his operations from Santa Fe to Stockton was logical. His ability to transport the two mails in the same stages to Santa Fe and back may explain why his bid was so much lower than the others. On August 14, 1858, Hall's Kansas City-Stockton contract was transferred to John E. Barrow, James Porter (Hall's partner on the Independence-Santa Fe line), and A. L. H. Crenshaw, all of Independence, with no change in the contractual terms.[40]

Service started on schedule at the Kansas City end but was a month late in starting from Stockton. The mail party left Stockton in an eight-passenger, six-mule, Concord mud-wagon, with no passengers and some fifty or sixty letters. They took no extra mules, and there were no relay stations. Fear of Indians turned them back to Fort Tejon, but the mail from Kansas City came through unscathed. Both parties went up to Stockton, reaching there on November 14.[41] For some reason, the first mail to get through from Stockton to Kansas City did not arrive until March 1, 1859.[42]

A "Kansas City and Stockton Overland Mail" left at noon on February 1, 1859. The coaches carried a heavy mail and a number of passengers in charge of M. Porter. How much of the load was left after Santa Fe and Albuquerque is not known; in fact, the run may not have been completed. Perhaps the run that left Kansas City on April 1 and reached Stockton on May 29 in just under fifty-five days is more representative. No night travel meant that a little over twenty-seven days was taken in actual travel time.[43] Somewhere along Beale's route (35th parallel) west of Albuquerque, the mail party passed the eastbound mail that arrived in Santa Fe on May 2 at 5 A.M.[44]

The eastbound mail party that left Stockton on June 1, in charge of a man named Cooper, came into Kansas City on July 23, after a fifty-one day trip (twenty-five days of travel time), nine days within the scheduled maximum.[45] There is a strong inference that the mail was carried by pack mules over part of the rugged miles between Albuquerque and Fort

Tejon. The June 1-July 23 trip from Stockton to Kansas City was the last one on that route; the *Kansas City Daily Western Journal of Commerce* noted with regret that "the best route across the continent" was being disbanded just as trouble with the Mojave Indians ended.[46] The precise number of round trips is uncertain, but their irregularity is clearly indicated by records showing only five completed from October 1858 to July 1859.[47]

The Neosho-Albuquerque line began operation as scheduled on October 15, 1858. At Neosho, in the extreme southwestern corner of Missouri, the venture was suitably launched by a big supper and numerous speeches. In charge of R. Frank Green, the mail party was guided by John Britton of Neosho, whose presence indicates just how confused most people were about just where the route lay. A San Francisco paper said Green intended to meet up with Lieutenant (Edward Fitzgerald) Beale's survey party and then follow along the 35th parallel.[48] Green's mail party and some immigrant groups joined Lieutenant Beale's expedition, which had a military escort of 130 men and two pieces of artillery, to have protection across Comanche country,[49] but it was so long before reliable word got back to Missouri that people accepted a report filtered through from New Mexico telling of the mail party's destruction by the Comanche. That brought a demand for a military post somewhere on the Canadian River to control Comanche and Kiowa.[50] Then Green and his men showed up about January 1, 1859, at Anton Chico on the Pecos River southeast of Santa Fe. Apparently the mail party was alone, having pressed on ahead of Beale's force through the most dangerous country, and at Anton Chico the mail wagons followed the left fork of the road across to Albuquerque.[51]

The volume of the October mail from Albuquerque—two letters and one newspaper—was certainly not encouraging for the line's future,[52] and it may not have reached Neosho. The November westbound mail never did get through. It consisted of four or five pounds of letters and papers and was carried by John Hall, who was alone on muleback trying to overtake Lieutenant Beale and his escort, who were eight or ten days ahead in company with Green and his mail party. Before he could catch up, Hall was attacked by about forty Comanche and severely wounded in leg and side by arrows. His mule was shot dead, and the mail was destroyed. As a prisoner he was prostrate for several weeks, and, when he recovered, he had to follow his captors about on the plains. In mid-February he escaped on an Indian horse, gaining the settlements to the east after traveling four days and nights.[53]

Apparently that was the end of service on the Neosho-Albuquerque mail route. The way was difficult and patronage was slight, so much so that a departmental order in February instructed the postmaster in St. Louis to see that document mails for New Mexico be divided to give the line its proper portion of the business.[54] Not much more could be said for the Kansas City-Stockton line in terms of investment versus revenue. Postmaster General Brown was liberal in policies of developing mail connections with the Pacific coast,[55] but his generosity was molded by pro-South sympathies and his strong antipathy for the central route. Brown's death on March 8, 1859, brought a new man to his cabinet position.

President Buchanan's second postmaster general was Joseph Holt of Kentucky, who unlike Brown was averse to uneconomical post roads, regardless of whatever else might be put forward in their favor.[56] As a part of Holt's policy of retrenchment to make the Post Office Department as nearly self-sufficient as possible, the Neosho-Albuquerque and Kansas City-Stockton mail routes were discontinued beginning July 1, 1859, although both contractors were allowed an extra month's pay to compensate for their inability to shut down that quickly.[57] The departmental orders for discontinuing the two lines were issued on May 11,[58] and a newspaper dispatch under a Washington dateline gave some idea of the late postmaster general's view of them, when it spoke of the Butterfield Overland Mail routes between Neosho and Kansas City and Stockton.[59] Brown had regarded them as part of a system that gave preeminence to the South in Pacific mail connections.

A contractual peculiarity saved the Butterfield Overland Mail from Holt's curtailments, but he slashed away at many other lines, discontinuing them altogether or reducing service and compensation. One of the hardest hit by the economies was Jacob Hall's former partner John Hockaday, who was practically ruined financially.[60]

The Independence-Santa Fe mail line was one that received Joseph Holt's approval. As far as Jacob Hall was concerned, the chief effect of the postmaster general's businesslike approach to the problems of the Department was an order to reduce the running time of Hall's line from twenty to fifteen days.[61] Hall started operating the faster timetable by August 22 and soon reported with satisfaction that the mail usually arrived within fourteen days.[62] Monday departures were retained, but at midnight rather than 8 A.M. Also, a special schedule of thirty days was allowed the contractor for book and document mail. Faster service meant greater costs for additional livestock and relay stations. To cover Hall's enlarged expenses, the Post Office Department granted him $15,000 more per annum, bringing his total compensation to $54,999.[63]

Hall and Porter's Difficult Years

1859-1860

IN THE SPRING OF 1859 there were disturbing signs that the gold rush to the Rocky Mountains was petering out. Jacob Hall, returning from a trip over his mail route, reported having passed 2,500 wagons on their way back from Pike's Peak. This discouraging trend was noted in the *Kansas City Daily Western Journal of Commerce* under the heading: "The Ebb of the Gold Tide."[1] The slowdown was not personally worrisome to Hall, of course, because Hall and Porter's mail stages did not run to the gold camps.

He was much more interested in the future implications of the removal of the Leavenworth and Pike's Peak Express Company's recently opened route from Leavenworth through Junction City, along the Republican River to the mouth of Cherry Creek. Because that company had acquired Hockaday and Liggett's unexpired Salt Lake City contract, the Post Office Department required the line to be moved father north to the Overland Trail along the Platte River.[2] The *Leavenworth Times* stated: "Some more of Jones and Russell's Pike's Peak coaches arrived in the city on Saturday. An agent has gone out on the route to break up the stations."[3]

Disillusionment over the Pike's Peak prospects was erased a short time later by news of John H. Gregory's discovery of lode gold in the mountains west of Denver City, soon augmented by reports of George A. Jackson's big placer find.[4] As the summer wore on, reports arrived of new gold strikes in the Clear Creek area west of Denver City and of an extension of the gold-producing area to South Park and the headwaters of the Arkansas and the Rio Grande[5]—information eagerly received by boosters of the Arkansas River route.

Part of the route was already experiencing an unprecedented volume of merchandise going to Santa Fe and large wool shipments coming back.[6] To clog the "best natural road in the world" with a fresh surge of gold-seekers was a pleasant thought for merchants and shippers. In praise of the Arkansas route, the Westport *Border Star* quoted the late Colonel Thomas Hart Benton[7] on its naturalness, saying that its originators, the buffalo, were the best engineers on the continent.[8]

With the probable development of gold camps and trading centers around the headwaters of the Arkansas, Hall and Porter were in a very favorable position to extend their service in that direction, especially since the Leavenworth and Pike's Peak Express line had withdrawn from the closest competitive route. It would take time to make such an arrangement, particularly to supplement the mail contract. In the meantime, their current operations took most of their attention.

That spring Hall and Porter changed some fares and rates, which are given here with the old ones noted in parentheses: through fare from November 1 to May 1, $140 ($150); from May 1 to November 1, $125 (the same); forty pounds per passenger baggage allowance, with extra baggage rate at 40 cents (35 cents in summer) per pound and 50 cents in winter. Monday departures from each end of the line were retained.[9]

Improvements along the line were always a matter of concern. The old Diamond Spring station (established by Waldo, Hall and Company) was given a post office on July 21, 1859,[10] and a company mail station was established and maintained by George Smith at Lost Spring about the same time.[11] The *Kansas City Daily Western Journal of Commerce* told its readers that Lost Spring was the first place on the Trail where travelers would find buffalo chips, the *bois de vache* so important to plains cookery.[12]

The need for frequent stations along the line was emphasized by the Post Office Department order to reduce the maximum running time from twenty to fifteen days, focusing attention on the unrelieved miles from Allison's Ranche (Walnut Creek) to Fort Union. Hall and Porter met the new schedule but at considerable cost in livestock as the extra $15,000 compensation demonstrated.

Some temporary help came that summer from the three companies of the First Cavalry camped at the site of Fort Atkinson under the command of Captain William De Saussure. And Jacob Hall was determined to set up a mail station on the Pawnee Fork of the Arkansas, about thirty-five miles west of Walnut Creek, even though the Kiowa and Comanche had clearly indicated that they would resist such an intrusion when he tried to establish one there the previous spring.[13]

Hall and Porter's conductor William Milligan, in charge of the eastbound June mail, reported a big gathering of Kiowa, Comanche, Cheyenne, and Arapaho north of the Arkansas on the Smoky Hill River. Milligan told of meeting troops about 168 miles from Kansas City at the Cottonwood mail station; the men probably were those of Captain De Saussure's force on their way from Fort Riley to the summer camp to guard the Trail against Kiowa and Comanche.[14] The suggestion of massive hostilities by Cheyenne and Arapaho is questionable; William Bent, recently appointed to be head of the Upper Arkansas Agency, remarked upon their peaceful inclinations despite their concerns about increasing white inroads.[15] Perhaps some Kiowa and Comanche chiefs were trying to pull them into an alliance against both federal troops and Texas forces,[16] an alarming possibility.

Jacob Hall persisted in his plan for a mail station on Pawnee Fork and was not deterred by the likelihood of Kiowa-Comanche violence. Postmaster General Holt agreed; his regard for efficiency made him deplore Hall's $12,000 loss in livestock because of a dearth of relay stations. Secretary of the Interior Jacob Thompson and Acting Secretary of War William R. Drinkard received letters from the postmaster general vouching for the need for a mail station on Pawnee Fork. Holt believed that the great trunk route from New Mexico to the valley of the Mississippi had to be kept open.[17] The outcome of that and other correspondence was the stationing of one of Captain De Saussure's companies on Pawnee Fork for the rest of the summer, although Colonel Sumner thought that the mail company's station at Walnut Creek was a better location for the detachment.[18]

Hall and Porter sent out seven wagons and a number of employees from Independence, in charge of William Butze,[19] to erect buildings and corrals and to cut hay beside the Pawnee Fork. But as the work party moved slowly westward, other developments changed the cast of events. Jacob Hall knew that the War Department planned to recall the troops on the Trail in Kansas to Fort Riley in the autumn, and he urged Colonel Sumner to permit the company at Pawnee Fork to remain at least until November when, hopefully, the mail station would be ready for the winter.[20] His plea was ignored, and Captain De Saussure began his withdrawal from the Fort Atkinson site on September 14, reaching Pawnee Fork on the 17th. There, Buffalo Hump and another Comanche chief, along with four or five Kiowa chiefs, came in to talk, and they agreed not to molest a mail station. De Saussure then went to talk with the major Kiowa chief, To-ha-san (Little Mountain), who was sick in his lodge near Walnut Creek. His main force (including Captain Edward W. B. Newby's company from Pawnee Fork) went on to the Big Bend of the Arkansas. De Saussure joined them there, and the entire command proceeded eastward to Cow Creek. They found a small wagon train encamped there with Major James L. Donaldson, Quartermaster's Department.

Major Donaldson and his party went on to Walnut Creek the next morning. At Allison's Ranche he learned of (or perhaps may have witnessed) threats against a couple of men by two Kiowa subchiefs, Satanke and Pawnee—said to be the brother of To-ha-san. Major Donaldson, apparently fearing an attack in force, sent an express to Captain De Saussure at Cow Creek. The messenger arrived during the night, and by 6 A.M., Captain William S. Walker with Companies G and K, First Cavalry, under orders from Captain De Saussure, reached the trading post on Walnut Creek. Donaldson's train had departed, and Pawnee, the Kiowa, had returned alone and sober. The Indian was placed under arrest, allegedly to keep him as a witness and to prevent him from warning the Kiowa of the presence of troops at Allison's place. Pawnee tried to escape on horseback and was shot to death by a young second lieutenant, who, according to military reports, gave the Kiowa ample warning to return.[21]

Captain De Saussure returned to Walnut Creek with the rest of his command on the night of September 23, after receiving a dispatch from Captain Walker. A short time later, Hall and Porter's westbound mail wagon arrived, in charge of Conductor Michael Smith, who, with his brother, Lawrence, and William Cole (no passengers) had left Independence at noon on September 19. Naturally, Conductor Smith was apprehensive when he saw the cavalrymen and learned of the shooting of Pawnee. He told De Saussure that he would turn back unless he could have an escort at least as far as Pawnee Fork. De Saussure agreed and sent First Lieutenant Elmer Otis and thirty men with the mail party the next morning. About 1 P.M. on September 24, they arrived at Pawnee Fork, where the escort left them and returned to Walnut Creek.

After eating dinner and grazing the mules, the mail party hitched up and started on their way about 4:30 P.M. Less than six miles along, the mail party was accosted by about fifteen mounted Kiowa, who galloped out of a ravine which the mail wagon had just passed. The Indians appeared friendly enough in their demands for sugar and crackers, which were given to them as was customary. But their demands became more insistent and their manner more insolent until the situation exploded into a running fight with the Kiowa. Armed as they were with guns as well as bows and arrows, the Kiowa killed the two Smiths and lost only one of their warriors. William Cole managed to escape into the tall grass, where he spent the night, and reached the cavalrymen the following morning. Lieutenant Otis and his men returned with Cole to the scene of the fight, buried Michael and Lawrence Smith, and recovered the letter mail, which they left with the postmaster at Beach Valley.[22]

The rest of the First Cavalry units under Captain De Saussure had reached Lost Spring on their way to Fort Riley. There they met the Hall and Porter work party and wagons in charge of William Butze, and they were joined by Lieutenant Otis and his men with William Cole. That night, September 30, William Butze wrote an account of the mail stage disaster for Jacob Hall. On the following night at Diamond Spring, Butze wrote again, relating an unsubstantiated report that the eastbound mail party had been destroyed. Captain De Saussure left forty men to escort the next westbound mail, in charge of Peter Kelly, as far as the crossing of the Arkansas. But Butze believed Kelly would turn back because of the dangers. The Hall and Porter foreman also said he and his men would turn back westward as far as Big Cow Creek, where he would await instructions if they had not already arrived.[23]

An army surgeon extracted a slug from William Cole's arm and dressed other wounds, and the surviving member of the three-man mail party reached Independence on the evening of October 5.[24] His eyewitness account and Butze's reports disturbed Jacob Hall, who sent a telegram to the postmaster general the next day.[25] Hall was alarmed by the rumor that the eastbound mail stage may have been lost. Aboard were his partner, Judge Porter, and A. L. H. Crenshaw (both formerly associated with the Kansas City-Stockton line), as well as Miguel A. Otero, delegate from New Mexico to the Thirty-sixth Congress, with his family, and Judge John S. Watts, with his son and family, of Santa Fe.[26]

The missing mail stage to Independence did get through, late but safe, on October 9. Conductor Matthew Kelly and four hands had been responsible for the mail and the distinguished passengers. Hall learned that they reached Big Coon Creek, on the other side of Pawnee Fork, ahead of schedule. There they met a train of Mexican buffalo hunters, from whom they learned of the recent killing of the Smiths at a point not far ahead. One of the hunters recognized Otero and told him of Kiowa threats to kill all Americans. That information brought a decision to accompany the hunters back along the Trail until they met an eastbound Majors, Russell and Company[27] train, which they had passed. They accompanied the wagon train for five days before they felt safe enough to push ahead on their own. During that slow progress, they found the bodies of three murdered Pike's Peakers beside the road, presumably victims of the Kiowa.[28]

Later it was learned that the westbound mail had reached Santa Fe without mishap. Conductor Peter Kelly did not turn back as William Butze had predicted. James Brice was a helper on that trip.[29]

Indian Agent William Bent believed that the attacks on the mail party and the Pike's Peakers were "solely attributable" to the killing of the Kiowa, Pawnee, at Walnut Creek.[30] But valid as Bent's explanation probably was, the killing appeared to Jacob Hall in Independence as simple proof of the need for military escorts on the Santa Fe road. Hall strongly urged the Post Office Department and the military to provide escorts, and he got results.[31]

His cause was supported by a letter to Secretary of War J. B. Floyd from one of Missouri's representatives in Congress, Samuel H. Woodson, who happened to be in his home town of Independence when William Cole and the delayed mail stage bearing Delegate Otero reached there. Woodson informed the secretary of war that plains tribes on both sides of the Arkansas were said to be hostile and posed a grave threat to the annual $1,500,000 commerce with New Mexico involving about 5,000 American citizens. As the representative of a part of the country vitally concerned with that trade, Woodson called for an adequate number of troops and military posts along the more exposed portions of the route. He suggested that Allison's trading post had sufficient corrals and living quarters for troops, which could be used free of charge for the winter.[32]

In St. Louis, Colonel Sumner reacted quickly by informing Jacob Hall, in a letter dated October 4, that a company of cavalry would be sent back to Pawnee Fork.[33] Then he ordered Captain De Saussure, who had not

yet gone into Fort Riley, to station a company on Pawnee Fork indef-
initely and to arrange for supplies to be sent out from Fort Riley.[34] In a
letter directly to De Saussure, Sumner ordered, "If you should hear that
any of the murderers of the mail party are within striking distance, make
a dash at them."[35]

The failure of Michael Smith's mail party to reach Santa Fe also had
repercussions there, causing Colonel B. L. E. Bonneville, commanding
the Department of New Mexico, to issue orders for a thirty-five man
escort, in charge of Lieutenant Andrew Jackson, to guard the next mail
stage leaving Fort Union for Independence. He was to stay with it as far
as he thought necessary, or until he should meet the incoming mail.
Vague reports of trouble on the Arkansas resulted in an increase in the
escort to fifty men with extra provisions and additional instructions to
aid any wagon trains that might be in danger.[36]

A few days before the flurry of military correspondence between Santa
Fe and Fort Union, a Hall and Porter mail stage in charge of J. W. Woodruff left the fort for Independence. Woodruff reached Cold Spring on the
Cimarron Cutoff without meeting the westbound mail. His concern was
strengthened at the spring when he learned, probably from a wagon train,
of the killings near Pawnee Fork. Responsible not only for the mail but
also for his passengers (three men, a woman, and two children), he returned to Fort Union. When an incoming mail (probably Peter Kelly's)
reached there on October 19, Conductor Woodruff decided to try again.
By this time, three eastbound mails had accumulated. Woodruff's mail
wagons were accompanied by seventy-five troopers of the Regiment of
Mounted Riflemen under the command of Captain Robert M. Morris.[37]

One of Woodruff's three male passengers was a representative of the
Westport mercantile firm of J. and W. R. Bernard and Company, T. K.
McCutchen, who kept an account of the journey. It was toward the end
of the season for commercial traffic on the Trail, and the trains headed
for Fort Union, Las Vegas, and Santa Fe were probably making their
last trip from the States. The Woodruff party met a westbound mail stage
at Cottonwood Creek or Spring.[38] Accompanying the mail party was Colonel Thomas T. Fauntleroy, First Dragoons, who was on his way to take
command of the Military Department of New Mexico from Colonel
Bonneville. Their combined train consisted of eight wagons, four carriages, eighty mules, and twenty-five mounted troopers. Members of the
party included Captain John Porter Hatch and Captain George McLane

(both of the Mounted Riflemen), with their families, who were probably headed for Fort Union.[39]

Colonel Fauntleroy and his entourage had witnessed a violent and unusual incident near the Dry Cimarron a short time before. They had seen a party of five Kiowa, who rode parallel to the train in a friendly enough fashion about three-quarters of a mile away. A young employee of the mail company, who was riding a mule beside the wagon, suddenly dashed off in the direction of the Indians, who, apparently frightened by his precipitate approach, shot and killed him after he had fired at them first.[40] One version says he wanted to persuade the Kiowa to come and talk with Fauntleroy; when they refused, the young man drew a pistol and they killed him with arrows.[41]

When Fauntleroy's train met the eastbound mail escorted by Captain Morris and his men, the colonel immediately assumed command of the department without waiting for formalities with Colonel Bonneville in Santa Fe. He modified Morris's orders to relieve him of escort duty to return to Fort Union. Lieutenant Andrew Jackson was ordered to continue with thirty-five men as escort for the eastbound mail to the Arkansas River, if necessary, or at least until he might meet the westbound mail south of the river.[42]

Conductor Woodruff's mail wagons then resumed their eastward journey. Lieutenant Jackson and his men halted at the Arkansas, and the mail party went on alone to Pawnee Fork, where they found a company of the First Cavalry under Captain George N. Steuart, along with a Hall and Porter work party (presumably William Butze's), busily building a small fortification and a mail station. Steuart was having problems with escorts for mail stages; grass was poor and the forage from Fort Riley almost gone, so he was sending escorts out in wagons to conserve the dwindling forage. One of the wagon-escorts took Woodruff's mail party east to Cow Creek.[43]

A westbound Hall and Porter mail stage was waiting at Cow Creek to go with the returning escort to Pawnee Fork. Woodruff took his three passengers and three overdue mails into Independence, arriving there on November 9. It was then revealed that also on board was $2,000 in gold for J. and W. R. Bernard and Company of Westport, which had been shipped from Denver via Fort Union.[44] That cargo may have had something to do with Woodruff's extreme reluctance to travel the dangerous stretches without escort, and it certainly must have made businessmen more aware of the possible advantages of a more direct connection with the gold camps up the Arkansas River.

The military and mail installations on Pawnee Fork partially fulfilled Jacob Hall's prerequisites for a safer and more efficient operation of the Independence-Santa Fe mail. The government, however, showed no signs of complying with his proposal for another military post on the "upper Simeron,"[45] apparently meaning the Dry Cimarron. But the vacillating policy of the War Department and the shock of the killings near Pawnee Fork delayed mail and passenger service, which in turn generated public impatience.

Not all public criticism was directed at the mail contractor. One feature article dwelt sympathetically on the high cost of operation—$52,000 per annum, which someone figured out to be $65 per mile.[46] No basis was given for the total figure. Hall's contract currently called for $39,-999.[47] A few days later the same paper published a complaint about the delays, not blaming the contractor, Indians, or the weather, but the Democratic administration of President James Buchanan. However, a letter from Santa Fe published in the Westport paper assumed that the contractor did not care about the disruptions since he received his pay anyway.[48] None of the criticism was substantial, but it revealed the state of public information and ignorance.

The next mail from Santa Fe departed on October 24. Upon reaching Fort Union, the conductor learned that the previous mail (Woodruff's) had left under escort only three days before. The conductor hoped to overtake them, but when he reached Mud Creek, fifty miles out from the fort, he heard from someone on the Trail that Woodruff was at least 100 miles ahead. With no chance of overtaking Woodruff before reaching the Arkansas, the conductor returned to Fort Union. At the post was Captain John N. Macomb with a small party of Topographical Engineers about to leave in the direction of Pawnee Fork. The captain had laid out a road between Santa Fe and Fort Union, going through San Jose, Tecolote, and Las Vegas, widening it from a single track to thirty-three feet, macadamizing a steep hill near Tecolote and bridging an arroyo in Apache Canyon with an eighteen-foot span.[49] Hall and Porter's man decided to accompany the small military unit.

Macomb, however, had to stop near the crossing of the Cimarron for several days in connection with his work. The mail party and others who had joined the group went on by themselves. They traveled along the

Cimarron Cutoff for three days without incident, but on the third night they were attacked by Indians. The red men were repelled, but the mail party and the others hastily returned to Captain Macomb and his men and stayed with them as they moved slowly toward Pawnee Fork. November 24 was the date of their arrival at the mail station and the small post[50] that had been named Camp on Pawnee Fork.[51]

The westbound mail to Santa Fe was also disrupted.[52] One of Hall and Porter's November stages, however, made it through in a somewhat unorthodox way. James Brice, by then a conductor, asked for a military escort from Camp on Pawnee Fork but was told by Lieutenant David Bell, second in command, that he did not have men to spare.[53] One company of the First Cavalry at the camp was a small garrison, half of whom were constantly engaged in escort duty. Captain Steuart was evidently with an escort when Brice's stage arrived. The rest of the garrison could not be spared from caring for the horses, cutting hay, and constructing sod quarters for the winter.[54]

Apparently there was a fair chance that Mounted Riflemen from Fort Union would be waiting at the Cimarron Crossing, so Brice decided to go on without an escort. It was his luck that no cavalrymen greeted him at the crossing. Brice was hesitant to go back to Camp on Pawnee Fork, but he was not pleased at the thought of trying the Cimarron Cutoff alone. In a state of great indecision, he took his mail party across the Arkansas and headed down the cutoff. He thought better of it after a short distance and returned to the north bank of the river. Then he decided to follow the Mountain, or Bent's Fort, Branch of the Santa Fe Trail over the Raton Pass to Fort Union.[55]

In other words, on that trip Brice used the old military road of 1846, which had also known express riders and some freighters, as well as mountain men and Indian traders. In his recollections, Brice cited a few of the features along the route, first mentioning Pleasant Encampment, which was also known as Pretty Encampment.[56] Then came Sand Creek —seven years later the scene, upstream, of the Sand Creek Massacre of the Cheyenne and Arapaho. Bent's New Fort, on its low bluff on the north side of the Arkansas, was headquarters for the Upper Arkansas Indian Agency. Thirty-five miles west of there, Brice forded the river near Bent's Old Fort.[57] He probably stopped at Iron Spring and then, after about fifty miles, forded the "Picket Wire" (Purgatoire) at the site of present-day Trinidad, Colorado. From there, he crossed the "Ratone" Mountains

(Pass) to Maxwell's Ranch on the Rayado. Below Maxwell's place he came to Calhoun's Ranch at the crossing of Ocate Creek, and six miles north of Fort Union his mail stage came to the junction with the "regular mail route." Brice reached both Fort Union and Santa Fe on schedule, with the distinction of being the first man to take a regular mail stage, although unofficially, over the Mountain Branch of the Trail.[58]

Inclement weather caused one of the eastbound November mail stages to take a month to make the trip, and the party brought in a report that some troops had been withdrawn from Camp on Pawnee Fork, meaning there would be no more escorts for the mails or anyone else from that point east.[59] That was not quite accurate. Captain Steuart with part of the little garrison had returned to Fort Riley. Lieutenant Bell was left at Camp on Pawnee Fork with only thirty men.[60] He did the best he could under such severe limitations, informing his superiors that he could provide an escort for the entire distance from Cow Creek to the Cimarron Crossing only once every two weeks.[61]

Because of the restricted escort duty, Hall and Porter vehicles bunched up at Pawnee Fork. Colonel Sumner requested that Hall and Porter temporarily cut their service from weekly to semimonthly;[62] that happened anyway when Lieutenant Bell furnished an escort every two weeks from Pawnee Fork to the crossing of the Arkansas.[63] The camp was in good condition with an adequate corral, sufficient hay for the winter, and comfortable sod quarters for the men.[64] What Bell needed was more men. In December he was informed that a detachment of twenty men from the Second Infantry at Fort Riley was on its way in three six-mule wagons with rations and forage, all in charge of a lieutenant.[65]

Part of the problem was the uncertainty of meeting cavalry detachments from Fort Union at the crossing of the Arkansas. An escort from Pawnee Fork accompanied Conductor J. W. Woodruff's mail stage arriving at the Cimarron Crossing on November 28, only to find that the Fort Union escort had gone back down the Cimarron Cutoff two days before. Woodruff decided to try to overtake it, which he did sixty miles along. The escort was composed of seventeen Mounted Riflemen. The mail stage had gone another eighty miles with them, and all were camped at Cold Spring, when about midnight they were attacked by Kiowa— estimates ranged from twenty to a hundred. The fight continued intermittently until daybreak, when the Kiowa, having sustained several losses, withdrew among the rocks and hills. There were no casualties in the mail party, and only one trooper was slightly wounded.[66]

On his return trip to Independence, Conductor Woodruff decided to follow the lead of his colleague James Brice and avoid the dangers of the Cimarron Cutoff by taking the Mountain Branch of the Trail. The detour was without notable incident, except that the party had a chance to admire the distant view of Pike's Peak from the top of the Raton Pass.[67] Apparently, Woodruff was the first man to take a regular mail stage northward on the Mountain Branch of the Santa Fe Trail. The driver was a former Ohioan and Wells Fargo employee, Henry George.[68]

Change of Hands, Change of Route

1860-1861

DURING THE SPRING OF 1860, the mail service between Fort Union and Camp Alert—the new name for Camp on Pawnee Fork after February 1, 1860[1]—was very poor, despite Lieutenant David Bell's efforts to regularize it. Six late mails arrived together in Independence on April 4, and the conductors said they saw no Indians en route.[2] On that same date, near the other end of the line, a train of nineteen wagons belonging to Ceran St. Vrain left Mora, New Mexico (north of Las Vegas), and arrived at Westport on May 8. They encountered no Indians, yet on the entire trip they saw only one mail party, moving slowly with a military escort.[3] A mail came into Independence from Pawnee Fork on May 22, but it had nothing from west of the little post and mail station.

Seven weekly mails were overdue from Santa Fe, and exasperation was growing rapidly among those in the Missouri towns waiting for letters, newspapers, and packages. They reacted with rising tempers to continued reports that no Indians had been seen along the Santa Fe road.

Criticism had been mounting for six months. As early as December 1, 1859, a disgusted resident of Santa Fe had written that "no ox trains have come in for the last three weeks and therefore no mail."[4] By May 1860, citizens were saying flatly that there was no reason for the delay since the Indians were not active.[5] Some of the anger may have come from public knowledge that on January 31 the Post Office Department approved an additional compensation of $15,000 to Jacob Hall, retroactive to the previous August.[6] At any rate, Judge Porter said that he would do everything he could to put the mails through on time. He laid the blame on timid drivers and said that "men of more grit have been employed."[7] It is not known whether that explanation was valid.

Probably some of the castigation of the mail company was unfair. Certainly the absence of Indians may have been partly attributable to the presence of military escorts and to wagon trains large enough that the Indians would not dare to attack. That the War Department did not have enough troops on the scene to move the mails quickly and regularly was hardly the fault of Hall and Porter.

The perils and problems of mail transportation on the Santa Fe route that spring and sumer were not unusual or spectacular enough to elicit general interest and attention. The public gaze was fixed upon the central route to the Pacific, where the exciting experiment of the Pony Express achieved success and fame, only to be replaced about eighteen months later by the much faster but less appealing transcontinental telegraph wires. But along the Arkansas and the Cimarron Cutoff, events continued on their more prosaic but scarcely less important course.

The War Department did not regard the Kiowa and Comanche as pacified. A campaign was ordered against them as soon as spring grass was adequate, and a force under Major John Sedgwick, First Cavalry, assembled at the post on Pawnee Fork—renamed again and called Fort Larned.[8] His command included four companies of the First Cavalry and two companies of the Second Dragoons. They made a sweep south to the North Fork of the Canadian and along it to a point south of Bent's New Fort. From there they moved north to the Cimarron and on to the Arkansas just above Chouteau's Island.[9] In their 500-mile June swing they saw no Kiowa or Comanche.[10] In July, however, a smaller cavalry force did attack a band of Kiowa on the Arkansas above Bent's New Fort, killing two Indians and taking some prisoners.[11]

In June 1860, the War Department made an important decision about matters along the Arkansas route west of the Cimarron Crossing. A new fort was ordered at Big Timbers, and even before its precise location was determined, supplies were rolling toward the general locale. It was not long before it was known that the still unbuilt post was to be named Fort Wise, in honor of Governor Henry A. Wise of Virginia. Fifty wagons belonging to Alexander Majors left Kansas City for Big Timbers on June 25, with a stop scheduled at Topeka to load corn for the new post. In early August, he sent out twenty-five wagons, and later that month both Majors and J. C. Irwin and Company sent out twenty-five corn-laden wagons each.[12]

Finally, Major Sedgwick, with four companies of the First Cavalry arrived, and on September 1 a site was chosen a short distance west of Bent's New Fort.[13] At the time of ground-breaking on the distant upper Arkansas, the nation was gripped by a divisive political campaign in which Abraham Lincoln and the young Republican Party were hoping for a November victory over the split Democrats and a third party challenge.

Certain Kansas City interests pointed out that Hall and Porter were part of a California connection that gave the town quicker communication with the West Coast than did the southern Butterfield Overland Mail Line. Mail and express from California could be transferred from the Butterfield line at El Paso to mail stages for Santa Fe operated by the mercantile and freighting firm of Elsberg and Amberg,[14] whose wagons were well known on the Santa Fe Trail. Hall and Porter mail stages from Santa Fe brought the weekly mail into Independence sometimes as much as ten days ahead of that brought by the Overland California into St. Louis and from there back west to Kansas City.[15] Daily service linking Independence and Kansas City was provided by the Missouri Stage Company, whose coach left Kansas City every afternoon upon the arrival of the Missouri River steam packet of the Hannibal and St. Joseph Railroad Company.[16]

The new post of Fort Wise on the upper Arkansas was an added inducement to Hall and Porter's germinating plans for a major change in the route to Santa Fe. The firm proposed to the postmaster general that they shift their service to the Mountain Branch of the Santa Fe Trail with a running schedule of thirteen days and twenty-two hours. Included in their projection was an extension of a branch line to Colorado City, hopefully with a parallel expansion of Jacob Hall's mail contract.[17] That settlement (later named Colorado Springs) seemed to be a key connection for the gold camps of the Pike's Peak and upper Arkansas regions.[18] Their abandonment of the Cimarron Cutoff would deprive no community of mail service.

Their plans were complicated by a degree of competition with Russell, Majors and Waddell's Central Overland California and Pike's Peak Express Company, successor to the Leavenworth and Pike's Peak Express Company,[19] and the Western Stage Company, both of which operated into Denver from the northeast via Julesburg and the South Platte River.[20] Here was an example of Missouri River town rivalries for control of contacts with the Rocky Mountain gold regions. Colorado City had a weekly mail connection north to Denver City through a Post Office Department contract with Harmon G. Weibling dated June 16, 1860.[21] And Hall and Porter, as well as other boosters of the Arkansas River route, hoped to divert some of the business going through Denver to the "best natural road in the world."

In August, criticism of Hall and Porter's service flared again. The editor of the *Council Grove Press* (the *Kansas Press* renamed) termed it a "nuisance." His dissatisfaction stemmed from a schedule change which he claimed made it impossible to correlate publication of his paper with mail stage arrivals from the West.[22] Departures at each end of the line changed from Monday at midnight to Saturday at midnight, effective August 3.[23] The *Santa Fe Weekly Gazette* declared several months later that Hall and Porter were "culpably negligent in transporting the mails across the plains during the winter season."[24]

Indian interference and violence occurred at widely separate points in the last four months of 1860. In the southern part of New Mexico Territory at Ojo del Muerto on the Santa Fe-El Paso line, Indians killed the stage driver and his assistant in September.[25] And at about the same time in Kansas Territory, some Kiowa destroyed Peacock's Ranch (formerly Allison's) on Walnut Creek.[26]

In December, Santa Fe's Postmaster Whiting, a through passenger to Independence, reported that the unescorted mail party was stopped by thirty Comanche, well armed with rifles, at McNees' Creek on the Cimarron Cutoff. Nobody was hurt, and after about an hour the stage was allowed to go on. Conductor Coon decided that the wisest course, however, was to join a wagon train which they had passed a few miles back. Whiting also said that between McNees' Creek and Pawnee Fork it was common to see Indians on the high ridges every day, and he found that the westbound mail had turned back to Pawnee Fork because of the danger.[27]

Two days before Christmas 1860, critics and well-wishers in Kansas City and Independence read a public announcement that Hall and Porter had sold their vehicles and livestock for carrying "the great Santa Fe Mail" to the Missouri Stage Company headed by Preston Roberts, Jr. Within a fortnight the change was general knowledge in Santa Fe. The *Daily Kansas City Journal of Commerce* also asserted that Hall's unexpired mail contract went to the Missouri Stage Company, but that was an error.[28] The contract was not reassigned, and Jacob Hall was the sole contractor for the Independence-Santa Fe mail until his contract expired in 1862.[29] He undoubtedly received financial consideration for working with the Missouri Stage Company.

Preston Roberts, Jr., was a man of ample experience in the transportation business. In 1844, at the age of nineteen, he was manager of his father's stage routes based in Steubenville, Ohio, and then he engaged in Ohio River shipping at Cincinnati, becoming part owner and captain of a river steamer. Following that he developed the first boat line from New Orleans to Montgomery, Alabama, via Mobile. It was in 1857 that he became interested in mail contracts in southern and western states, and his successful bid of $9,349 to carry the daily Independence-St. Joseph mail in four-horse coaches was accepted on April 24, 1858.[30]

Expansion was the keynote under Roberts' direction. In the summer of 1859, the Missouri Stage Company inaugurated a new line of stages from Kansas City via Independence, Liberty, and Plattsburg to Osborn, where connections were made with the Hannibal and St. Joseph Railroad and the Northern Missouri Railroad. That combination of railroad and stagecoach made it possible for mail and newspapers from St. Louis to reach Kansas City in twenty-four hours. Fare for the fifty-six mile trip to Osborn was $4.[31] From Independence, the company also had a line to Wilmington, Lexington, Dover, Jonesboro, and Boonesville—a run of 136 miles for $6.[32] And the Missouri Stage Company offered special conveniences; in September, 1860, for example, it advertisd two daily coaches between Kansas City and Independence, where a week-long fair was being held. Round trip was $1.50, with the return from Independence to be at any time suitable to the patrons.[33]

Takeover of the Independence-Santa Fe line was a major enlargement, and the Missouri Stage Company immediately announced that it would also establish an express connection up the Arkansas with Canon City, Tarryall, Colorado City, and Denver City in the extreme western part of Kansas Territory, a plan comparable to Hall and Porter's. The branch line was planned to be competitive with the Platte route in the express business to the mountain mining camps, but regular U.S. mail service westward from the Cimarron Crossing of the Arkansas would have to wait until a contract could be secured to cover the extension. The circumstances are not clear, but evidently Preston Roberts sought financial assistance to develop his plans. Associated with him was W. G. Barkley, of the Trail freighting firm of McCarty and Barkley, Kansas City.[34]

The new management and the old mail contractor had to cope with recurring Indian hostilities. Conductor William Basham brought in the Santa Fe mail for the Missouri Stage Company on January 23, 1861, after a rugged trip of twenty-three days. His most exciting news was of a six-hour fight at Cimarron Springs, on the Cimarron Cutoff, involving the Kiowa and units of the Regiment of Mounted Riflemen under Lieutenant Colonel George B. Crittenden, commandant at Fort Union.[35] According to Basham, only four soldiers were wounded, while probably fifty to seventy-five Kiowa warriors were killed.[36] His version differs markedly from official reports.

Other accounts put the scene of action about ten miles north of Cold Spring, which, as an estimated distance, could have been near Upper Cimarron Spring. Colonel Crittenden and his detachment of eighty-eight Mounted Riflemen surprised a Kiowa-Comanche village of about 175 lodges on January 2, 1861. As often happened, the biggest discrepancies involved reported casualties; official figures showed three cavalrymen injured, and the Indian losses were given as at least ten dead and an unknown number wounded,[37] instead of fifty to seventy-five killed.

Indian troubles on the Cimarron Cutoff made the Mountain Branch of the Santa Fe Trail more attractive as a possible mail route, although there was no guarantee that Indians would not menace that road. As a matter of fact, Colonel Crittenden and his force had left Fort Union because of a report that Kiowa and Comanche were showing hostility on the Mountain Branch about seventy miles to the north. But when they arrived, they found that the combined bands had moved eastward to the Cimarron Cutoff.[38]

A short time later, the *Canon City Times,* published in that little Arkansas River mining town, carried an item about a fight with Arapaho along the middle reaches of the "Picket-Wah" (Purgatoire) River, where the Mountain Branch passed. The story was picked up by the *Daily Kansas City Western Journal of Commerce,* which told its readers that troops from Fort Wise had killed twelve Arapaho near the Raton Mountains, with the loss of one soldier.[39] Since the post returns of Fort Wise show no troops on detached service on the Purgatoire at that time and no record of an officer or enlisted man wounded or killed,[40] the story is questionable.

The Mountain Branch of the Trail sometimes presented another kind of problem to anyone concerned with keeping a regular time schedule. Snow in the Raton Mountains could stop all traffic. Alexander Majors found that out in December 1860 when four of his wagon trains bogged down in it with more than 300 tons of provisions and groceries for the Fort Union and civilian markets. The wagons were left under guard, and Majors returned to Fort Wise with the oxen until the grip of winter eased.[41]

A powerful influence in favor of an official mail service along the upper Arkansas was the collective voice of the garrison at Fort Wise, and Major Sedgwick was active in promoting the change of route.[42] The government finally consented, and on February 14, 1861, Preston Roberts, Jr., announced that the Post Office Department had approved the route change to include the new military post. He also announced that his company would be prepared by the end of the month to begin operating its express line from Kansas City and Independence up the Arkansas to the gold diggings.[43]

Roberts's press release followed a departmental order of February 7 for the change, which added eighty-seven miles to the Independence-Santa Fe line by way of the Mountain Branch of the Trail instead of the Cimarron Cutoff. For the new arrangement, additional compensation of $5,000 was allowed, bringing the total annual figure to $65,695, but there was no change in the contractual running time of fifteen days. Service over the Mountain Branch began at each end of the line with the February 16 departures, and the two mail stages reached Fort Wise—a quadrangle of mud and stone buildings without exterior wall or stockade —on the same day, February 22. The stage from Santa Fe was accompanied by a military escort. Dr. F. B. Culver boarded the stage, headed for Washington with a copy of the Treaty of Fort Wise.[44]

Just four days before the Missouri Stage Company made its first runs into Fort Wise, Arapaho and Cheyenne chiefs signed a treaty there, giving up claims to the high plains country except in the wide angle between the Sandy Fork (Big Sandy or Sand Creek), a northern tributary of the Arkansas, and the southern tributary known as the Purgatoire. The western edge of the reservation was set as a north-south line five miles east of the junction of the Huerfano River with the Arkansas. Colonel Albert G. Boone, grandson of Daniel Boone and Indian agent for the Upper Arkansas Agency,[45] and Dr. F. B. Culver, commissioner and special agent, signed for the government.[46] Together with agreements Boone had concluded earlier with Kiowa and Comanche,[47] the treaty gave added attraction and a false sense of security to the Mountain Branch route.[48]

Ten days after the negotiations with some of the Arapaho and Cheyenne bands, the Congress of the United States passed the Organic Act of February 28, 1861, creating Colorado Territory.[49] Not only did Fort Wise come within the boundaries of the new Territory, but the northern boundary of New Mexico was placed at the 37th parallel instead of the 38th, so that the Mountain Branch of the Santa Fe Trail now crossed into New Mexico about at the crest of the Raton Pass.

Employees of the Missouri Stage Company along the Arkansas River renovated stage stations or built new ones, completing the work as far as Bent's Old Fort by mid-February.[50] It is probable that the Missouri Stage Company also set up the Iron Spring stage station, about forty miles south of Bent's Old Fort, in early 1861. About forty-seven miles beyond that, James S. Gray, a Kentuckian, settled on the Purgatoire at the mouth of the Rito San Lorenzo (Gray Creek) in April 1861. Gray's Ranch, about four miles east of the site of Trinidad, Colorado, became a stage station in July.[51] Near the south end of the Raton Pass, at Willow Spring, the government had established a forage station in 1860, and it was used by the stage line as a water stop.[52] The Iron Spring station and Gray's Ranch significantly narrowed the uninhabited stretch of the Mountain Branch of the Trail. The distance from Gray's Ranch to Lucien B. Maxwell's place at Cimarron, north of Rayado, was about sixty-seven miles.

Promoters of Canon City, the settlement on the Arkansas River at the foot of the mountains, expected the little town to provide services to nearby mining camps similar to those provided by Denver City and Colorado City. They were elated by the change of the Santa Fe mail route and by the plans of the Missouri Stage Company to run a branch express line to their town.[53] The States seemed much closer to them when they learned that the regular mail from Santa Fe made it from Fort Wise to Kansas City in only six days.[54] Running time was calculated from Fort Wise, because it was the closest post office on the main Independence-Santa Fe line.

Until the spring of 1861, communication with Canon City was mainly by the northern route via Denver City and Colorado City. The connection was not very reliable, and the editor of the *Canon Times* complained on one occasion that twenty-five sacks of mail were still stranded at Jules-burg, probably with his newspaper exchanges among them.[55] A pony express between Canon City and Denver was maintained at that time by Messrs. McGregor and Evans, leaving every Monday morning from Canon City and arriving from Denver every Saturday night.[56]

The lack of regular transportation of express packages and passengers was overcome in late October 1860, when a four-horse coach began operations between the two places.[57] In about a month arrangements were made for the coach from Canon City to connect with a line already running between Colorado City and Denver, for which Harmon G. Weib-ling had the mail contract.[58] Miller and Evans, proprietors of the express coach, announced on December 1 that "having made arrangements with the well-known Express company of Hinkley & Co., we are now prepared to transport gold dust and light freight to and from Canon City to any part of the United States or Europe at reduced rates." This ambitious service was to be by means of Miller and Evans' Friday coach to Colorado City, making connection the same day with a coach of Harrison's line to Denver. Passengers and freight could leave Denver for Canon City every Friday from the office of Hinkley and Company.[59]

All that pull to the north did not give Canon City the more direct east-ern connections which its business interests wanted, nor did it provide the closer contact with New Mexico wanted by enterprising men in both Denver and Canon City. The big gap in connections began at the Ar-kansas River. As early as January 11, 1860, Denver's *Rocky Mountain News* confessed surprise that no one had established an express line join-ing Auraria and Denver with Santa Fe by way of Colorado City, Foun-tain City (Pueblo's predecessor), Taos, Las Vegas, and Fort Union. There were arrivals in Denver from New Mexico nearly every day by private conveyance, and the paper expressed the opinion that nearly everyone would prefer to use a comfortable line of hacks. Best of all, such an express line would reduce the distance for mail from Denver to Santa Fe to 500 miles. The current route was 1,600 miles, because the mail went from Denver to the States and then by overland mail (the Independence-Santa Fe line) to Santa Fe.[60]

Mail contact with New Mexico was not entirely lacking, but it was neither public nor regular. Private travelers sometimes carried letters, and military expresses often brought letters and newspapers. On the evening of March 19, 1861, a military express from Santa Fe to Denver brought a March 9 edition of the *Santa Fe Gazette,* a total of only ten days in transit instead of the usual forty required to go to Missouri and then to Denver on the Platte River route, if one patronized the Post Office Department. Faster delivery of newspaper exchanges was a boon to an editor, and the greatly shortened time was a convenience to people along the route from Denver to "the Mexican towns."[61] That express came up through Fort Union and Fort Wise; there was another which came eastward over the Sangre de Cristo Pass from Fort Garland to Canon City, where it made weekly connection with the private pony express northward to Denver.[62]

The kind of service that Canon City wanted, however, was transportation of mail, passengers, and express as directly as possible to and from New Mexico and the States. For those actively promoting it, an express line up the Arkansas was preliminary to establishment of a regular mail route. So, when it was reported that Colonel A. G. Boone had returned from Washington with commissions for postmasters along the Arkansas route, attainment of the goal seemed to be in sight.[63]

But matters did not move that quickly, and, as it turned out, a semi-competitive development emerged before the stage connection with the east was established. A public meeting, sponsored by community business interests, promoted a semiweekly Pony Express between Canon City and Denver. Operating on a fourteen-hour schedule, the Pony Express also connected at Canon City with the military express to Fort Garland and the private express to the mining camps. The Canon City editor observed that "this is a fast age, and our citizens should do all they can for an enterprise so prolific of good." Agents for the new Pony Express were St. James and Waggaman, whose offices were at the warehouse of A. Majors, the freighter.[64]

The same agents represented the stage company when the first express coach finally rolled into Canon City on the afternoon of Monday, May 13, 1861. Four white mules pulled the vehicle on that special occasion. Only two passengers were aboard, but the *Canon City Times* hastened to predict that the stage was the forerunner of full coaches that would begin to arrive weekly from the States. That night the "grand festivities" were capped by a "splendid fete" at the Jenks House. A buffet in the supper room, hung with evergreens, was succeeded by dancing until dawn.[65]

The only notable change in the proposed Canon City-Kansas City connection, now a reality, was in proprietorship. The new firm of Slemmons,

Roberts and Company took over from the Missouri Stage Company. Mail contractor Jacob Hall was evidently active in the change of control, but the interrelationships are obscure. It is a matter of record that Hall, as of April 25, 1861, asked that his correspondence be addressed to him in care of Samuel Slemmons, of Cadiz, Harrison County, Ohio. Preston Roberts, Jr., the former head of the Missouri Stage Company, also continued his business interest. The new man, Slemmons, was very much involved at the time in mail route contracts in Missouri and Kansas.[66]

Expansion by Slemmons, Roberts and Company brought a new, descriptively inclusive name to the enterprise—the Kansas City, Santa Fe and Canon City Fast Line. Bent's Old Fort was the division point where connections could be made for all points in New Mexico and for Kansas City and all eastern lines, with the U.S. Express Company mentioned specifically. Coaches left Canon City every Friday at 4 A.M.[67] An advertisement at the eastern end of the line proclaimed departures "for Pike's Peak, New Mexico & Arizona" by means of the Kansas City, Santa Fe and Canon City Fast Line, carrying express and U.S. Mail along the Arkansas River, "the best natural road in the world." The line was prepared to carry gold dust and valuable packages. In Santa Fe connections could be made for western Texas and Arizona, and from Canon City express coaches ran to California Gulch and Denver City.[68]

Although Kansas City was advertised as the eastern terminus, the prevailing mail contract was still Jacob Hall's secured in 1858, for the Independence-Santa Fe route.[69] The first eastbound stage left Canon City on Friday, May 17, with two passengers, a heavy mail, and $7,000 in valuables. The mail included 500 letters (100 of them for Kansas City) and uncounted newspapers, including the *Canon City Times* edition describing the appearance of the line's first coach there. The trip from Canon City took less than eight days.[70] The second Kansas City departure of Slemmons, Roberts and Company's Kansas City, Santa Fe, and Canon City Fast Line was on the same date, May 17, with five passengers. It is not known if they were through passengers to Canon City or Santa Fe.[71]

As far as Council Grove, on the more heavily settled eastern portion of the line, Slemmons, Roberts and Company put on a semiweekly express coach, leaving Kansas City and Independence on Mondays and Fridays and returning from Council Grove on Tuesdays and Fridays. The towns benefiting from the more frequent service were Olathe, Gardner, McCarnish, Union Town, Lanesfield, Black Jack, Willow Springs, Burlingame, Havanna, and Wilmington, in addition to Council Grove, Independence, and Kansas City.

Safety and quality of service were stressed by telling the public that Slemmons, Roberts and Company employed "good sober drivers and reliable messengers." John Anders was general road agent for the line, which was represented in Independence by H. V. Harris, in Westport by J. and W. Bernard and Company, and in Kansas City by James Roberts,[72] who does not appear to have been related to Preston Roberts, Jr. James Roberts was a general booking and ticket agent for most of the stage lines in Kansas City, and railroad and steamship tickets also were available from him.[73] Many of the stage lines had offices in the same building with him on the corner of Delaware and Levee Streets. Such was the case with Slemmons, Roberts and Company.[74]

Most of the mail to Canon City from the east still came in over the central route to Denver and then south,[75] but most of the outbound mail went by way of the Arkansas route to Kansas City. The K.S.F. & C.C. Express Co.—the usual abbreviation found in the Canon City paper—was managed by Agent D. Hood. Under his supervision, the company built a fine office, stables, and corral at the Canon City end of the branch line.[76] Express and mail service were also projected to California Gulch and other mining camps.[77]

Civil War and the Santa Fe Mail

1861-1863

THE CHANGES IN ROUTE AND MANAGEMENT came about during a time of grave national crisis. Abraham Lincoln's electoral victory in 1860 intensified the sectional angers which split the country. Admission of Kansas as a free state and Colorado as a free territory in early 1861 was overshadowed by secession of the seven states of the lower South. With the firing on Fort Sumter and the completion of the Confederacy by the four states of the upper South, the issue was clearly drawn.

Missouri's ambivalence toward the civil conflict was less noticeable in Kansas City where, despite a strong pro-South element in the population, city government was in northern hands, strengthened by the presence of federal troops. Often, southern guerrillas (bushwhackers) dominated the ten miles between Kansas City and Independence, but the garrisoned river towns were generally safe from any serious Confederate threat.[1] Across the Missouri River in Kansas, the events which had given it the name of Bleeding Kansas were past, and that new state was in the Union column.

The Territories of Colorado and New Mexico soon showed symptoms of divided loyalties. A Confederate flag appeared briefly on a Denver store building about twelve days after the attack on Fort Sumter,[2] and the Stars and Stripes flew over Canon City, although it had some southern sympathizers.[3] Colorado was mainly pro-Union, an official line proclaimed by William Gilpin, President Lincoln's choice as first territorial governor, upon his arrival in Denver in late May.[4]

Predicting the course of New Mexico was more difficult. Passage of a slave code by the territorial legislature in 1859 had seemed to link New

Mexico to the South, a position that had been abetted by Miguel A. Otero, the delegate to Congress. But John S. Watts succeeded Otero in the Thirty-seventh Congress, and Governor Abraham Rencher, a North Carolinian, remained loyal to the Union. Yet many citizens evidently adopted a wait-and-see attitude. Because of her contiguity with a seceded state (Texas), New Mexico was in a position of vulnerability not unlike Missouri's.[5] One of the most obvious examples of national division was among the officers of the United States Army; notable defections to the Confederacy occurred at Fort Marcy (Santa Fe), Fort Union, and Fort Wise on the route of the Independence-Santa Fe mail.[6]

Amid the signs of spreading civil war, business was good enough on the Santa Fe and Canon City runs to warrant thinking about increasing the services to semiweekly or even triweekly,[7] and Washington approved an additional $5,000 for contractor Jacob Hall to carry the mail on the branch to Canon City. Deliveries under the extended contract were weekly over the 142 miles from Fort Wise via Haynes Ranch and Colorado City to Canon City, with the first mail reaching Canon City on June 14, 1861. Inclusion of Colorado City which was off the route, may have been the result of geographical ignorance; at any rate, by an order of July 2, Pueblo replaced Colorado City.[8]

The *Rocky Mountain News* in Denver advised its patrons that mail for New Mexico should be sent to Canon City in care of the Kansas City, Canon City, and Santa Fe Express.[9] Weibling, the Denver mail agent, went down to Canon City to examine the business opportunities. He then announced that he and other parties would start an express coach from Colorado City through Canon City to the mining camp of California Gulch on July 1.[10] When that information reached Kansas City, a Slemmons, Roberts and Company man named Andrew Stewart prepared to leave for Canon City to plan an extension of the Kansas City, Santa Fe, and Canon City service to California Gulch.[11] It does not appear that the Weibling competition ever came into existence, but his interest indicates that Miller and Evans's Canon City and Denver express coach was no longer running, although the semiweekly pony express was still operating.[12]

To report accurately on Canon City's new line of communication, the editor of the local paper rode the mail stage to Bent's Old Fort and back in early July. Leaving late on a warm, cloudy night, they arrived just before dawn in Pueblo—a dozen houses and one store surrounded by "the luxuriance of verdure" of the Arkansas River bottoms; across the tributary Fontaine qui Bouille was the Mexican town of Fountain City, with its log and adobe structures. After the mule team was changed, the stage followed the winding road along the north bank of the Arkansas, where the reporter was impressed by the amount of agriculture and live-stock and the number of farm houses below Pueblo. The party ate sub-stantial breakfast at the Haynes Ranch, where the team was again changed. They saw more fine ranches and met several emigrant wagons moving upriver. The road was excellent all the way, and the mail stage reached Bent's Old Fort "in time for a regular pioneer supper" (un-fortunately not described). Only three rooms remained in the crumbling place, and all were utilized by the stage company. The old trading post had no post office at the time, although its location near the forks of the Santa Fe road made it an important place on the line.

The coach from Santa Fe was waiting there. One of its passengers was Judge John S. Watts, New Mexico's delegate to Congress, who told the Canon City newsman and others that Colorado Territory's Governor Gil-pin had received orders to raise two companies of volunteers to be sta-tioned at Fort Garland in the San Luis Valley, a reminder to everyone present that the horrors of the Civil War might not always be far from the local scene. The return trip was delayed because mail stages from the east were late due to rain and muddy roads, and the run to Canon City was slowed by the rain, hail, and swollen streams.[13]

Andrew Stewart, of the firm of Slemmons, Roberts and Company, had to delay his trip to Canon City because of a near-fatal accident. He shot himself when he knocked a pistol off the bureau in his hotel room at Council Grove, Kansas. The ball struck him in the cheek and glanced upward, giving him a brain concussion.[14] But when the mail stage ar-rived in Canon City early on Sunday, September 1, 1861, Stewart alighted, quite recovered. Reports in Canon City said that more buffalo had been encountered on their trip along the Arkansas route than in years and that the party had to fire on them constantly to keep them off the road, but weather was fine, grass was good, and Indians were friendly. Stewart left for New Mexico on Thursday, pleased with the company's increased volume of business.[15] Unfortunately, the data do not give sup-porting figures.

Andrew Stewart's visit to Santa Fe doubtless involved more than in-spection. The Civil War in the Southwest brought both problems and opportunities. When Texas and the other states of the lower South seceded in February, the prospects of the Butterfield Overland Mail line from St. Louis to El Paso and on to California were jeopardized. Very soon afterward, property of the Butterfield Overland Mail Company was expropriated by Texans at Fort Chadbourne.[16] With a large portion of the line in Confederate hands, naturally there was concern about mail connections with California. The circumstances revived the hopes of the men who had long sought better congressional support for the central route to California. On March 2, 1861, Congress passed a post roads bill which discontinued Route No. 12578—the Butterfield line.[17] For Slemmons, Roberts and Company the question was how to maintain an El Paso connection and how best to anticipate a Confederate military thrust northward to Santa Fe and beyond. Andrew Stewart was searching for the answers.

By the time he reached Santa Fe, it was common knowledge that his company was having problems. Texans were reported to have seized the livestock and vehicles of the Santa Fe-El Paso stage line, and it was certain that Fort Fillmore had been abandoned after Major Isaac Lynde surrendered his force of about 500 regular troops to 300 Texans.[18]

Evidence of Confederate relations with the Indians also came to light. The Confederates had appointed Albert Pike as commissioner to the Indians, and he was apparently trying to arrange treaties with the Comanche and other Plains tribes. This information was relayed by Indian Agent Albert G. Boone to his superiors in Washington.[19] Pike's success along the Santa Fe Trail was minimal. Perhaps overstating the case, one of Slemmons, Roberts and Company's drivers, William H. Ryus, who drove the Long Route from Fort Larned to Fort Wise, said the Indians were so peaceful during much of 1861 and 1862 that one could go right into a village and be received kindly with dancing and choice buffalo meat or venison.[20]

As the Confederates moved north, preparations were made to evacuate Santa Fe, and on March 3, 140 wagons loaded with government stores arrived at Fort Union. Volunteer troops were raised hastily in Colorado. An eastbound mail stage encountered three companies of infantry under Lieutenant Colonel Samuel F. Tappan at Hole-in-the-Rock, a well-known watering place on the Mountain Branch about fifty-five miles southwest of Bent's Old Fort. The troops were headed for Fort Union from Fort Wise, and they expected to join seven other companies, which were marching south from Denver, on the Purgatoire River.[21] The forces joined in the snow near Gray's Ranch, the stage station where the Denver-Fort Union road joined the Bent's Fort road about ninety miles south of the old trading post.[22]

The combined force under Colonel John P. Slough hastened over the Raton Pass to Fort Union. A contemporary report said that Slough's men had marched 160 miles in four days, on one day making an astonishing fifty-one miles.[23] They knew that a Union force under Colonel Edward R. S. Canby had been defeated at Valverde, New Mexico, and while they were in bivouac on the southern slope of the Raton Mountains, word came through that Albuquerque and Santa Fe had fallen to Confederate troops commanded by Colonel Henry H. Sibley, former commandant at Fort Union.[24]

New Mexico's civil government was set up at Las Vegas,[25] but Slemmons, Roberts and Company decided to use Fort Union, north of Las Vegas, as the stage line's terminus.[26] At the same time that mail and passenger service were cut off south of Fort Union, the Kansas, Santa Fe and Canon City Express announced extension of service westward from Canon City to the new gold mines at Buckskin Joe, advertised as the richest yet in Colorado Territory.[27]

Victory came to the Colorado troops in decisive engagements at La Glorieta and Apache Canyon, March 26 to 28, 1862, and within the month the Confederate threat to New Mexico and Colorado was largely removed.[28] Santa Fe was restored as the territorial capital, and Slemmons, Roberts and Company resumed service to the ancient town. The editor of the *Daily Kansas City Western Journal of Commerce* advised merchants not to forget to place some of their advertisements in Spanish, as he would be sending a large number of papers to New Mexico with every mail.[29] Passengers and shippers were reminded that Santa Fe was only twelve days away, while Canon City could be reached in nine days and the mountain mining camps in ten. A through ticket to Santa Fe cost $125, and one to Buckskin Joe cost $85.[30]

The Confederate presence in New Mexico had curtailed the transportation of provisions and merchandise into the Territory and, of course, had severely hampered its export trade. With the coming of spring 1862, one of the largest volumes of freighting business was expected over the Santa Fe Trail to replenish markets at each end.[31] That spring was also mail contract time.

87

Independence and Westport continued to languish as commercial centers for the Santa Fe and Southwest trade, and the war slowed down that kind of activity in Kansas City.[32] Perhaps influenced somewhat by those circumstances, the Post Office Department said that bids for mail service starting elsewhere than Independence would be considered, along with proposals to service Fort Riley, Kansas. Ten bidders responded, and Kansas City, Missouri, and Leavenworth and Atchison, Kansas, were proposed as starting points. Both Jacob Hall and Samuel Slemmons were among the bidders, but on April 24, 1862 the contract for the Santa Fe route (now No. 10547) was awarded to George H. Vickroy and Thomas J. Barnum (who was listed as from Canon City, Fremont County, Colorado Territory).[33] They offered to start from Kansas City and supply Fort Riley for $37,415 or from Leavenworth or Atchison via Fort Riley for $34,900. The first proposition was accepted with the privilege of shifting to the other at any time.[34] Evidently, Kansas City's preeminence was not yet assured.

The contract for Route No. 10547 was transferred on May 3 to a group of five men: Mahlon Cottrill, George H. Vickroy, Bradley Barlow, Harvey M. Vaile, and Thomas J. Barnum. Vickroy and Barnum, of course, were the winners of the contract in the first place, while Cottrill and Barlow were unsuccessful bidders. The latter two had prior experience in the mail contracting business. In 1860, under the name of Cottrill, Moore, Barlow, and Sanderson, they had secured several small mail routes in Missouri, ranging from thirteen and a half to seventy miles in length.[35] Presumably Sanderson was Jared L. Sanderson, who came from Vermont to Missouri in 1860,[36] the year in which he became involved in mail contracting with Messrs. Cottrill, Moore, and Barlow. Mahlon Cottrill and Bradley Barlow were also from Vermont—from Bridport and Fairfield respectively.[37] Cottrill, the senior partner, had been involved in mail contracting in the Green Mountain State in the early 1850s between Montpelier and Burlington,[38] and it appears likely that Jared Sanderson, who drove stage in and out of Burlington about that time,[39] may have worked for Cottrill.

The three Vermonters were the nucleus of the group, and Jared Sanderson may have played a more important part then the official record indicates. The only known business correspondence of the later Barlow, Sanderson and Company—a letter to Postmaster General John A. J. Cresswell, dated May 1869—says that substantially the same mail service to New Mexico and beyond had been performed by the undersigned (Barlow, Sanderson and Company) for nearly seven years, which points to the beginning of mail contracts on July 1, 1862.[40] From this it seems reasonable that Barlow and Sanderson controlled the group which acquired the Santa Fe contract in 1862, but the name Barlow, Sanderson and Company was a later development. The only Independence man involved was Harvey M. Vaile.[41] George H. Vickroy probably came from Johnstown, Pennsylvania.[42]

The same five partners (Cottrill, Vickroy, Barlow, Vaile, and Barnum) also received a transfer from George H. Vickroy of the contract for Route No. 14313 in Colorado, effective July 1, 1862. His bid of $2,890 per annum had been accepted on April 24, and the group paid him $2,174 for it. The route, for which Harmon Weibling and Samuel Slemmons also bid, was a weekly one from Pueblo to Beaver Creek, Canon City, Kellar's Bar, Fairplay, California Gulch, Cash Creek, Georgia Gulch, Buckskin Joe, Laurette, Hamilton, and Breckinridge—125 miles one way.

The line did not remain stable for long. Breckinridge was dropped on November 1, terminating the line at Hamilton. That shortened the line eighteen miles round trip, for which $416 per year was deducted from the contract. Another departmental order in late November called for the omission of Kellar's Bar, California Gulch, Cash Creek, Georgia Gulch, and Hamilton. The line was then from Pueblo to Beaver Creek, Canon City, Fairplay, and Laurette, but because the distance was about the same, there was no adjustment in payments.[43] Those curtailments may have come about, in part, because of the powerful influence of Ben Holladay, who projected his lines southward through the mountains to Breckinridge, Fairplay, Buckskin Joe, and other towns.[44]

A short time before the Pueblo-Breckinridge contract was let, Ben Holladay acquired the Central Overland California and Pike's Peak Express Company route into Denver[45] and was providing real competition to mining camps on the headwaters of the Arkansas and the Blue. Another factor affecting Cottrill, Vickroy and Company's fortunes in serving the mining camps was a general slump in the Kansas City-Pike's Peak trade because of uncertain wartime conditions in Missouri. Wartime activity had benefited Omaha and other Nebraska towns, as well as the Santa Fe trade, especially after the Union victories at La Glorieta and Apache Canyon. Kansas City business interests expected the prosperity of the Santa Fe trade to continue and looked for the commerce with the gold camps to improve as Union forces gained the upper hand in Missouri.[46]

Cottrill, Vickroy and Company, as the enterprising quintet came to be known, enlarged their operations still further by providing an express coach service from Pueblo to Denver.[47] But they did not secure a mail contract between those two points,[48] which perhaps was another indication of the strength of Holladay and other proponents of the central overland route in keeping control of mail service in and out of Denver.[49] References in the press to the new Pueblo-Denver mail service imply that Cottrill, Vickroy and Company were private mail carriers on that line and probably expected to secure a U.S. mail contract in time. Apparently, the new services bypassed Colorado City, which was on Weibling's route and was the southern terminus of the mail line from Denver.[50]

Daniel J. Hayden, agent for Cottrill, Vickroy and Company, gave notice through the press that he planned to leave for Pueblo on July 10, making the trip in two days and connecting there with the company's coach for Fort Lyon or Fort Union and beyond. Anyone who wanted to send letters with him was instructed to direct them "via Russellville" and have them in the hands of Denver's postmaster before noon of the departure date. Hayden also announced that the line would be in regular operation within three or four weeks, providing the much-needed service between Colorado and New Mexico Territories.[51]

The members of the firm of Cottrill, Vickroy and Company were ambitious and confident as they prepared to furnish mail, express, and passenger service from Kansas City to Santa Fe, Denver, and some of the Colorado mining camps, over routes having a combined distance of 2,700 miles. One day early in June, the river steamer *War Eagle* tied up at the Kansas City Levee and unloaded fine horses, coaches, and other gear consigned to them.[52] It is possible that the new vehicles were Concord coaches, but they may have been celerity wagons, mud wagons, or Troy coaches.[53] The last mail brought in by Slemmons, Roberts and Company from Santa Fe to Kansas City arrived twelve hours ahead of schedule on June 28,[54] and the first mail from Santa Fe under Cottrill, Vickroy and Company's contract was right on schedule on July 5.[55] The new contractors planned to reduce the running time between Kansas City and Santa Fe from twelve to ten days and to enhance the quality of service by having more and better stations, so that travelers could stop overnight if they wished.[56]

Kansas City boosters were jubilant that the line's terminus remained there; business interests in Leavenworth had sought to attract it. And the new contractors barely had their service in operation when the public learned that preliminary surveys west of Kansas City were to be started right away for the National Pacific Rail Road.[57]

It appears that Lyman H. Cottrill, Mahlon Cottrill's son,[58] assisted agent Daniel Hayden in getting the overall Denver-Santa Fe service organized that summer.[59] The season undoubtedly gave them qualms because of a flurry of Confederate guerrilla activity in southern Colorado, particularly the seizure of the Fort Garland mail at Cucharas.[60] Those risks were augmented by Indian harrassments along much of the Santa Fe Trail, circumstances which brought strengthened garrisons at Fort Larned and Fort Lyon (Fort Wise renamed to avoid association with former Governor of Virginia Henry A. Wise, who had become a Confederate). Military units patrolled the Raton Pass between Forts Lyon and Union, and a battalion of First Colorado Volunteers was stationed at the crossing of the Huerfano.[61]

At last, Cottrill, Vickroy and Company's first direct mail coach from Bent's Old Fort, via Pueblo and Russellville, reached Denver on September 28, 1862. Among the passengers were Lyman H. Cottrill and Thomas J. Barnum, both closely associated with the firm. Their first southbound stage pulled out of Denver on the morning of Tuesday, September 30. Afterward, a Cottrill, Vickroy coach left the Planter's House every Tuesday morning at 8 o'clock for Bent's Old Fort, where, according to advertisements, connection could be made with the Kansas City and Santa Fe Mail Line for Gray's Ranch, Maxwell's Ranch, Fort Union, and Santa Fe.[62] Reference to the Santa Fe terminus underscored the line's southward orientation out of Denver and indirectly reminded people of Denver's dependence on the Overland route along the Platte River for its regular U.S. mail service to the Missouri River and beyond. The line south from Denver functioned as a private letter carrier, and, of course, passengers and express could be transferred at Bent's Old Fort to Cottrill, Vickroy stages bound for Kansas City along the Arkansas Valley route.

Winter travel could be hazardous and uncomfortable. In early November 1862, the eastbound mail to Independence and Kansas City was delayed for two days because of a severe storm and resulting high water. The storm was reported as one of the most destructive in many years and was responsible for the loss of twenty-one oxen by Irwin, Jackson and Company, government freighters. Mail service was again disrupted later that month by heavy snow at Maxwell's Ranch, New Mexico, and in the Raton Mountains, astraddle the New Mexico-Colorado boundary. To save as much time as possible, the mail was packed over 200 miles on mules.

About a month after that, the mail coach skidded on ice and snow on the south side of the Ratons and slipped down an embankment, rolling over twice. None of the passengers was seriously injured because the vehicle was packed full, but the top of the coach was rather badly dented. High water and bad roads returned in February 1863, causing a delay of several days for some merchants who were on their way to Kansas City to buy their spring stocks of goods.[63]

Denver's *Rocky Mountain News* noted in the personal column of its March 31 edition that Cottrill and Barnum of the Southern Mail Company were in town.[64] In that brief item is the first known use of the term "Southern Mail" for any portion of their system. It appears to have been a local usage in that instance, indicating the Denver-Santa Fe connection. But it also points out that part of the Southern Overland Mail route, formerly used by the Butterfield Overland Mail, had been reopened by military action, and connections were again possible over that route with California.

A proposal had been made in late 1861 that California troops commanded by Colonel James H. Carleton attempt to clear the southern mail route by marching eastward through Fort Yuma to the Rio Grande and to recapture Forts Buchanan (Arizona), Thorn and Fillmore (New Mexico), and Bliss (Texas) from the Confederates. Carleton's California Column did not begin its march until April 1862, after the Confederate defeats at La Glorieta and Apache Canyon. Carleton was confident that stage coaches would be running from Independence to Los Angeles and San Francisco by way of Santa Fe, Fort Thorn, and Tucson before winter set in, but progress was slow. He reached Fort Thorn on the Rio Grande in mid-August after an arduous desert march, and in late September he was in Santa Fe, where he wrote that the Southern Overland Mail route had been freed of Confederate obstacles and the military posts in southern New Mexico and northwestern Texas had been recovered.[65]

Cottrill, Vickroy and Company's service was extended to Fort Fillmore soon after that post was retaken by federal troops. After the successful campaign of the California Column, the line was projected to Mesilla, Arizona,[66] with intermediate stops at Albuquerque, Peralta, and Fort Craig.[67] Reestablishment of a stage line south from Santa Fe by a company headquartered at Kansas City was another reason for thinking of it as the Southern Mail Company.

The dangerous realities of Civil War had faded from most of the areas that were tied together by the communication system of Cottrill, Vickroy and Company. Only in the extreme eastern portion—the Kansas City, Independence, Westport triangle—did a significant threat remain, and that was in the form of intensifying guerrilla warfare.

M. Cottrill and Company and the Indian Wars

1863-1864

HARVEY M. VAILE LEFT THE FIRM, and the Santa Fe and Pueblo-Laurette mail contracts were reassigned by departmental orders in early March 1863, retroactive to January 1, to the remaining partners—Barlow, Cottrill, Vickroy, and Barnum.[1] The star route register of those transfers gives Bradley Barlow's name first and indicates that the management headquarters were in St. Albans, Vermont, where he resided.[2] Perhaps he bought Vaile's interest; at any rate, it is reasonable to conclude that Barlow greatly strengthened his position in the company, although it came to be known officially as M. Cottrill and Company.[3] John R. Griffin, a carryover from the last days of Cottrill, Vickroy and Company, was retained as Kansas City agent for the line.[4]

While those changes were going on, Jared L. Sanderson (probably a silent partner) was doing well on his own as a mail contractor and proprietor of a stage line from Leavenworth, Kansas, and Kansas City, Missouri, to Fort Scott, Kansas. He was praised in the newspapers for his excellent service with four-horse coaches, which began making daily runs on March 15.[5]

By early summer two more deletions affected operation of the line to Santa Fe. For some time it had been rumored that the town of Independence would be dropped from the service, with Kansas City to be the official eastern terminus, although it had been the starting point for quite a while.[6] Permission for the contractors to do that was granted in a departmental order, effective June 15 and subject to revocation, with departure time set for Friday at 8 A.M. rather than midnight.[7]

The other change was a private one; George H. Vickroy gave up his membership in the firm,[8] leaving Mahlon Cottrill, Bradley Barlow, and Thomas J. Barnum as the principal owners. At that time, Barlow was acquiring prominence as a wool merchant in Kansas City, dealing heavily in New Mexico wool. It was said that he was shipping about 100,000 pounds per week, and he advertised unlimited facilities for storage and baling at his wool house in Jarboe's Building on the Kansas City Levee.[9] But for all that, he seems to have spent most of his time in Vermont, and Thomas J. Barnum was increasingly active in the management of the line.[10]

The parent organization, M. Cottrill and Company, advertised its off-spring as the Kansas, Santa Fe and Canon City Express,[11] but variations of the name soon circulated: Kansas City, Santa Fe and Denver Mail and Express Line; the Santa Fe Stage and Express; the Santa Fe Stage Company; and simply the Santa Fe Stage.[12] Reference to the "great Santa Fe mail"[13] suggests that the Santa Fe division of the system was regarded as the more important.

There were a few changes along the line, although the number of new post offices in Kansas sharply declined. None had been added east of Council Grove, a circumstance undoubtedly derived from depressed conditions following the panic of 1857 and continued by the restraints on large-scale immigration imposed by the Civil War.[14] Only the name of Palmyra had been changed to Baldwin City. West of Council Grove, the Diamond Spring station had been moved a few miles east to Six Mile Creek, and a new office appeared on Muddy Creek, west of Lost Spring. Pawnee Fork was retained as the name of the post office at Fort Larned,[15] and improvements were planned for the Long Route from there to Fort Lyon. A forlorn stretch of over 200 miles, including the Dry Route cut-off, the Long Route required travel time of four to five days in good weather, much of it often through vast herds of buffalo. Camp was made at night, with buffalo and antelope steaks and strong coffee prepared over a buffalo-chip fire.[16] M. Cottrill and Company sought to alleviate the discomforts by adding seven new stations to the two already on the Long Route (one being at old Fort Atkinson and the other probably on Coon Creek). Each new station was to be 80 by 40 feet, with adobe walls 9 feet high and 2 feet thick.[17]

Fort Lyon—formerly Fort Wise—had a post office, and the stage station there was probably fairly typical. The agent for "the Santa Fe Stage

Company" was a man named Lambert, who, with his wife, was responsible for various chores. Normally, there were three relay drivers at the station, and Lambert had to oversee their care of the livestock. He had charge of grain supplies brought in by company wagons, in addition to the summer hay that was cut in the river bottoms nearby. As soon as a coach came in, express and private packages were in his custody. Because Fort Lyon was a home station, the Lamberts had to provide board. They could set their own prices for food sold to passengers, but they had to feed company employees at rates set by the company. Supplies could be obtained from the post commissary through the stage company, and the Lamberts were entitled to government protection because of the company's contract to carry the mail.[18]

A post office was opened on June 4, 1863 at Bent's Old Fort, where the Denver branch split off from the main Santa Fe road. Lewis Barnum, apparently Thomas J.'s brother, was postmaster. He brought his bride, Emma, the daughter of Van Daniel Boone and great-granddaughter of Daniel Boone, to the living quarters in the semiruined trading post.[19] Farther up the Arkansas, the Haynes Ranch post office had been discontinued, and one had been established at Booneville. There, Emma Barnum's father and his brother, Colonel Albert G. Boone, had settled on a 1400-acre tract, formerly the property of the big freighting firm of Russell, Majors and Waddell, with whom the colonel had been associated.[20]

Forty miles south of Bent's Old Fort on the Mountain Branch of the Santa Fe Trail, the Iron Spring stage station (no post office) was operated by Henry C. Withers, who lived there with his family. His son Gus herded mules for the stage company at $10 per month. The station was small and simple—a little house surrounded by a high wall, which served as a barricade against Indians.[21]

About forty-five miles farther on, Gray's Ranch, close to the junction of the Mountain Branch with the Denver-Fort Union road, was given a post office in September. But the one at Trinidad, at the foot of the Raton Pass, was discontinued.[22] A post office had been in operation since September 3, 1861 at Cimarron (Maxwell's Ranch), New Mexico.[23] Those additions and changes on the main and branch lines of M. Cottrill and Company's contracts were authorized by Abraham Lincoln's postmaster general, Montgomery Blair.

A shadow of impending trouble was cast on the Nine Mile Ridge, west of Fort Larned, in January 1863. A small, eastbound wagon train was making camp when a band of Indians (not identified) approached and begged for food. The wagonmaster refused. As the wagons were being corralled, one of them nearly tipped over, and a nervous teamster shot and killed one of the Indians. The Indians hastily disappeared but returned about dawn for a surprise attack in which all but one of the wagon crew were killed. Vegetation beside the Arkansas shielded the survivor, and from his refuge he watched as the wagons were destroyed and the animals driven off. The fortunate teamster said later that nothing would have happened if the wagonmaster had given the Indians the food, but a Santa Fe stage driver felt that the clash on Nine Mile Ridge was really the beginning of the Indian War that reached a climax in 1864.[24]

That same winter another incident showed the other side of relations with the Indians on the plains. About eight miles west of the site of Dodge City, Kansas, the eastbound mail from Fort Lyon bogged down in the snow. One of the mules froze to death after being unhitched from the wagon. One of the drivers started on muleback to report to James Brice, by then the station agent at Pawnee Fork near Fort Larned. Two army officers—passengers—gave the driver a letter to the commandant at Fort Larned, asking for help.

In about four or five miles the driver's mule gave out, but after a while the man saw a flickering camp fire on the south bank of the Arkansas. He managed to cross the frozen river, but by the time he reached what turned out to be an Indian camp, his hands and feet were frozen. The Indians (unidentified) cut off his boots and wrapped his feet in a buffalo robe, but they were unable to remove his gloves. His benefactors then recovered his mule and took the man over the bleak miles to the mail station.

Agent Brice sent out men and mules, and fuel was transported from the fort. The rest of the party survived their icy experience and made it to Fort Larned, but one of the wagons was left to be recovered later. When Brice went out for it in more clement weather, the wagon had disappeared. Before long it was located on Pawnee Creek about sixty miles from the fort, where it was being uniquely employed. Indian squaws had made harnesses for themselves from strips of buffalo hide and pulled the wagon, with papooses riding in it, from camp to camp.[25]

At least for the summer, the Santa Fe stages were drawn by horses. On June 26, for example, the stage left Kansas City at 11 A.M. and was pulled by six fine bays. On board for that trip was Mahlon Cottrill, who was going as far as Pawnee Fork.[26] The line was well patronized that summer, which was in keeping with the huge volume of trade with New Mexico—the largest ever.[27] Cottrill returned to Kansas City on July 11, reporting that everything was in excellent order along the line to Pawnee Fork. The only hint of trouble came from a large gathering of Indians at Pawnee Fork, who had assembled for an annual buffalo hunt.[28] The buffalo were so thick around Fort Larned in the summers of 1862 and 1863 that soldiers were ordered to fire blanks to frighten them off the military reservation to preserve the grass for the post livestock.[29]

The real danger that summer was at the eastern end of the mail route. Probes and attacks by southern guerrillas mounted, and there was a successful ambush of federal cavalry at Westport, Missouri, on June 17.[30] Between Westport and Council Grove one could see the charred remains of many buildings, and even as far west as Diamond Spring, the guerrillas burned buildings and killed inhabitants.[31]

Jared L. Sanderson found it advisable to publicly reassure his customers that the Kansas City and Fort Scott Daily Stage Line was no longer in danger from bushwhackers and that perfect safety had been restored.[32] The culmination of guerrilla warfare was the destruction of Lawrence, Kansas, and 150 of its residents by bushwhackers led by William Clarke Quantrill on August 21.[33] The location, of course, was some miles north of the Santa Fe Trail, but Quantrill's Raiders had passed through the Trail village of Gardner, Kansas, on their way to Lawrence the night before.[34] There is no indication, however, that M. Cottrill and Company's service was ever more than delayed.

A far more durable, long-range threat to mail stage lines was being talked about, although no railroad had yet reached Kansas City. There was discussion of a proposed railroad from Kansas City to Fort Scott,[35] which would put Sanderson's stage line out of business. In noting arrival on September 12 of the Santa Fe coach filled with passengers, the editor of the *Kansas City Daily Journal of Commerce* foretold that "the glory of stage coaches is passing away, and the locomotive with its train will soon bear our merchandise westward."[36]

The Kansas City editor was confident of the future, no matter how men and merchandise traveled westward. On October 10, he wrote that "the Santa Fe stage went out yesterday with a load of passengers for the cities of the Plains. The southern route is in fine order—grass and water plenty, while buffalo abound in droves."[37] His confidence was substantiated when the stage from Santa Fe arrived on October 17 with news of rich gold strikes in Arizona.[38]

As usual, autumn brought an end to such ideal travel conditions. A severe and widespread blizzard swept over the plains in November, delaying the Santa Fe coach into Kansas City well beyond contract specifications. When it finally did arrive, it was learned that the mail stage had upset a short distance east of the Raton Mountains and its distinguished passengers were somewhat shaken. On board were (Lieutenant) Colonel Francisco Perea, veteran of the battle of Glorieta Pass and new delegate from New Mexico to the Thirty-eighth Congress, and his wife, accompanied by outgoing delegate Judge John S. Watts and his daughter.[39]

That winter the office of M. Cottrill and Company was moved to quarters under (presumably in the basement of) the Mechanics Bank in Kansas City, where the office of Jared L. Sanderson's Kansas City and Fort Scott line was also housed.[40] Reports came in of matured plans to open mail service between Mesilla, New Mexico Territory, and Tucson, Arizona Territory.[41] And the editor of the *Kansas City Daily Journal of Commerce* called for a daily mail service on the Santa Fe route. Proof of such a need, he said, was represented by the fact that the Santa Fe stage left on February 27 with at least twelve sacks of mail (apparently a common occurrence).[42]

In the midst of that talk was growing interest in the city concerning the prospects of railroad construction by the Union Pacific Eastern Division westward from St. Louis, hopefully to span the Missouri River at Kansas City and ultimately to cross the plains.[43] Former Santa Fe mail contractor Slemmons, Roberts and Company made connections with the Pacific Railroad in western Missouri at Dresden and ran mail coaches to St. Louis in fifty hours. The firm also ran four-horse coaches from Sedalia to Warsaw, Quincey, Bolivar, and Springfield.[44]

Good weather set in for a short time after the first of the year so that "the coaches [were] making as good time as in the summer." That observation was part of a boost given to M. Cottrill and Company by the *Kansas City Daily Journal of Commerce*: "The promptness with which this great mail, passenger and express line is run, is worthy of all praise."[45] But another big storm hit the Raton Mountains in March. The eastbound mail stage was extricated from snowdrifts by men from a passing wagon train, and the conductor and driver of the westbound mail did everything possible to ease the discomfort of their passengers, according to a letter of thanks sent from Santa Fe.[46]

"Loaded down as usual" described the departure of the Santa Fe stage from Kansas City on March 25, 1864.[47] No doubt, some of the passengers, mail, and express packages were destined for points along the Denver branch from Bent's Old Fort. That portion of the system was under the management of Thomas J. Barnum, whose jurisdiction also extended over the Mountain Branch of the Trail to Fort Union.[48]

The Denver schedule of stages to and from the south was a Monday arrival and a Wednesday departure. When the weather was good the mail sometimes came in as much as twenty-four hours ahead of schedule,[49] which must have made it a bit awkward for anyone wanting to board the stage at a way station. The twenty-four hour delay of the mail into Denver in the first week of January was notable, because it was the first disruption of the service by snow and severe cold. The most difficult spot on the branch line was the Divide separating the Arkansas and Platte drainages. The coach that came into Denver on March 14 had experienced an especially cold trip over the divide; passengers were division superintendent Thomas J. Barnum, Fort Garland's sutler, and several army officers who made the trip from Santa Fe. The officers asked the *Rocky Mountain News* to publish their appreciation of the care of passengers by division superintendents and conductors on the way.[50] Convenience was not the only company policy appreciated by customers; an attractive rate of $75 was offered to travelers for the through trip from Denver to Kansas City along the Arkansas route.[51] Further details could be obtained from George E. Crater, still the stage company's agent in Brown's Banking House, Denver.[52]

The expected large-scale outbreaks of Indian hostilities did not happen in the summer and fall of 1863. So far as M. Cottrill and Company's employees and patrons were concerned, the only dangerous incident had been an attack in August on the mail stage below Santa Fe in the jurisdiction of David R. Knox, superintendent from Fort Union to El Paso.[53] A band of eighty Indians rushed the stage about forty miles below Fort McRae, the recently established post near Ojo del Muerto. After throwing off the mail and express (and probably the passengers' baggage, too), the mail party managed to reach the fort.[54] A greater problem was an intense drought on the central plains—one report said the upper Arkansas was dry for 200 miles. It was one of the reasons why trouble was

100

expected from the Indians, but government annuities or supplies relieved the situation.[55]

When the fighting began in April 1864, the opening scenes were on the Platte River, where the Cheyenne raided ranches and stage stations of the line operated by Ben Holladay. By summer, however, the plains tribes were generally on the warpath across the plains of eastern Colorado and western Kansas. The first reported violence on the Trail concerned Kiowa attacks on wagon trains near Fort Larned. In mid-May the Cow Creek stage station, about thirty miles east of Fort Larned, was attacked by Cheyenne, who ran off the relay mules. Settlers were fleeing the country.[56] Reports of destruction by Comanche of the Santa Fe mail stage and its passengers and drivers west of Fort Larned appear to have been false,[57] and the stage from Santa Fe in late May brought in thirteen passengers—mostly New Mexico traders—without mishap.[58]

The garrisons at Forts Larned and Lyon were numerically inadequate for protecting the mail stages and wagon trains on the Santa Fe Trail. Reinforcements from Fort Riley and by Colorado troops soon made it possible to reestablish military escorts for the mail stages and many of the wagon trains.[59] That broke the bottleneck at the Pawnee Fork stage station (Fort Larned), where the agent, James Brice, had detained westbound mails. Four stages filled with passengers, together with six baggage wagons, left with a twenty-five man escort. On the second day out, the vehicles had to be corralled because of Indians, who surrounded the train but succeeded only in wounding a few mules with arrows. The travelers later had a bad scare at Pretty Encampment where they came upon a big Indian village. But to their great surprise and relief, "Barnum himself" (Thomas or Lewis) and Dan Hayden emerged from the camp, which belonged to friendly Arapaho under Chief Left Hand.[60]

The Trail was kept open all the way from Council Grove to Fort Union on both the Cimarron Cutoff and the Mountain Branch as military efforts were enlarged and better coordinated. In addition to the forts, special military camps were set up at the Cimarron Crossing of the Arkansas, the Upper and Lower Cimarron springs (both on the Cutoff), and at Gray's Ranch on the Purgatoire to help protect the mail stages on the Mountain Branch between Fort Lyon and Maxwell's Ranch. But the number of troops available was never sufficient to protect every vehicle that moved over the Trail. Depredations were numerous and often serious.[61] Even with protection, the mail stages were not completely safe, but they were able to beat off attacks.[62]

The more isolated stage stations still were vulnerable. Cheyenne burned the Iron Spring station south of Bent's Old Fort, and Henry Withers and his family barely escaped to Trinidad.[63] Company animals were driven off from the Cow Creek station. The keeper of the Cottonwood Springs station was killed and the livestock were run off. Ten men were killed at Walnut Creek.[64] The old Walnut Creek trading post was operated then by Charles Rath, who stored thousands of buffalo robes there. The place also had a new post office designated as Kiowa.[65] And Kiowa Indians raided close to Fort Larned, capturing a number of government animals. In an major effort to tighten control, Major General Samuel R. Curtis with troops from Fort Riley established the new post of Fort Zarah, at the Trail's crossing of Walnut Creek.[66]

Not all marauding could be attributed to Indians. Antonio Manuel Otero's wagon train was held up near the Raton Mountains and robbed of money and animals. The robbers professed to be Texans, a story which Kansas City and Santa Fe papers discredited but which may have been true. The Reynolds gang, rebels from Texas, were operating in southern Colorado.[67]

No one could deny, however, that a major Confederate threat to Kansas City was developing. Volunteers to help defend the city were called for as early as mid-June,[68] although it was not until fall that the campaign reached its climax. Major General Curtis, based at Fort Leavenworth, took charge of the defense against the Confederate force commanded by Major General Sterling Price. The Confederates swung westward from Jefferson City and took Independence. But the Union troops were victorious in the Battle of Westport, October 23, 1864, an engagement which was called the Gettysburg of the West and which effectively ended Confederate aggression in that part of the country.[69]

The brunt of Indian hostilities fell on the Platte River route, where the Overland Company withdrew its agents, livestock, and coaches near Fort Kearny, Nebraska. Service was not restored for more than a month.[70] For a while Denver was so tightly sealed off from eastern contacts over that route that mail from the east came via the Isthmus of Panama and California, then by Overland Stage east to Denver. Mail that ordinarily would have gone east by the Platte route also made the circuitous trip, which caused the editor of the *Rocky Mountain News* to comment on one occasion that the mail left by way of "Salt Lake, Carson Valley, San Francisco, the isles of the Pacific, the isthmus of Darien, Cape Horn and God knows where all!"[71]

That also implies that little if any States mail in and out of Denver was transported over the Arkansas route. People were conditioned to using the Overland line, which was a little shorter and was the official U.S. mail connection. M. Cottrill and Company's operation as a private carrier south from Denver was primarily one to Santa Fe and back. That part of the Cottrill line from Denver to Bent's Old Fort was fairly close to the fighting on the east-central plains of Colorado; some of the gravest threats were along that segment.

In early July, a family of four was killed about thirty-five miles south of Denver. In mid-August a party of four men and two women was attacked on the Arkansas about fifteen miles below Colonel Boone's station and post office; the men were killed and the women carried off.[72] On August 21, the bodies of two men, scalped, were found eighteen miles west of Fort Lyon. They were employees on the Haynes Ranch above Bent's Old Fort.[73] Arrows brought into Fort Lyon were identified as Arapaho. There was said to be a large Arapaho encampment at the head of Sand Creek.[74] The stages continued to operate because of military protection, although the slow pace of escorts sometimes delayed them.[75]

But despite the double danger of the Civil War and the Indian Wars, M. Cottrill and Company's lines to Santa Fe and Denver were not greatly curtailed. There were some casualties among its employees, and the losses of livestock, supplies, and equipment added up to a considerable dollar total.[76] Nonetheless, during that perilous summer the company sought to improve the quality of its service. On June 24, the river steamer *Emilie* tied up at the Kansas City Levee, and six splendid coaches from Concord, New Hampshire, were unloaded for M. Cottrill and Company.[77] This is the first certain data as to when the Concord coach was introduced on the Santa Fe line. The new vehicles were put into operation all the way to El Paso, and Thomas Barnum and David Knox were given much of the credit.[78]

The Indians were much quieter along the Trail by October, and business boomed for M. Cottrill and Company. The coach which came into Kansas City on October 11 had probably the largest number of passengers ever carried on the line, including ten through passengers. The next coach came in loaded and had served many passengers along the way as well. Messenger (conductor) J. Gerrold said that forty persons were waiting at Fort Union for seats on the eastbound coaches. Military escorts for the mail were still employed from the Purgatoire River to Fort Larned.[79]

Senior partner Mahlon Cottrill died in Kansas City on October 20, at the age of about seventy.[80] There was no immediately apparent reorganization of the company. Advertisements continued to appear under the old name, and experienced employees like A. J. Anthony, Jeff. Nesbit, J. Gerrold, and Peter Kelly[81] prepared for winter discomforts along the route. By November, winter snows were heavy in southern Colorado. Deep drifts were encountered on the branch from Bent's Old Fort to Denver, and crossing the divide between the Arkansas and the Platte was especially difficult and treacherous.[82]

Delays due to weather were common, but one slowdown occurred for quite a different reason. The coach was not permitted to get ahead of the Third Regiment of the Colorado Volunteer Cavalry, which was marching down the Arkansas valley to Fort Lyon.[83] The commanding officer, Colonel John M. Chivington, was trying in every way possible to prevent advance notice of his approach. Their destiny, of course, was the Cheyenne-Arapaho village to the northeast of the fort on Sand Creek, which was the site of the massacre of the Indians by Chivington's men on November 29, 1864.[84] That controversial action was one of the most devastating blows struck against Plains tribes along the Santa Fe Trail.

9

The Santa Fe Stage Company

1865-1866

THE FIRST PUBLIC SIGN of company reorganization appeared in a January 21, 1865 advertisement, which simply replaced the name of M. Cottrill and Company with that of the Santa Fe Stage Company.[1] A few days later, a new ad informed readers that the Santa Fe Stage Company was the only company that carried the U.S. mail and express weekly to Santa Fe. Connections were available in Santa Fe for Fort Craig, Mesilla, and El Paso. Mail and express service was provided also to the gold mines—meaning those on the upper Arkansas, in South Park, and on the headwaters of the Blue River in Colorado. The Denver City connection was advertised as an express line with rates 25 cents less per pound than those on any other route. The use of military escorts through Indian country was particularly emphasized, and semiweekly service between Kansas City and Council Grove was mentioned.

In another column, it was noted that "Mr. J. P. (L.) Sanderson, one of the most successful stage men in the west, has lately become connected with this company. It is a good thing for all concerned."[2] The observation probably meant only that Sanderson became more directly involved in management; he had been associated with the firm for about two years.

Business promotion in Denver was supervised by George E. Crater, agent, from his office in George W. Brown's banking house on Larimer Street. As might be expected, attention was focused on express coaches which left Denver every Wednesday and Kansas City every Friday. The rate to or from Kansas City was 75 cents per pound, and the usual running time was twelve days. Eastern shippers were cautioned to mark their commodities: *In Care of Santa Fe Stage Company, Kansas City,*

105

Missouri. Crater was an agent only part time—his main employment was at the Branch Mint—and he was in the stage line office to accept fares and freight only on Tuesdays from 2 to 8 P.M. The *Rocky Mountain News* urged that the Santa Fe Stage Company advertisement be read by all who were going to Kansas City; Santa Fe; El Paso; Chihuahua, Mexico; or the new gold mines of Arizona.[3]

Volume of business for the Santa Fe Stage Company maintained its growth. Colonel Matt Foster, the Kansas City postmaster, said that the coach which left on February 24, 1865 carried more mail than had any other coach.[4] And the increasing inadequacy of the weekly mail service was emphasized by New Mexico Territory's Secretary W. F. M. Arny, who stopped over in Kansas City on his way to Washington. Arny said that in the capital he would press for a triweekly mail service to New Mexico. That goal had the full approval of the editor of the *Kansas City Daily Journal of Commerce,* who observed that the government had appropriated money by the millions for mail service to Colorado, Salt Lake, and California, while the people of New Mexico were put off with a deficient weekly service.[5]

Talk was again circulating that Leavenworth, Kansas, might be made the terminus of the Santa Fe line. It had been heard before, and Secretary Arny thought that proponents of the change would not be successful. That opinion was punctuated by the Kansas City editor, who said that the service rendered by the present Santa Fe mail contractors was superior to anything that would be offered by the Kansas Stage Company,[6] presumably the company that would take over if the terminus were changed.

With the sprouting of spring grass on the plains came the annual revival of commerce over the Santa Fe Trail, and many hoped that 1865 might be a record year.[7] The seasonal surge also aroused the dangers to wagon trains and stagecoaches from Indians. Santa Fe Stage Company officials were apprehensive when the mail stage from Santa Fe failed to come during the last week in April; only a coach from Fort Larned arrived.[8] But the risks did not interrupt stage departures.

For the moment the Indian activity was commonplace—like the theft of seventeen mules from the stage station at Fort Larned.[9] Also, the Army's anticipation of Indian hostilities by systematizing military escorts of wagon trains between Forts Larned and Union was reassuring to travelers. The plan, beginning March 1, was to allow an escorted train to leave Fort Union on the 1st and 15th of each month, alternating between the Cimarron Cutoff and Mountain Branch routes. The returning military units would accompany the wagons that had collected at Fort Larned. Similar arrangements were made for wagon trains east of Fort Larned. Plan and performance, however, were two different matters, and after about two months the tightly planned escort service was abandoned because of lack of troops.[10]

On June 9, "Colonel" Sanderson sent out a Santa Fe coach from Kansas City "full of passengers and express freight," and it turned out that the Santa Fe Stage Company's patrons on that trip were in for a thrill. Somewhere along the route another coach, carrying military personnel, joined them, although the two vehicles did not travel close together. The mail coach had an escort of six men from the Second Colorado Cavalry commanded by Lieutenant R. W. Jenkins. Three days out on Tuesday, June 12, at a spot three miles west of the Cow Creek station (east of Fort Larned), about fifty mounted Indians (unidentified) made a dash to intercept the mail coach. The driver had seen them soon enough to wheel his mules around and head at top speed back to the Cow Creek station. Pursuit by the Indians was warded off by Lieutenant Jenkins and his men. When the Indians gave up and veered toward the Arkansas River, the cavalrymen followed and inflicted some casualties.[11]

Veteran conductor Peter Kelly said in Kansas City that in his years of experience he had never seen worse conditions along the Trail. His opinion was strengthened by a report that Indians had run off all government livestock except ten head at the new Fort Dodge and had killed and scalped several people along the route.[12] The uncompleted post was just west of where the "wet" and "dry" routes from Fort Larned merged. Its location was strategic because it was between two principal places where Indians forded the Arkansas River—the Cimarron Crossing to the west and the Mulberry Creek crossing to the east. At the time of the alleged loss of livestock, the soldiers at Fort Dodge were quartered in dugouts along the bank of the Arkansas.[13] Close by was the stage company's Adkins Ranch station, established in 1863 and burned by Indians in 1864.[14]

During July and August 1865, the military escorted mail stages between Fort Lyon and Fort Larned.[15] Along the Purgatoire River an extremely heavy rainstorm caused flooding that destroyed sheep and goats which belonged to settlers who had recently come into that valley.[16]

107

South of the Raton Mountains an incident occurred that, on first report, appeared serious. Presumably, Cimarron's distinguished resident and alleged owner of the Beaubien and Miranda (Maxwell) Land Grant, Lucien B. Maxwell, and two soldiers were killed by Ute Indians. But the Santa Fe Stage Line's agent at Cimarron, a man named Mills (probably Melvin W.), corrected the story, saying that the Ute had surrounded Maxwell and his family but he talked their way out of a dangerous situation.[17]

Along the Santa Fe Stage Company's routes there were a few changes in facilities. The Beach Valley station, between Big Turkey Creek and Fort Zarah, was reestablished after a post office discontinuation of over a year, and the Kiowa office was renamed Fort Zarah. Those were in Kansas. In New Mexico, below Las Vegas, San Miguel was given a post office after being without one since 1859. At the same time the San Jose office was closed.[18]

New developments also occurred in Colorado on the main line and the Arkansas River branch. At the Gray's Ranch station and post office on the Purgatoire, Dan L. Taylor, former hotel keeper at Fort Union, opened a general store.[19] But the major development on the main line in the summer of 1865 was a road improvement at the highest point—the Raton Pass, south of Trinidad. "Uncle Dick" Wootton (Richens Lacy Wootton), prominent scout, Indian fighter, and trader, had been permitted by an act of the Colorado territorial legislature to incorporate the "Trinidad and Ratoon [sic] Mountain Wagon Road Company,"[20] and his hired hands labored long and hard to get the twenty-seven miles of improved road ready for use. Wootton said that he also obtained a similar charter from the New Mexico legislature to build and operate a toll into New Mexico as far as Red River.[21]

On the branch line up the Arkansas River from Bent's Old Fort, a transportation of U.S. mail over the forty-four miles between Pueblo and Canon City was terminated by departmental order, effective August 31, 1865.[22] The cut in service was probably brought about by the sharp decline in Canon City's population during the Civil War years.[23] That contraction resulted in an annual deduction in pay to the Santa Fe Stage Company of $1,672, bringing the total annual compensation from $37,415 to $35,743. Not far below Bent's Old Fort on the main line, the Point of Rocks post office (established in May 1864) was discontinued early in the year.[24]

The year 1865 was a poor one for the Post Office Department in terms of money received on the Kansas City-Santa Fe line. President Andrew Johnson's postmaster general, William Dennison, said he recognized the vital national objectives of such a service and the public approval that it commanded, but he did not think that the heavy costs should be charged wholly to the postal fund, which belonged to those who contributed to it. Dennison submitted the following figures in making his point:

	Pay	Receipts	Excess of Pay[25]
Kansas City to Santa Fe	$35,743.00	$6,536.57	$29,206.43

In another sense, the Post Office Department fared well during the summer of 1865. Measures taken by the War Department—escorts and new forts—greatly reduced the number and severity of Indian attacks on mail stages and wagon trains. To cope with the possibilities of a major uprising, two small temporary forts were founded along the Trail. Camp Nichols was established by Colonel Kit Carson near Cold Spring on the Cimarron Cutoff and was in use from May until November.[26] The other was Fort Aubry, located on a site recommended originally by the well-known trader and Trail rider Francis X. Aubry[27] and intended to protect the Aubry Cutoff and the Mountain Branch of the Santa Fe Trail. The site chosen was on the Arkansas River in Kansas, not far from the Colorado line. Fort Aubry was occupied from September 1865, to April 1866. A post office was in operation there from January to October 1866.[28]

An anonymous passenger recorded some interesting facts about a trip on the Santa Fe Stage line from Denver to Bent's Old Fort. Leaving Denver at 8:45 A.M., January 3, 1866, the coach arrived at Franktown for the midday meal, and the passengers had supper at Colorado City.[29] The run had taken ten hours for a distance of seventy-two miles, which was thought to be "pretty good staging." Cold weather prevailed, and snow was deep on the summit of the divide. After the supper stop, travel was resumed through the snow, and the Fontaine qui Bouille (Fountain) was reached at daybreak. There was no great rush on the trip from Pueblo because the coach from Santa Fe was expected to be late by half a day or more in reaching Bent's Old Fort. Snow lay on the ground for thirty or forty miles down the Arkansas and then disappeared until about fifteen or twenty miles from the old trading post.

The observant passenger was impressed by the number of irrigated farms along the river below Pueblo, but he said there was an almost un-limited supply of good land that was still covered with greasewood and sagebrush. About ten miles below Booneville at the stage station near the former Civil War Camp Fillmore, he was annoyed to see about 1,500 tons of hay put up for the government, with no government animals to eat it. Cows of local farmers were the main beneficiaries. Many buffalo had recently come into the valley of the Arkansas near Spring Bottom, an-other stage station about twenty miles above Bent's Old Fort,[30] where hunters were killing them for their bones, hearts, and tongues, which were marketable in Denver.

The coach arrived at Bent's Old Fort a little before 10 P.M.; the one from Santa Fe had come in five hours before. Looking with interest upon the thick adobe walls and remnants of bastions and other defenses, the passenger-writer noted that the stage company had converted the fort into "a very complete and comfortable station," and he had nothing but praise for Messenger Arthur Hill, who had charge of the coach from Den-ver. The passenger departed on the eastbound coach in the morning.[31]

Words of praise for Messenger Hill, particularly for his "fish horn solo" announcing the coach's approach to a station, were expressed by another passenger two weeks later, but this one had nothing to say for the Santa Fe Stage Line's accommodations at Bent's Old Fort. This time the correspondent for the *Rocky Mountain News* was a man of some literary pretentions named Russell, who was a correspondent for *Harper's Magazine*.[32] Perhaps his outlook was soured a bit by the fact that he had to wait some time for the coach coming from Kansas City to Santa Fe. Or, perhaps Russell's memory of the generous dinner at Booneville and the company of the colonel's pretty daughters distorted his view of things. At any rate, he reported that it was "an absolute impossibility" for the stage from the States to make close connection at Bent's Old Fort with the one from Denver. The Denver-Santa Fe passenger also questioned the liberality of the stage company. While he was there, the coach from Santa Fe left for the east in a driving snowstorm.[33]

The weather was generally severe along the Trail in southern Colorado and northern New Mexico. An eastbound coach, perhaps the one watched by Russell at Bent's Old Fort, encountered several snowbound wagon trains, each of which had sustained heavy loss of livestock. Nine men with one train were badly frozen, and three government trains lost over 300 head of livestock. All of this bad fortune was caused by a covering of snow from one to two feet deep, topped by a hard crust, over much of the country between Red River and the Arkansas.[34]

In the opinion of correspondent Russell, the next station below Bent's Old Fort, Iron Spring, was a more comfortable place, where "the landlord can 'keep a station.' " He was quite curious about the spring, with its water of high iron content flowing at a rate of several gallons per minute. However, he found Raton Pass a disappointment in not being nearly so high and grand as he had imagined.[35] It may have been Russell who sent a special dispatch to the *Rocky Mountain News* about an interesting circumstance at "Uncle Dick" Wootton's stage station in the pass. A southern Kansas editor by the name of Sam Wood was there with a broken leg. He said an old trapper had told him about a spring of almost pure tar boiling out of the earth. Wood hoped to see it, thinking it was probably petroleum, and he generalized on what he thought was the enormous wealth of coal and oil in the Raton Pass country. It was enough to pay the national debt, he said, and he called for a geological survey of the area.[36]

The *Harper's* man was quite impressed by Lucien B. Maxwell and his establishment on the Cimarron, with its Pennsylvania-type barn and recently completed flour mill. Two Navajo squaws in the small building next to the house wove a blanket every two weeks and were currently working on one that Maxwell planned to give to the secretary of the interior.

Russell spoke of Rayado as the first Mexican town on the route. They stopped there to eat, and the fowl placed upon the table caused another passenger to ask "if they had many petrifactions like it in the region." They reached Fort Union at midnight. There the Santa Fe Stage Line's Thomas J. Barnum climbed aboard and made the trip into Santa Fe, where he took Russell and his traveling companion, General William R. Brewster, to La Fonda and showed them around the town a bit.[37] Russell did not say whether Barnum was fully aware of the general's identity or the purpose of his journey, but it is difficult to imagine that Barnum was ignorant.

Military rank—brigadier general of volunteers for service before Richmond[38]—was not Brewster's only distinction; he was then vice-president of David A. Butterfield's Overland Despatch Company. The company, originally a freight and express line, recently reorganized to compete with Ben Holladay's Overland line mail and passenger service west of

the Missouri River and to challenge the Santa Fe Stage Company's monopoly over service to Santa Fe.[39] Butterfield's Overland Despatch had
reopened the Smoky Hill Trail, which was roughly midway between the
Platte River and Arkansas River roads, and Holladay responded by
slashing rates and fares and by tough harrassments, apparently even to
the point of physical attacks (disguised as Indian raids) on Overland
Despatch people and vehicles.[40] There is no evidence that the Santa Fe
Stage Company planned similar reactions. In fact, Barnum's presence
on the coach from Fort Union to Santa Fe, and his attention to Brewster
and Russell in showing them some of the sights of Santa Fe, strongly suggest that business consultations took place some time during the visit.

General Brewster was on a fact-finding tour. Among the plans of the
B.O.D., as the Butterfield Overland Despatch Company was commonly
known, was a line from Denver to Santa Fe that would be a hundred miles
shorter than that used by the Santa Fe Stage Company.[41] The Overland
Despatch people were undoubtedly thinking in terms of cutting straight
south from Pueblo via the old Denver-Fort Union Road to Gray's Ranch,
Trinidad, and the Raton Pass, thus eliminating the long, eastward jog to
Bent's Old Fort and back—a sensible proposal. Their major proposition,
however, was for B.O.D. coaches to cut south from the Smoky Hill route
at Pond Creek, Kansas, to Fort Lyon, Colorado. Surveyors who had been
out in December 1865 determined that their line would cut seventy miles
from the Missouri River to the New Mexico capital.[42]

Basic to the whole concept of successfully competing against Holladay's Overland Mail line and the Santa Fe Stage Company was the westward construction of the Union Pacific Eastern Division Railroad from
Kansas City. Track laying had begun in late 1863[43] and extended forty
miles by mid-July 1864.[44] Soon, daily trains were running in and out of
Lawrence, Kansas. Leavenworth, the terminus of Holladay's stage line,
was without a railroad, and before long the Santa Fe Stage line would
not need to go all the way into Kansas City. The B.O.D. proposed to begin
from successive railhead towns. Therefore, its routes to Denver and Santa
Fe and beyond would get shorter and shorter,[45] which would bring competition to terms or extinction. One contemporary observer expected that
by 1865 mail from Santa Fe would be going from Fort Riley to New York
City with only one change of cars.[46] In early 1866, when the tracks were
approaching Junction City, Kansas, near Fort Riley, the impact of the

railroad on the Santa Fe line was expressed a little differently; the combined modes of transportation would put Santa Fe within eight or nine days of travel time from St. Louis.[47] That a Santa Fe Stage Company coach made a record trip of eleven days from Kansas City to Santa Fe in March 1866[48] soon would be irrelevant.

Ben Holladay would not topple easily. On February 5, 1866, about a fortnight after Colorado's territorial legislature passed an act incorporating the "Butterfield Overland Dispatch [sic] Company," it also granted a charter to the Holladay Overland Mail and Express Company.[49]

There is no indication whether the Santa Fe Stage Company's officials were greatly disturbed by the possible takeover. Both Bradley Barlow and Jared L. Sanderson followed the normal course of events and submitted bids for the Santa Fe mail contract in the spring of 1866. Among the fifteen other bidders were Isaac E. Eaton, James B. Kitchen, and E. F. Hooker.[50] Presumably, Eaton was the retired army officer who had made a survey of the Smoky Hill route for David A. Butterfield,[51] and Kitchen may have been related to W. E. Kitchen, treasurer of the Butterfield Overland Despatch.[52] One or both of them may have been acting for that company. E. F. Hooker was undoubtedly the former superintendent of the Kansas Stage Company, another loser in the fight against Holladay's aggressive tactics.[53] Of the remaining twelve bidders, no one is identifiable as a Holladay representative. Two of them—Samuel Slemmons and Harvey M. Vaile—had former Santa Fe line associations. Denver mail contractor Harmon G. Weibling made a proposal, and the man listed as Francis Perea[54] was in all likehood Francisco Perea, former delegate from New Mexico to the U.S. Congress.

Jared L. Sanderson's offer to carry the mail three times a week from the railhead at Lawrence, Kansas, to Santa Fe, New Mexico, and return for $47,700 per annum was accepted on April 13, 1866. Five days later a Post Office Department order directed that Bradley Barlow be associated with Sanderson as mail contractor for the line, beginning July 1, 1866.[55] It is curious that one contemporary notice of the award said that the Santa Fe mail contract had been let to Barlow, the old contractor.[56] This may have been an example of collusion known as straw bidding. If not, it was a case of careful planning. True, Sanderson's bid was the lowest of those based on triweekly service. One of Barlow's proposals ($85,000) was for triweekly service on a shortened running time, and

113

the other ($57,000) was for triweekly service on the main and once a week on a branch,[57] presumably meaning from Bent's Old Fort to Pueblo and possibly on to Denver.

Even before the Lawrence-Santa Fe contract was awarded to Sanderson, the problem of competition with the Butterfield Overland Despatch Company disappeared. Ben Holladay bought out the B.O.D. in March, once again monopolizing the stagecoach services between the Missouri River and Salt Lake City.[58] It was first reported that Holladay would abandon the Smoky Hill route, but that was soon disproved.[59] By early April the Smoky Hill line was being stocked from both ends, and a lumber train left Denver for construction of stations along the way. It was expected that mail would be transported by April 15, with passenger and express service already under way.[60] On May 4 the *Rocky Mountain News* recorded that an Overland Mail and Express coach had come from Atchison, Kansas, over the Smoky Hill route to Denver in only five days and twelve hours.[61] For all the Overland Company's use of the Smoky Hill route, however, evidence is lacking that Ben Holladay had marked the Santa Fe line for conquest. If he entertained the idea, his own immediate problems relegated it to the background.

In the spring bidding on contracts, Jared L. Sanderson had tried to secure the Colorado Route No. 17001 from Denver to Pueblo. He failed, and the contract went to Daniel Witter, who proposed a round-trip service twice a week for an annual compensation of $4,440.[62] Witter was a prominent Denver figure, who had been a member of the lower house of Colorado's first territorial legislature and candidate for governor in the 1864 abortive attempt to achieve statehood for Colorado.[63] He was also the brother-in-law of Schuyler Colfax, then speaker of the House of Representatives in Washington, former chairman of the House Committee on Post Offices and Post Roads, and the man who introduced a bill (1859) to create Colona Territory, the first attempt to organize the gold region of western Kansas Territory into a separate unit.[64] Witter may have been a front man for more powerful interests, but the available data do not confirm this.

10

The Emergence of Barlow and Sanderson

1866-1867

FOR SEVERAL YEARS Bradley Barlow had been a major figure in the operation of companies providing mail, express, and passenger service on the Santa Fe line and its branches. The death of Mahlon Cottrill in October 1864 probably clinched Barlow's position in the former Cottrill company and opened the way for Jared L. Sanderson's move into the top management group. The order of April 18, 1866 simply gave official sanction to Sanderson and Barlow[1] already *de facto* partners, as mail contractors.

In the closing days under the 1862 contract, of course, the Santa Fe stages continued to use Kansas City as the eastern terminus, and one of their conductors, George Richards, was quoted as saying that New Mexico merchants were determined to return to Kansas City.[2] He probably meant only that most of them would continue to patronize Kansas City jobbers and wholesalers even though their wagons no longer came into the city. And the people on the coaches brought in reports of familiar conditions along the way—Indians were amicable and a two-foot snow in the Raton Mountains had delayed the coach for twenty-four hours.[3]

Evidently the mail that left Santa Fe in mid-June was treated as the first conveyed under the new contract. Although originally directed to Lawrence, it went to Junction City, at the confluence of the Smoky Hill and Republican Rivers. A departmental order of June 20 provided that Junction City, the new terminus of the Union Pacific Eastern Division Railroad, would be the official end of the 805-mile stage line, beginning July 1.

The first mail for Santa Fe under the new arrangement departed from Junction City on July 2, traveling through Detroit, Abilene, Solomon

115

City, Salina, and Ellsworth (near Fort Harker). The route to Ellsworth was the same as that used by the Holladay Overland Mail coaches on their way to Denver. From Ellsworth the new Santa Fe mail route cut south to Fort Zarah, on the Santa Fe Trail near the juncture of Walnut Creek with the Arkansas River.[4] That meant, of course, that all the stage stations and post offices east of the Big Bend of the Arkansas on the Santa Fe Trail were no longer served by the "great Santa Fe mail."

A questionable story from the *Council Grove Democrat*, copied by the *Junction City Union* shortly after the change of route, said that when the Santa Fe Stage Company had drawn off its stock and coaches, over two tons of mail had been left in the old stage barn at Council Grove. Some of it had been there for quite a while; some of it was addressed to *His Excellency, the Governor of New Mexico*. The item ended with the comment: "Faithful mail contractors they are indeed."[5]

The postal route changes in Kansas also resulted in the transfer of the operational headquarters of the Santa Fe Stage Company to Junction City.[6] Sanderson kept an office in Kansas City for his Kansas City and Fort Scott stage line. His son, J. L. Sanderson, Jr. assisted him in that line, but it is not known whether Bradley Barlow had an interest.[7]

For some time before the new Santa Fe contract began, company officials were preparing the line for the new triweekly service. On May 29, 1866, they sent out twenty-six men in three coaches and three wagons to build new stations and corrals. There were probably other work parties; the overall job was sufficiently large to take most of the summer and fall to complete. Much of their effort was expended on the Long Route between Fort Larned and Fort Lyon. In the 230-mile distance, habitations were sparse—nothing in the 110 miles from Fort Dodge to abandoned Fort Aubry, for example.[8]

Seven stations were put up along the Arkansas east of Fort Lyon on locations recommended by Robert M. Wright. Those built under his supervision were rather simple structures. The road was on the north bank of the river. Low bluffs that could be excavated were chosen. The dugouts were fronted by sod or adobe walls over which poles were laid and covered with hay and dirt. Wright was also employed to harvest local hay for the stations, as well as to bring in grain by mule trains from as far away as the Missouri River. One of his stations was at the well-known point on the Mountain Branch known as Pretty Encampment, and Fred Schmidt was its first keeper.[9]

Other men were distributed along the Mountain Branch below Bent's Old Fort. From there to Gray's Ranch, just east of Trinidad on the Purgatoire, there were no settlements except the isolated little station at Iron Spring. Alex Taylor and George Boyles were placed as stage drivers over the forty-five miles from Gray's Ranch to Iron Spring and back. Three months later (about late September), Taylor received instructions to build a new station between those points at Hole-in-the-Prairie,[10] an old camping place on the Mountain Branch of the Trail. It is probable that a station was established about the same time at Hole-in-the-Rock, at the head of Timpas Creek about half way from Hole-in-the-Prairie to Iron Spring.[11]

Transfer of the post office from Gray's Ranch back to Trinidad in early 1866[12] restored the status Trinidad had lost when the post office was moved to Gray's Ranch almost three years before. On November 26, 1866, Barlow, Sanderson and Company, U.S. mail contractors, leased space in a small hotel on Main Street, Trinidad, belonging to William R. Walker,[13] "Uncle Dick" Wootton's son-in-law. This is the first documented use of the name "Barlow, Sanderson and Company" found so far. During the summer, far south of Santa Fe, Thomas J. Barnum was setting up new mail stations between Mesilla, New Mexico, and Tucson, Arizona.[14]

Under the 1866 contract for Route No. 14020, the Santa Fe Stage Company continued to serve the branch line up the Arkansas from Bent's Old Fort to Pueblo,[15] but Jared L. Sanderson's failure to obtain the contract for Route No. 17001 from Pueblo to Denver meant that the Santa Fe Stage Company's service to Denver would be for express and passengers only. Daniel Witter had secured that contract for $4,440 per annum,[16] but he sublet it to William Jones—known also as "One-armed" Jones—who announced in late June that he would carry the semiweekly mail from Denver to Pueblo and back in two-horse hacks, converting to four-horse coaches as soon as business justified.

Jones also procured a contract to transport a weekly mail from Pueblo to Santa Fe by way of the mountain route over the Sangre de Cristo Pass and through the San Luis Valley. The points to be served en route by his two-mule buckboards (for mail, express freight, and passengers) were south from Pueblo to the settlement on the St. Charles River (Rio San Carlos) and Hermosilla on the Huerfano River, from there west over the pass to Fort Garland in the San Luis Valley, and then south through San

Luis, Costilla, Taos, an unnamed post office, and on to Santa Fe. He publicized that his route was 150 miles and two days shorter than any other line.[17]

Proprietor William Jones called his venture the Denver and Santa Fe Stage Line, somewhat of an overstatement. Beginning August 1, a departmental order increased the service to Pueblo from twice to three times weekly, with an additional compensation of $2,220, evidently to make connection with the triweekly Santa Fe Stage Company coaches.[18] For $20 a passenger could board one of Jones's vehicles and reach Pueblo in twenty hours, barring unforeseen difficulties.

The Denver office of the line was at 76 F Street, with William S. Walker as agent. The address was also that of A. Jacobs and Company's clothing store, and it appears that Walker was the manager of that business.[19] When the new Denver-Pueblo line became operational, the old Santa Fe Stage Company, then controlled by Messrs. Barlow and Sanderson, abandoned its service between the two towns.[20]

On his route from Pueblo to Santa Fe, Jones met with troubles at once. Controversy developed with the postmaster at Pueblo, who felt that Jones should carry the mail for Santa Fe; Jones insisted that he was expected to carry only mail for points along the way and that the line was stocked for carrying just that by horseback. The *Rocky Mountain News* said that Mr. Barnum, of the other route—meaning the Barlow and Sanderson contract from Pueblo to Bent's Old Fort and Santa Fe—believed that Jones should carry it, but the paper emphasized that Barnum was not a direct party to the controversy.[21] If so, then it appears that Barnum was hoping to maneuver Jones into a responsibility to restock that he could not handle financially, forcing him to give up the Pueblo-Santa Fe route. To avoid indefinite detention of the mail, Jones made an agreement with Barnum for Barnum to carry the mail to Santa Fe. Jones then asked the Post Office Department for a ruling, which was made in his favor; it was ordered that the through mail to Santa Fe would go by "Barnum's route" on the roundabout way via Bent's Old Fort, which was 137 miles farther according to the distances published in the Denver paper.[22]

A new post office had been established at Excelsior, on the Bent's Old Fort-Pueblo branch, and at the Pawnee Fork office, renamed Fort Larned before Barlow and Sanderson became the line's mail contractor. Afterward, they were directed to serve Chapman's Creek, Kansas, between

Junction City and Detroit, without change of pay. But the most important departmental order affecting them was that to reduce the running time on the main line, beginning July 16, 1866, from fourteen days to ten from April 1 to December 1, and to twelve days from December 1 to April 1. Their coaches still adhered to Monday, Wednesday, Friday departures, leaving Junction City at 8 A.M. and Santa Fe at midnight.[23]

Indian relations along the Santa Fe Trail were the most peaceful in years, mainly due to a series of treaties concluded with Plains tribes the previous autumn.[24] There was some worrisome unrest, however, among the Ute and Jicarilla Apache in southern Colorado and northern New Mexico during the summer. In June, a few Tabeguache Ute were on the Huerfano, far east of where they should have been,[25] and the next month a mixed band of Ute and Jicarilla Apache raided livestock near Trinidad.[26] The climax came in early October when the Mohuache Ute under their Chief Ka-ni-ache clashed a few miles west of Trinidad with Company G, Third Cavalry, commanded by Lieutenant Colonel Andrew J. Alexander. When the Ute withdrew, they raided and killed settlers on the upper Cucharas and Huerfano rivers.[27]

Trouble for the stage line came from other sources, one of them internal. An outbound Santa Fe coach, with Peter Kelly as conductor and Frank Simcox as driver, arrived at Gray's Ranch on the Purgatoire one day in October. Simcox quit, drew his pay, and started back on an eastbound coach conducted by Charles Richards. It was not until later that Kelly, perhaps suspicious because of the driver's abrupt termination, discovered that Simcox had probably stolen company funds. Instead of having the stage pursued, Kelly sent a messenger to Denver with instructions to telegraph to Junction City asking for Simcox's arrest there. When the ex-driver stepped off the coach, he was arrested with $1,803 of company money on him, and he was lodged in the town jail.[28]

On the last day of October, a coach bound for Santa Fe experienced an attempted holdup as it passed through Arroyo Hondo, a short distance outside the city. Five men sprang from the bushes by the roadside and tried to stop the mules, but the lead mules were spirited animals and sprang forward, leaving the would-be robbers in the dust. It was believed that the men were army deserters, who later gave themselves up.[29]

The next day, November 1, 1866, was significant in the history of American stage lines. There was a great merger of the Holladay Overland Mail and Express Company with Wells, Fargo and Company and other express companies. The merger was accomplished under the terms of the Colorado charter obtained by Holladay in 1865, but Wells, Fargo and Company was the name of the consolidated giant, because that firm was in financial control.[30] Wells, Fargo and Company now dominated every stage line of importance between the Missouri River and California, with the exception of the Santa Fe Stage Company operating from Junction City to Santa Fe and beyond.

Not long after its near-monopoly of western staging began, Wells, Fargo and Company allowed the United States Express Company to run the Smoky Hill line into Denver. Superintendent was W. H. Cottrill,[31] who may have been the son of the late Mahlon Cottrill,[32] onetime controlling factor in the Santa Fe line. The Wells, Fargo and Company subsidiary and the Santa Fe Stage Company apparently coexisted in amity on that segment of the Smoky Hill route from Junction City to Ellsworth, since both lines had to face the advancing competition of the Union Pacific Eastern Division Railroad. Occasionally, the two stage lines cooperated. On Washington's Birthday, 1867, the Smoky Hill coach came into Denver with several sacks of Santa Fe mail on board because of an interruption on the Santa Fe line—probably high water.[33]

The usual, sporadically harsh, spring weather prevailed in 1867, but one incident was rather extreme. President Andrew Johnson's appointee as governor of New Mexico, Robert B. Mitchell, was returning on the regular mail stage to Santa Fe, when a terrific twelve-hour windstorm lashed the Cimarron area. The wind was so strong that the driver was blown from his seat—a published account said for forty feet—and the coach had to be held on the ground by chains.[34]

The companion danger to bad weather—the Indian—was still evident despite the relative peacefulness of recent months. Shortly after the turn of the New Year, a band of "friendlies," in this case a mixed group of Cheyenne and Arapaho, intercepted the Santa Fe coach near the Cimarron Crossing of the Arkansas and asked for tobacco and other provisions, which were given to them. On hearing of the incident, the editor of the *Junction City Weekly Union* commented: "That kind of robbery on the plains is becoming as frequent as it is incommodious, and should have a stop put to it in some way."

About the same time, the Santa Fe *New Mexican* noted that Conductor Quinby brought in the eastern mail from Junction City on January 14 after a record trip of only six days and nineteen hours.[35] But the people of Junction City were very much concerned about the approaching end of their prosperous days in a railhead town. W. S. Stone, agent for the Santa Fe Stage Company and the Merchants Union Express, had hardly established a general railroad ticket office in Junction City when attention began to turn more and more to the future benefits that would accrue to the town of Ellsworth and its nearby fort, recently renamed Fort Harker.[36]

Before Junction City became just another station on the railroad and the terminals of the Santa Fe and Smoky Hill lines were moved westward, the Post Office Department issued an order in April to Barlow, Sanderson and Company and their Santa Fe Stage Company to reduce the running time from ten to seven days for eight months of the year and from twelve to eight days for the four winter months. An additional $28,620 pay per annum was allowed, "the Department having satisfactory evidence that this additional compensation does not bear a greater proportion to the additional stock, or carriers, rendered necessary, than the sum stipulated in the original contract bears to the stock and carriers necessarily employed in its execution." That brought the mail contractors' total annual pay up to $85,860.[37] Former New Mexico delegate to Congress John S. Watts was credited with having arranged for the time reduction, assisted by Senator Samuel C. Pomeroy of Kansas.[38]

Then came the order of July 13, 1867 to shift the terminus of the stage line westward about eighty miles to Fort Harker, about four miles east of the town of Ellsworth.[39] Probably the bulk of the Santa Fe Stage Company's business was centered in the railhead town of Ellsworth, but the Department officially designated the fort as the terminus, because it was not directly on the railroad. No reduction of pay was made because the Department stipulated that, although all post offices between Junction City and Ellsworth on the railroad would not require the stage line's service, places like Solomon City, Salina, and Fort Harker (not on the railroad) would still be supplied by the stage company. Operating out of the new terminus reduced the running time to Santa Fe by thirty-six hours.[40]

In September a passenger on a Santa Fe coach reported that the body of a scalped and mutilated man was found near Plum Creek, about eighteen miles west of Fort Harker. It was thought he had been dead for only about a half hour and was killed by a small band of Cheyenne. The coach was probably not molested because it had a military escort. The picket house at the stage station at Cow Creek was heavily barricaded, with a woman, two men, and a dead man inside. A begging group of Cheyenne had surrounded the place about an hour before the coach's arrival. When the occupants refused to let the Indians come in, a Cheyenne thrust a revolver through the pickets and managed to mortally wound one of the men. The approach of the coach and escort caused the Indians to flee. When the mail party, augmented by the people at the Cow Creek station, reached Coon Creek they found that Indians had driven off seven mules from the station corral. At Fort Dodge the next day they heard of numerous raids in the vicinity, and later at the Cimarron Crossing of the Arkansas they found that Indians had attacked a large Mexican train, running off about 280 mules including two that were attached to a mowing machine belonging to Robert Wright. In accounts of that kind, narrators often digressed to condemn do-gooders, frequently Washington officials, who thought of the Indian in terms of the noble savage. In this instance, the person so criticized was William Hepworth Dixon, well-known English writer who had spent the summer and autumn of 1866 in the United States and whose book *New America* (1867) aroused the stage passenger's ire because of its facile recommendations that Indians should be employed in agriculture. Seizure of Bob Wright's mowing machine was evidently the basis for the complaint.[41]

On the Arkansas above Fort Dodge the Indians were less active, supposedly because of the presence of cholera, which the Indians tried to avoid.[42] In support of that theory it was reported that "several bodies of Indians have lately been discovered on both the Smoky and Santa Fe routes. They appear to have died from disease, as there were no marks of violence on the bodies. It is thought the cholera is among them."[43]

But even that area did not escape entirely. A short distance west of the Cimarron Crossing on Nine Mile Ridge, a U.S. paymaster with an escort of sixty men repulsed about seventy-five Indians in a four-hour fight.[44] Hope was raised for an end to depredations when representatives of most of the Plains tribes along the Santa Fe Trail signed the Medicine Lodge treaties in October, but there was also skepticism that neither whites nor Indians would stand by the agreements.[45] Postmaster General Alexander Randall, in his annual report for 1867, stated that Barlow, Sanderson and Company service was much less interrupted than that on the line to the north operated by Wells, Fargo and Company.[46]

Ellsworth's days as a railhead town were few. During the late summer

122

and early fall of 1867 the Union Pacific Eastern Division Railroad built about sixty miles of track across the plains to the recently relocated Fort Hays, where another town sprang up.[47] A departmental order of October 28, 1867 directed that Barlow, Sanderson and Company begin their service from Hays City on November 1.[48] The short time given for the transfer suggests that the order was simply official approval of something that was already a matter of practice. Apparently, there was no change in pay. The cutback meant more than simply lopping off some miles in the progression from one railhead town to the next. It also resulted in abandonment by the stage line of that segment of the Santa Fe Trail between Fort Zarah and Fort Dodge, including Fort Larned—the former Camp on Pawnee Fork.[49] The line dropped south from Hays City to Fort Dodge, and from there west along the Arkansas to Fort Lyon and on over the Mountain Branch to Santa Fe. That put Santa Fe only four and a half days from the railhead and nine days from New York City. By mid-December the run from the New Mexican capital to Hays City was being made in four days and eleven hours.[50] Mail stages left from each end of the line at 8 A.M. on Monday, Wednesday, and Friday.[51]

There is little personal information about Bradley Barlow and Jared Sanderson, the principal partners in Barlow, Sanderson and Company, and on Sanderson the record is contradictory and confusing. Their contracts give Kansas City as their place of business, but it is doubtful that Barlow spent much time there or on the line. Barlow continued to serve as cashier of the Vermont National Bank in St. Albans and as treasurer of Franklin County in 1867. In 1868 he was elected a senator from Franklin County to the Vermont legislature.[52]

There is no doubt that Jared Sanderson was actively engaged in management of the partnership's staging operations, but precisely when and how much are debatable. On January 21, 1865, the *Kansas City Daily Journal of Commerce* noted that "Mr. J. P. [L.] Sanderson, one of the most successful stage men in the west, has lately become connected with this company [the Santa Fe Stage Company]."[53] That makes his statement (in 1903) that he and his wife moved into the stage station at Bent's Old Fort in 1861 and lived there for twenty years open to serious challenge;[54] even more questionable is the assertion, apparently his, that he carried the first mail into Denver in 1860.[55] And quite insupportable is the claim in one of his obituaries (1915) that "he organized the first stage freight, passenger and mail line from Kansas City to all parts of the

Southwest and the Pacific Coast."[56] There is no agreement as to when he retired from the staging business—1880, 1885, or 1890.[57]

Sanderson's use of "colonel," which first appeared in the record in June 1865,[58] was probably at most a courtesy title. His obituary (1915) contained the unsubstantiated and implausible explanation that the government bestowed it in 1861 for his distinguished service in protecting U.S. property.[59] There is a possible speculative explanation. The Kansas City newspaper item that noted his connection with the Santa Fe Stage Company referred to him incorrectly as J. P. Sanderson, and after that, the title of "colonel" came into use. There was a Colonel J. P. (John Philip) Sanderson, provost marshal of the Department of the Missouri, who died in October 1864.[60] Perhaps some misidentification transferred the title from the deceased J. P. Sanderson to the living J. L. Sanderson.

11

The Southern Overland Mail and Express Company

1867-1869

ALTHOUGH THE NAME "Southern Mail Company" is found as early as 1863,[1] it appears to have been of local use in reference to Cottrill, Vickroy and Company and M. Cottrill and Company, both of which carried the mail south from Denver in 1862 and 1863. But the key word "Overland" was not appropriated by Barlow and Sanderson until some time after they obtained contracts in 1866 to carry mail from Kansas to California.[2]

Primarily connoting a line from the Mississippi or the Missouri to the Pacific coast, "Overland" appeared in the name of the Overland Mail Company (John Butterfield's line) in 1857.[3] Its rivalry with promoters of the central route was obvious with organization of the Central Overland California and Pike's Peak Express Company in 1859.[4] The Civil War put an end to the southern line, but the Overland Mail Company secured a mail contract to California over the central route in 1861.

About the same time, it obtained control of the ailing Central Overland California,[5] which provided service as far west as Salt Lake City. In 1862, however, Ben Holladay took over the Central Overland California,[6] and from then until 1866 he dominated the central route as far as Salt Lake City,[7] with only a brief bout of competition with David Butterfield's Overland Despatch on the Smoky Hill route.[8] His operation went under the name of the Holladay Overland Mail and Express Company.[9] When Wells Fargo took over the entire central route in 1866, the firm did not incorporate the word "overland" in its name, although it advertised as sole proprietor of the "Great Overland Mail Route."[10]

In a sense the word became available at a time when Barlow, Sanderson and Company held mail contracts from a Kansas railhead to Santa Fe, El Paso, Tucson, San Diego, and Los Angeles,[11] making their line an overland one in the accepted meaning of the term. Although they might have used the word anyway, the new circumstances enabled them to use it without challenge as the Southern Overland Mail and Express Company over a route that, from El Paso west, was essentially a restoration of Butterfield's Overland Mail line.

Barlow, Sanderson and Company now controlled one of the two so-called transcontinental mail, express, and passenger routes to California, which had been established by the Post Office Department's extension of Route No. 17408 westward from Tucson.[12] The extension was made on a *pro rata* basis. Barlow and Sanderson's compensation was increased from $24,909 to $44,091, and the service was increased to three times a week,[13] in conformity with the company's schedules all the way back to the Kansas railhead.

On the mail line south and west of Santa Fe, Barlow, Sanderson and Company sublet contracts. For example, in 1868 the Southern Overland Mail was carried from Santa Fe to El Paso and Tucson by Shaw and Cook's Stage Line, and in 1870 J. F. Bennett and Company carried it from Mesilla, New Mexico, to Tucson, Arizona.[14]

Although still dwarfed by the scale of the Wells Fargo operations to the north and west, Barlow, Sanderson and Company had developed a major communication and transportation system by the late 1860s. Their service covered about 2,000 miles, and its maintenance required about 1,200 animals and more than 200 regular employees as well as many others in incidental employment.[15] In its most expansive period, part of the system included three Missouri routes: Nos. 10697, 10699, and 14013 (the Kansas City-Fort Scott line,[16] which Sanderson had owned for several years). But the main portions of the service were in Kansas, Colorado, and New Mexico.

In January 1868 coaches of the Southern Overland Mail line still adhered to 8 A.M. Monday, Wednesday, and Friday departures from each end of the Hays City-Santa Fe run, with the same running time of four and a half days.[17] There was room for nine passengers on three inside seats in the big red Concord coaches, and another passenger could be put on the box with the driver and the conductor. Luggage was stowed on top and in the front and rear boots. Leather aprons were stretched over the boots for protection. If space permitted, other passengers could sit on top of the coach.[18] Peculiar to the Southern Overland Mail line, and reflecting the cultural impact of the Southwest, was the five-mule hitch—two on the wheel (or at the pole) and three abreast in the lead—a slight variation of the two and four hitch common in Mexico.[19] That arrangement was not popular among all the drivers. One Jehu, as stage drivers were commonly known,[20] called it "one of them d—d three cornered teams."[21]

The country through which the Santa Fe mail passed was still sparsely populated. There were only two counties in the western fourth of Kansas, both of them astraddle the right-of-way of the westward-building Union Pacific Eastern Division Railroad. Most of the residents of western Kansas, aside from the Indians, were employees of the railroad, the stage line, or the federal government (soldiers).[22] From Fort Hays to Fort Dodge the stage line followed the government freight road that was laid out in 1867. The road passed through county subdivisions, but there were hardly any settlers. West of Fort Dodge (in Ford County) there were even fewer.[23] Similarly, in Colorado, the route traversed only two big counties with very few people. From Fort Lyon on the Arkansas to the New Mexico line atop the Raton Pass the journey was entirely within the boundaries of a single county.

A correspondent of Denver's *Rocky Mountain News*, William Russell Thomas,[24] was in Trinidad in late January 1868 with Acting Governor Frank Hall, who went there from Denver in the aftermath of a serious ethnic (Mexican-Anglo) collision known as the Trinidad War, which had erupted on New Year's Day.[25] It started over a wrestling match involving a Barlow, Sanderson and Company driver by the name of Frank Blue, but it was only a catalyst for long-standing grievances and frictions. Southern Overland Mail coaches were not detained, but during the height of the trouble they were not permitted to stop in Trinidad, apparently so that an appeal could not be sent to either Fort Union or Fort Lyon. That precaution was easily circumvented when a nearby rancher rode to the Hole-in-the-Prairie stage station and told the keeper, Alex Taylor, who immediately wrote a letter to Brevet Brigadier General William H. Penrose, commandant at Fort Lyon.[26] Cavalry units from there and Fort Reynolds, recently established (July 3, 1867) on the right bank of the Arkansas between the St. Charles and the Huerfano,[27] rode through the bitter cold to Trinidad on January 5, and squelched the disturbance.[28]

127

The acting governor and the reporter boarded a five-mule Southern Overland Mail coach in Trinidad at 11 P.M. on Saturday, February 1. Their destination was Fort Lyon, about 125 miles to the northeast, which they reached at 4 P.M. the next day. That division of the line was managed by Lew Barnum. After leaving the valley of the Purgatoire below Gray's Ranch (probably at the point where it was crossed by Kearny's Army of the West in 1846), they made the forlorn trip over to the Timpas drainage and on to Bent's Old Fort. There were no habitations between stage stations, and the only living things they saw were a few gray wolves. They reached the Arkansas about eight miles above Bent's Old Fort, but did not cross the river to the north bank until they reached the fort. Passengers found a comfortable home station in the fort, which had been purchased by Messrs. Holbrook and Lander as headquarters for their cattle business.

Eighteen miles below was the "new" Fort Lyon, so called because much of the original post (about twenty miles down the Arkansas) was washed away in a flood in June 1867. The new fort was located on the north bank of the Arkansas a short distance below the mouth of the Purgatoire.[29] By early 1868 the second Fort Lyon was taking shape in structures of stone and adobe, and there were four companies stationed there: two of the Third Infantry, one of the Fifth Infantry, and one of the Seventh Cavalry, all under the command of Brevet Brigadier General William H. Penrose, Third Infantry.[30]

That southeastern Colorado still was Indian country was impressed upon Thomas while he was at Fort Lyon. A band of Arapaho, under their chiefs Black Wolf and Little Raven, were there being questioned about threats recently made at a stage station upstream (not identified). The Arapaho were on their way west to raid the Ute in the mountains, but General Penrose informed them that the Ute chiefs were in Washington and therefore all the Ute were under military protection.[31]

Acting Governor Hall and W. R. Thomas returned to Trinidad and then took a Denver and Santa Fe Stage Line coach north to Pueblo and Denver (for an account of this line, see Chapter 12, p. 138). Perhaps they did that because of their business, but the chance is good that they did so because Barlow, Sanderson and Company had taken their coaches off the Arkansas River run from Bent's Old Fort to Pueblo. The Denver and Santa Fe line had opened a direct, north-south connection between

Pueblo and Trinidad, and passenger traffic along the Arkansas River had sharply declined.[32]

In early 1868 the tariffs of the Southern Overland Mail and Express Company were published: through trip from Hays City to Santa Fe, $110; way rate, 25 cents per mile; express rate charged for each passenger's baggage in excess of forty pounds. A new time schedule was also put into effect. The maximum time was set up from four and a half days to five and a half days (six and a half days for the winter months). The only apparent reason for the change was the inclusion of the little town of Ocate (and possibly Las Gallinas) in the service. To reach Ocate one had to turn west from the regular stage road at Calhoun's Crossing of Ocate Creek, follow the creek to the town(s), and then follow another road to rejoin the old road just north of Fort Union.[33]

Some incidents that spring on the plains suggested that the Medicine Lodge treaties of the previous year had failed. Passengers alighting from a Southern Overland Mail coach in Hays City told of Cheyenne stealing mules about twenty-five miles west of Fort Dodge.[34] About the same time another coach from Santa Fe and an ambulance from Fort Union rolled into Fort Lyon with a party of San Francisco and Santa Fe bankers. Because of the Indian danger on the plains east of the fort, General Penrose ordered that the coach and a Fort Lyon ambulance be escorted to Fort Dodge by a sergeant, corporal, and twenty men riding in three six-mule wagons. Sergeant Luke Cahill, Company A, Fifth Infantry was in charge, and the journey was to be made at night.

The trip was extremely unpleasant and difficult because one of the passengers from Santa Fe objected to night travel. The mail party started without the man, but he later changed his mind and overtook them with a cavalry escort about midnight. In the meantime Sergeant Cahill and his men had quelled an attempt by the man's traveling companions and the driver of the coach to return to Fort Lyon.

Just before daylight the escorted vehicles pulled into camp near the mouth of the Big Sandy, a northern tributary of the Arkansas. During the day, bands of Indians were seen moving north, but they gave no trouble. Soldiers killed two buffalo heifers, two antelope, and a deer for fresh meat. Cahill remarked that the buffalo and antelope were so numerous that they looked like large herds of sheep. Deer were less plentiful and stayed close to the river and tall grass. Wolves howled around the

129

camp, and coyotes were everywhere.

The second night the man protested so strongly that the sergeant had him put in irons and fastened him to the erstwhile driver, threatening them both with abandonment on the plains. They were offered their freedom if they would promise to make no more trouble, and they agreed.

At Fort Dodge, Sergeant Cahill's conduct was exonerated. "Colonel" Sanderson, of Barlow, Sanderson and Company, was at the fort, and he felt it necessary to conduct a hearing on the sergeant's unauthorized restraint of a passenger. During the testimony Cahill's actions were so strongly supported by a lieutenant colonel, who had been among the passengers, that Sanderson was convinced the noncommissioned officer's decisions had been good for the company. Afterward Sanderson asked Sergeant Cahill and his men to come that afternoon to the stage station, where he thanked each one and gave him a five-dollar bill. As a further mark of commendation Sanderson offered Cahill employment when he left the army.[35]

The Union Pacific Eastern Division Railroad was in service by June 5 to Monument, a former Smoky Hill stage station and small military post called Monument Station in Kansas.[36] The Southern Overland Mail people, watching that progress and planning ahead, picked the old Smoky Hill's Pond Creek station, forty-seven miles southwest of Monument, for its new terminus in western Kansas.[37] Close by was Fort Wallace, established in 1865 as Camp Pond Creek, which was a major base for military confrontations with the Plains tribes.[38] Division superintendent, Lew Barnum, and "Colonel" Sanderson supervised removal of their stage station and office to Pond Creek, from which, Barnum announced, there would be daily service to Santa Fe after July 1.[39] The increase in service had been ordered for that date by the Post Office Department as early as March 31.[40] Undoubtedly the coaches went into Fort Wallace also. That post, about two miles east of the station, had a post office from October of 1866, but one was not established at Pond Creek until November 20, 1868.[41]

Evidently Pond Creek was regarded as a place that would remain a commercial point for some time. It was reported that "Uncle Dick" Wootton, who had the toll gate on Raton Pass, was laying out a road from Pond Creek to Bent's Old Fort. It was first indicated that the stage line would go west from Fort Wallace to Cheyenne Wells, a former Smoky Hill station in Colorado thirty-six miles beyond Pond Creek Station, and from there south to Bent's Old Fort. That would have dropped Fort Lyon from the stage route because of an alleged lack of water between that post and Fort Wallace.[42] Apparently, the change was not made, but the terminus at Pond Creek-Fort Wallace caused the mail line's abandonment of another segment of the Santa Fe Trail—from Fort Dodge to Fort Lyon.[43]

The route of the Southern Overland Mail was projected south from Cheyenne Wells to Fort Lyon, requiring stations and other facilities and possibly even a road. It was fourteen miles from the old Smoky Hill station to the Big Sandy, fifteen miles from there to Rush Creek, twenty-two miles to Kiowa Springs, twelve miles to Well No. 2, fifteen miles to Well No. 1, and then seven miles into Fort Lyon.[44]

When the service of the Southern Overland Mail and Express Company was increased to six departures a week (daily except Sunday) from each end of the line, the contractually allowable time for a trip was four days (five in winter). But since the stages ordinarily made it in less time, Lew Barnum advertised the journey as taking only three days.[45] And it was customary to speak of it as a daily service. Of course, Barnum was talking about Route No. 14020 from Kansas to Santa Fe, but the service also was increased to six times a week on Barlow and Sanderson's Route No. 17401 to El Paso. Inauguration of daily service from Kansas to Texas resulted from strong pressures by influential people in New Mexico and especially by the congressional delegations from Kansas and Missouri. The Missouri delegation was interested in stimulating commerce with Colorado, New Mexico, Arizona, and the northern Mexican states.[46]

A significant addition to Route No. 14020 in New Mexico also became operative on July 1. A branch line was opened by Barlow, Sanderson and Company providing daily service from Cimarron to Virginia City, and from there to Taos once a week.[47] Since 1867 gold prospectors had piled into the Sangre de Cristo Mountains west of Cimarron on land said to be part of the Beaubien and Miranda (Maxwell) Land Grant. Others had organized stagecoach service over those lines to accommodate the mining boom,[48] but the Post Office Department gave official recognition to Barlow, Sanderson and Company, by adding $85,860 per annum to their contract starting July 1, 1868. The increase made a total compensation for Route No. 14020 of $171,720.[49] And there was a minor change along the route in New Mexico below Fort Union; it was a new post office in La Junta (later Watrous) at the juncture of the Mora and Sapello rivers.[50]

Union Pacific Eastern Division railheads in western Kansas stimulated hope and speculation about the road's future course of construction. It was generally believed that extension of the railroad would follow the Santa Fe Trail (Mountain Branch) and go from there to California. The activities of survey parties strengthened that belief, and the citizens of Trinidad, for example, were excited about their chances.[51] Then, too, the growing proximity of the railroad to Trinidad (and probably elsewhere) fostered comparisons that were unfavorable to the stage line. Someone wrote to the editor of Pueblo's *Colorado Chieftain* complaining that the rail fare from Kansas City to the railhead was only ten cents per mile, while the stagecoach rate from the terminus of the railroad to Santa Fe was twenty-five cents per mile.[52]

Another type of competition for the Southern Overland Mail and Express Company appeared in 1867-1868. It had commercial importance and was particularly favorable to isolated newspaper editors. In the summer of 1867 a group of Denver capitalists organized the United States and Mexico Telegraph Company, and their first goal was to set up a line from Denver to Santa Fe.[53] Construction began in the winter. The men digging the holes were slowed down by snow storms, but by mid-May they were reported as somewhere between Trinidad and Fort Union. A few days later the poles were in place as far as Red River, and 30,000 pounds of wire (carried in twenty-mule wagons) had arrived at Trinidad from the railhead via Fort Lyon. Another shipment was expected in a few days. The telegraph line into Santa Fe was completed that summer.[54]

Constant progress by the work crews of the Union Pacific Eastern Division Railroad that summer brought the tracks closer to the new plains town of Phil Sheridan (also referred to simply as Sheridan), twelve miles northeast of Fort Wallace.[55] Because it was likely that the railhead would be there for some time, Barlow, Sanderson and Company removed their terminus to it. Whether their operations began from there in the summer of 1868 or in February of the next year, as indicated by Post Office Department records, is not clear.[56] In any event, Captain Charles H. Reynolds, formerly with the U.S. Army Quartermaster's Department,[57] and currently paymaster and agent for the Southern Overland Mail and Express Company, revealed in Santa Fe in July of 1868 that the line was stocked from Sheridan, which was 145 miles from Bent's Old Fort.[58]

Difficulties with the Plains Indians during the spring and first half of the summer of 1868 were minor, but hostilities that began in August soon made the country traversed by the Southern Overland Mail from Fort Wallace to Trinidad quite dangerous. Depredations also extended westward from Kansas along the Smoky Hill stage route and threatened the north-south Denver and Santa Fe Stage Line between Denver and Trinidad.[59]

Regular military escorts for the mail stages between Forts Wallace and Lyon were provided in a rather different way. A noncommissioned officer and ten men were located at each of the seven stations between the two posts. Those men as far north as Kiowa Station were furnished by Fort Wallace and those as far south as Rush Creek supplied by Fort Lyon. Four soldiers rode on top of a coach between stations, while the noncommissioned officers and five men remained to protect the stock tenders and company property at the stations.[60] There were serious disruptions elsewhere along the Southern Overland Mail line, and some of the stations were temporarily abandoned in response to raids made by Cheyenne, Arapaho, and Kiowa.

Strikes against ranches, wagon trains, mail stages, and even the military hit all around Fort Lyon, much to the distress of Brevet Brigadier General Penrose, who did not have sufficient cavalry to cope with them. Three Southern Overland coaches and a wagon train were molested near Bent's Old Fort on August 24, and several days earlier fifteen head of horses and mules and four cows were run off from that station.[61] In September the Kiowa were very active on the lower Purgatoire, driving off much livestock and causing settlers to congregate at Boggsville for mutual protection. General Penrose, with his lone cavalry unit, Company L, Seventh Cavalry, went in pursuit and caught up with the Indians on Rule Creek a few miles to the east. In a skirmish, four Indians and two troopers were killed, and several cavalry horses died from exhaustion in the chase. The Kiowa chief, One-eyed Bull, died in that encounter.[62]

The small infantry detachment at the Sand Creek stage station north of Fort Lyon repulsed an attack in early September.[63] On September 12 a band of Arapaho under Chief Little Raven raided a hay contractor's camp on the river bottoms east of Fort Lyon. The contractor was James Brice, former stage driver and station keeper at Fort Larned. He was baling hay for Southern Overland Mail stations in Colorado, and he estimated the raid cost him forty-five large mules, $3,000 to obtain an ox train to replace them, $3,900 in wages and maintenance, and a two-and-a-half-month delay.[64] And about the same time, the citizens of Trinidad were alarmed when a Southern Overland Mail conductor reported Indians only a few miles away at the Hole-in-the-Prairie station.[65]

Contemporary with these events was the well-known Beecher Island fight on the Arickaree Fork of the Republican River in northeastern Colorado. The culmination of the troubles came in General Sheridan's three-pronged, winter campaign against the Plains tribes, ending with their defeat in December on the Washita River, Indian Territory.[66] At the conclusion of the widespread disturbances in 1868, Barlow, Sanderson and Company's property losses and disruptions of their stage line totaled less than those sustained by the stage company on the Smoky Hill route into Denver. The brunt of the fighting and destruction was not along the line of the Southern Overland Mail, probably because the country through which it passed was still sparsely settled. What was left of the Santa Fe Trail retained the old characteristic of being more a commercial route than an emigrant one.

Nevertheless, Barlow, Sanderson and Company had prepared for more serious losses. They armed their drivers and conductors at company expense, and their pay scale for those categories ranged from $35 to $75 per month according to the comparative danger on their routes. About 200 horses and mules were lost, along with an unspecified amount of damage to stations and forage stocks, and, naturally, passenger revenues decreased as danger and attendant expenses grew.[67]

South of the Raton Mountains, the scale of depredations was less. The Plains tribes raided that close to the Sangre de Cristo Mountains less frequently, and the big military post of Fort Union was probably a deterrent. The difficulties north of the Ratons, however, were reflected in slower, more irregular arrivals of the mail in Santa Fe, which was relatively secure, and critical comments appeared in the press. Admitting that Barlow Sanderson coaches and wagons came in with "tolerable punctuality," indicating that delayed mails were not always the fault of the company, the editor of the *New Mexican*, nevertheless, made insinuations in his columns about willful inefficiency and even corruption—that the company had a contract for daily mail at twice the remuneration, but Santa Fe was getting less than a triweekly service. He also complained of the difficulty in sending out a daily paper, and protest was forwarded to the postmaster general.[68]

The appearance of company partner Thomas J. Barnum in Santa Fe, in response to the dissatisfactions there, apparently convinced the Santa

Fe editor that Indian troubles caused the disrupted service.[69] As winter set in and General Sheridan mounted his campaign against the tribes, the Southern Overland Mail line gradually returned to normal.[70] Problems were of a different nature, such as the stabbing death of driver Daniel Lehr at La Junta in Gregg's Tavern, where some of the Southern Overland employees stayed, or the complaint of a passenger that the conductor had refused to take him to the local hotel at Fort Union, depositing him instead at the post office over half a mile away.[71]

Winter travel was usually uneventful, except for sporadic hazards of the weather. At two o'clock on an early February morning, 1869, W. R. Thomas, the *Rocky Mountain News* correspondent, boarded a southbound Southern Overland Mail coach at Trinidad in a snowstorm that had already put a foot of snow on the ground. A slow trip over Raton Pass brought him to Red River station, New Mexico, by daylight. Thomas was the only passenger, so he and Conductor "Sandy" spent the trip inside the coach smoking cigars. They ate in Calhoun's Hotel at Maxwell's, and enjoyed a late evening supper with F. J. Ames at the Ocate stage station,[72] where they stayed the night because of the weather. A difficult road slowed them down; they had lunch at Sapello (probably meaning Gregg's Tavern at La Junta), ate supper at Tecolote, and did not pull up before the Exchange Hotel in Santa Fe until six o'clock in the morning.

Thomas's return trip was commonplace, but he did note that Lew Barnum managed the division from Red River station to Bent's Old Fort. A five-mule vehicle carried Thomas toward Bent's Old Fort at an average of six miles per hour. He had to stop over a day at the fort, the divisional headquarters, because the restored service to Pueblo was only triweekly. That segment was also under Barnum's supervision, and on the way Thomas observed that heavy settlement in the Arkansas Valley did not begin until about thirty-five miles below Pueblo, a circumstance which he attributed to the presence of the huge Vigil and St. Vrain (Las Animas) Grant on the south side of the river and a reservation for half-breed Indians on the north.[73] The branch to Pueblo was sixty miles long through South Side, Booneville, and Excelsior.[74]

The year 1869 may have been the best for the Southern Overland Mail and Express Company and its parent firm, Barlow, Sanderson and Company. Its government subsidies were the largest in its history. In addition to the $171,720 received for Route No. 14020 from Kansas to Santa Fe, it realized $100,000 for Route No. 17401 south from Santa Fe to El Paso and $213,194 for Route No. 17408 west from Mesilla.[75] The distance from Phil Sheridan, Kansas, to Los Angeles, California, was just under 1,700 miles. Including the branch lines the total came to about 2,000 miles over which company vehicles traveled about 18,000 miles each week. Mail carried exceeded 3,000 pounds per week, or about 500 pounds leaving Phil Sheridan daily. An estimated 200,000 people in Colorado, New Mexico, Arizona, and California were dependent on the service of the Southern Overland Mail, along with twenty-nine major and subordinate military posts.

Such were the statistics submitted by Barlow, Sanderson and Company to J. A. J. Cresswell, President Ulysses S. Grant's choice for postmaster general. The company was responding to reports that curtailment of its service was in the offing, and the letter was intended to convince the new postmaster general that expansion rather than contraction should be under consideration.[76] It was dated from Washington, D.C., May 1869, only two months after Cresswell took over, but by then at least the outlines of his policies were probably known. Cresswell wanted a rapid increase in railroad postal lines, and he aimed to destroy the practice of straw bidding[77]—bidding for contracts which, for various reasons, the bidder is unable or unwilling to fulfill.[78] The latter goal may have concerned Barlow, Sanderson and Company.[79]

Certainly the extension of railroad mail contracts had already entered into Barlow, Sanderson and Company's calculations. The Union Pacific Eastern Division Railroad had been renamed the Kansas Pacific, and its railhead in extreme western Kansas was still the town of Sheridan, 405 miles west of the Missouri River[80] and not far over the horizon from Pueblo and Denver, Colorado. Sheridan was about to go the way of many of its predecessors as the tracks were built beyond it, with construction only slightly impeded when Indians tore up the track.[81] Cheyenne Wells, in eastern Colorado, was the next temporary terminus and possibly a junction town. It was clear that the Kansas Pacific would build into Denver, but had not given up hope for a southwestern line to California.[82] Plans for the southwestern line were strengthened when members of the joint congressional committee on the Pacific Railroad were on an inspection trip in southern Colorado. A special Southern Overland Mail coach brought them into Pueblo on July 9.[83]

By the end of 1869 a new town was developing on the plains a few miles west of Cheyenne Wells and about ninety miles east of Pueblo.

Called Kit Carson after the famous frontiersman, it was in line to become the new railhead town on the Kansas Pacific and the terminus for stage and freighting lines into Colorado and New Mexico. Pueblo businessmen opened a new road to the town, which was described in December as having about 300 residents living mostly in tents, although six or eight frame buildings were under construction.[84]

12

The Denver and Santa Fe Line

1867-1870

WHILE BARLOW, SANDERSON AND COMPANY responded to the needs of the public for stagecoach service on the shortening route to Santa Fe, "One-armed" Jones's so-called Denver and Santa Fe Stage Line developed into real competition for the Southern Overland's Denver Branch. Jones took a partner named Abraham Jacobs, clothing merchant, who had opened his business in 1865 in the old National Bank quarters at 76 F Street, two doors from McGaa Street.[1] Jacobs' employee, William S. Walker, was agent for both the Denver and Santa Fe Stage Line and for the Santa Fe Stage Company (the old Barlow, Sanderson subsidiary), and he conducted the stage business on the store's premises. Apparently Jacobs was persuaded to put money into the line, and he soon became the dominant partner.

On April 3, 1867 the *Rocky Mountain News* carried the first advertisement of the Denver and Santa Fe Stage Line, announcing its most unique feature—direct service south from Pueblo to Trinidad.[2] The innovation eliminated the necessity for travelers between Denver and Santa Fe to go the extra miles eastward to Bent's Old Fort. More than a hundred miles were saved by using the Denver and Fort Union road south from Pueblo or north from Trinidad. It took thirty-six hours for the horse-drawn Concord hacks to make the trip either way between Denver and Trinidad, which was the southern terminus for connections to Santa Fe with Barlow, Sanderson and Company coaches at Davis and Barraclough's Hotel.[3] If one made connection with the southern coach at Trinidad, a two-day journey was still ahead. The overall time from Denver to Santa Fe was three and a half days.[4]

Joseph Davis, formerly a salesman in Jacobs's Denver store, had gone to Trinidad in March 1867, as advance man for the Denver and Santa Fe Line to arrange for the necessary facilities. He rented a house and stable on Main Street from William Hoehne for $40 per month, and soon he was joined by Henry A. Barraclough, ex-post-office employee in Denver. Together they opened a combined hotel, stage station, and general store in the little town with a population of about 200.[5]

It was necessary, of course, to put up stage stations on the Denver and Fort Union road between Pueblo and Trinidad, and the old stations north of Pueblo were improved so that "everything [would be] brought up to the highest standard of excellence."[6] Locations were chosen on streams that fed into the Arkansas from the south: the St. Charles (San Carlos), the Muddy, the Greenhorn, the Huerfano, the Santa Clara, the Apishapa, and the Chicosa, which was the last station before Trinidad on the Purgatoire. Access to this new portion of the line was made easier by the new bridge over the Arkansas at Pueblo.[7]

Jones and Jacobs did not use mules on their line. The *Rocky Mountain News* told its readers:

California horses are used on this route; small, wiry animals, very much like the Texas mustang. Their endurance is remarkable and their speed not to be despised. They frequently run the first route south from this city— seventeen miles—in one hour and twenty minutes, and they are just as keen to go at its close as when they start out.[8]

Post Office Department support for the new line was wanting, so Jones and Jacobs offered to carry the mail without compensation for a while until the Department might be convinced of its feasibility.[9] The proposition was accepted, and the Denver and Santa Fe Stage Company was still carrying it gratuitously over a year later, according to the new and only journalistic venture in Pueblo, Dr. Michael Beshoar's weekly *Colorado Chieftain*. In the event of such a Post Office decision, and because of a growing decline in the number of travelers to and from Denver via the Arkansas route,[10] Barlow, Sanderson and Company abandoned its branch from Bent's Old Fort to Denver. As a result, Wells, Fargo and Company announced that it made connections in Denver with the Denver and Santa Fe Line for all points in New Mexico.[11]

Service was suddenly interrupted at Trinidad on New Year's Day, 1868, by the Trinidad War, an ethnic clash between Anglos and Mexicans.[12] It began with an altercation on Christmas Day involving Frank Blue—a Barlow, Sanderson and Company driver, although his employment had nothing to do with it. The recurrence of trouble on New Year's Day resulted in a siege against many Anglos in Philo Sherman's Colorado Hotel (successor to Davis and Barraclough's), which was the southern terminus of the Denver and Santa Fe Stage Line. The besiegers refused to allow the regular Denver coach to leave, but it was permitted to go the next day because of fear of further obstruction of the U.S. mail. The scheduled driver, a man named Clark, was one of the men trapped in the hotel, so the coach was taken out by an inexperienced substitute, Joe Davis, who had opened the company's office in Trinidad less than a year before. Southern Overland Mail coaches were not stopped but were prevented from calling at Walker's Hotel, their station in the town.[13]

Under normal conditions Denver and Santa Fe Line departures were from each terminus—Denver or Trinidad—on Monday, Wednesday, and Friday mornings. Down-trip (from Denver) passengers ate supper at Colorado City,[14] where, in at least one person's opinion, was the worst food on the route. The hotel served bean soup as the staple at every meal, and a clean towel was a rarity.[15]

After the night trip along the Fountain River, those wanting breakfast could eat at Harry Pickard's Pueblo House (a supper stop on the return trip). For the gastronomically inclined, an excellent eating place was the station kept by Mr. and Mrs. George R. Miller on Muddy Creek, twenty-five miles south of Pueblo.[16] Pioneer Alexander (Zan) Hicklin's place on the Greenhorn was a swing station—that is, a relay station—for a change of horses.[17] Mail for Fort Garland was dropped off at the crossing of the Huerfano,[18] and the stop on the Apishapa (established on March 31, 1867) was also a swing station.

Zan Hicklin, Ed Turner, John Odenheimer, and his brother built a log cabin,[19] but not long afterward it was taken over by Captain and Mrs. James Foster, a Confederate veteran and his lady, who sometimes flew the Stars and Bars on commemorative occasions.[20]

Eleven o'clock at night was the scheduled arrival at the Colorado House in Trinidad.[21] The meals there were considered to be the best on the route, and the beds were the most comfortable.[22]

Early in 1868 three new vehicles were put in service between Denver and Pueblo. They were first referred to as Troy coaches and a short time later as the new Concord coaches.[23] A reasonable conclusion is that they

140

were of the Troy coach type—lighter than a Concord[24]—built by Abbott-Downing Company at Concord, New Hampshire. For travelers going on to Trinidad, the company furnished a good hack (stage wagon).[25] Contemporary descriptions indicate that the service was praiseworthy, and special commendation was given to Charles Bryant, a popular company messenger.[26] The company was regarded as well managed. Its coaches were usually full, and business was increasing.[27]

Plans were made to extend the line to the new gold mines in northern New Mexico around Virginia City and Elizabethtown by building a new road from Trinidad through Long's Canyon, at an estimated saving of forty miles. Abraham Jacobs, Joseph Davis, Henry A. Barraclough, and Washington G. Rifenburg incorporated the Trinidad and Moreno Valley Wagon Road Company on March 2, 1868.[28]

Trouble with Indians was minor, and occasionally white thieves would take livestock from a remote station.[29] But the biggest problem was snow on the Arkansas-South Platte divide. The coaches of all the lines due in Denver on the night of March 23 failed to appear because of a severe storm. The Denver and Santa Fe Line was the last to restore service. A Smoky Hill coach came in on April 2, but it was not until the morning of April 5 that a Santa Fe coach made it to Denver, followed by an accumulation of mail in an open wagon.[30]

Abraham Jacobs went east in the spring to buy equipment for his new extension to the Cimarron mines. By May 1 the Union Pacific Railroad brought harnesses into Cheyenne, Wyoming, and new coaches were expected in about ten days. Jacobs hoped to have them running from Trinidad to the mines in about three weeks.[31] Later in the month, Jacobs, now the sole proprietor of the Denver and Santa Fe Stage and Express Company,[32] went on a tour of inspection with his general superintendent, D. D. Ayers. Shortly afterward they announced "a number of spanking new Concord coaches for use on the Santa Fe line."[33]

A contract for carrying mail from Pueblo to Trinidad and return was never obtained by Abraham Jacobs, nor did he obtain one from Trinidad to Virginia City, although Congress authorized a post road between the two places in an act of March 30, 1868.[34] He was high bidder in the fall for a triweekly service on the Pueblo-Trinidad run. Both Thomas J. Barnum and Jared L. Sanderson also submitted bids, but the award went to William Craig,[35] agent for Ceran St. Vrain and the enormous Vigil and St. Vrain (Las Animas) Land Grant.[36]

It was planned that Craig would begin mail deliveries on October 2, and the route was shifted to the east to go by way of Craig's big Hermosilla Ranch on the Huerfano River, a road that was twenty miles shorter than by the regular Denver and Fort Union road used by Jacobs and Company's line.[37] The Hermosilla road was not often used, because the claimants to the Vigil and St. Vrain Grant did not encourage a public thoroughfare across their property.[38]

Buckboards were to be used at first, but coaches had not been put on by December, even though the fare was $10 through to Trinidad or 10 cents per mile to way stops. That caused the Pueblo *Chieftain* to remark, without elaboration, that if Jacobs would charge the same rates he would undoubtedly get all the passenger trade.[39]

At year's end the public learned that mail transportation had been discontinued between Pueblo and Trinidad, and that the mail was to be sent once again by the old and roundabout way via Bent's Old Fort. The Pueblo editor wondered if the change was made locally or if it was the "cussedness" of the Post Office Department.[40] It was soon confirmed that Craig had relinquished his mail route; in other words, his contract was annulled on December 31 for apparent nonfulfillment of his obligations.[41] News followed that Jacobs had closed down his line between Pueblo and Trinidad; it was thought, however, that he might resume operation in the spring.[42]

Rocky Mountain News correspondent W. R. Thomas gave the probable explanation for the shutdown in an article dated from Trinidad, February 3, 1869: "There are two causes for this act, first the lack of mail pay, and second the impossibility of running the line without such pay."[43] He also said that discontinuation of the service south of Pueblo was the government's fault,[44] an opinion that is difficult to validate from available evidence.

He was outraged that it would take from five to ten days to get a letter from Trinidad to Denver, via Bent's Old Fort. Businessmen in Trinidad could communicate faster with St. Louis. Newspapers from the south used to reach Denver in thirty-six hours, about the same time as exchanges from St. Louis, but now they would be from two to eight days behind the eastern papers.[45] Protests reached Washington, and George M. Chilcott, territorial delegate to Congress, returned assurances that the Post Office Department would advertise the Pueblo-Trinidad route for the next official bids.[46]

W. R. Thomas had gone down from Denver to Trinidad on the last coach to make the trip. Superintendent D. D. Ayers was on board, and business matters required him to hold up the coach's departure from Pueblo until 10 A.M. En route, the passengers did "full justice to one of Mrs. Miller's famous dinners at the Muddy" stage station.[47] Darkness overtook them at the crossing of the Huerfano, and they did not have supper until they reached the Santa Clara station.[48] Despite the cold wind blowing down from the Raton Peak, the travelers slept until the coach lurched to a stop in Trinidad at 3 A.M. The Southern Overland Mail coach had left for Santa Fe two hours before.[49]

A triweekly service between Bent's Old Fort and Pueblo was organized by Barlow, Sanderson and Company as soon as it seemed certain that Abraham Jacobs would pull his coaches off the Pueblo-Trinidad run. The old route along the Arkansas River was restored, and a Pueblo ticket office for the Southern Overland Mail was opened, with M. D. Thatcher as agent.[50] An order from the Post Office Department pressed the Southern Overland Mail to make close connections in Pueblo with Jacobs's line to Denver and at Bent's Old Fort with its main Fort Wallace-Santa Fe line.[51]

Predictions that Jacobs would be back in business were borne out by announcements that he would resume a triweekly service between Pueblo and Trinidad on April 21. Why he decided to do so is somewhat of a mystery. It appears that he believed that the line soon would be extended to the New Mexico mines, thereby making a triweekly link between them and Denver,[52] and he must have continued to hope that mail subsidies would come his way.

The situation became even more curious with private advice, which turned out to be correct, that a contract for the Pueblo-Trinidad route had been awarded to a Mr. Barnum. That meant, of course, Thomas J. Barnum, whose bid was for the Southern Overland Mail and Express.[53] The *Rocky Mountain News* said the contract was "for $3,800 per year, which is pretty cheap for tri-weekly service such as should be on that route."[54] Barnum's original bid was $3880; the Denver editor was simply using a round number in describing a transfer of contract concluded on April 5, 1869.[55]

Perhaps Jacobs had gone so far that he could not pull back from commitments. In early May he received twelve four-horse harnesses of the best Concord manufacture for his line to Elizabethtown, New Mexico, as well as an elegant, silver-mounted, six-horse harness for the teams pulling his coaches in and out of Denver.[56] But restoration of service to Trinidad was very slow.

In June the *Colorado Chieftain* asked what had happened to the promise of direct mail service to Santa Fe.[57] But a few days later it announced that the Southern Overland Mail Company's triweekly service had begun, saying that "the removal of the circuitous mail nuisance will be the occasion for general jubilation in Trinidad and Pueblo."[58] Early in July the rival lines were engaged in a rate war, with the Southern Overland Mail slashing its fare to $5 on the Pueblo-Trinidad run.[59] That was too rough for Abraham Jacobs, who took his stock and coaches off that segment of the line later in the month and abandoned his planned extension to the New Mexico mines. The Southern Overland Mail Company said it would keep its coaches operating with close connections in Pueblo and Trinidad, but with competition eliminated, it quickly restored the $15 fare.[60]

On the Denver-Pueblo line Abraham Jacobs continued the high-quality service for which he was so well regarded. He tried to stimulate business by special attractions and improvements. During the week of the agricultural fair at Denver in the late summer of 1869, for example, he offered the half-fare rate of $20 from Pueblo, with proportional reductions for points along the way and extra coaches if necessary.[61] Express service on the line was increased from once to three times per week.[62] Fast schedules were maintained as much as possible. On one of his trips as a driver, Johnny Shoemaker took a Jacobs coach over the seventy-five miles from Colorado City to Denver in a little less than twelve hours—an average of more than six miles per hour.[63]

Probably a typical trip south from Denver was described by *Rocky Mountain News* reporter W. R. Thomas. The coach rounded the corner to the stage line office on F Street, Denver. At the cry of "All aboard!" ten passengers took their seats (several on the outside). Their luggage was stored in the commodious boots, and the packet of mail for points along the way was handed up to the driver. Arthur Hill reined his team of bays through Denver and onto the hard, dry road that led south to the divide between the South Platte and the Arkansas. It was a bright morning on the bluff, so there was a view of Denver before the coach dropped into the valley of Cherry Creek, but clouds surrounded the summit of Pike's Peak, far to the south.

The bays kept to a five-mile-per-hour trot. Before the coach reached the crest of the divide, low clouds scudded into the March sky, followed by snow and a gusty wind. The outside passengers crowded into the coach and the curtains were buttoned down. The driver, Hill, drew a shawl closer about his shoulders, buckled down the coach's apron, and urged the horses along at a faster pace to Russellville, the end of the line for him.

Horses were changed and the mail for points en route was handled twice before they reached Russellville at 3 P.M. for dinner. After a meal served by the station keeper, Palmer, the coach moved off through the snow with a new driver on the box. Still climbing up the divide, the coach came to Spring Valley station, where the horses were changed again. After passing the crest, the four horses rolled the coach at a brisk eight miles per hour down to Colorado City. At 9 P.M., they stopped for supper at Ayers' Hotel,[64] operated by the general superintendent of the line, an old stagecoach hand himself. Blankets and other wrappings were issued in preparation for the night journey along the Fountain, and the passenger got off at the end of the line in Pueblo for breakfast.[65]

Passengers transferring to the Southern Overland Mail coach found that it departed from the Pacific House at 8:30 in the morning. Reporter Thomas rode with the driver as the mule-drawn mail stage climbed the bluff on the south side of the Arkansas. Before them was the panorama of Greenhorn and the rest of the Wet Mountain range, the Sangre de Cristos, and the Spanish Peaks (Huajatollas). Of the several tributaries of the Arkansas issuing from the mountains, the most promising for agriculture and colonization, in Thomas's opinion, was the valley of the Huerfano. He may have been aware that the valley was already fairly well settled, and that over 200 families, mostly from New Mexico, had come into the tributary valley of the lower Cucharas during the winter.

After supper and a change of mules at Captain Foster's station on the Apishapa, driver Roberts handled the reins on the night drive to Trinidad, doing the twenty miles at a round seven miles per hour. The night was cold and clear, and a full moon revealed the flat-topped bulk of the Raton (Fisher's) Peak. At midnight the travelers were greeted at the Sherman House by that establishment's junior partner, Fred Seilkin. The promise of a good bed and breakfast persuaded Thomas to spend the night, so the waiting Santa Fe coach left Trinidad without him.[66]

For undisclosed reasons, Abraham Jacobs disposed of his clothing

145

business in Denver in early February 1870,[67] and a little over four months later he sold the Denver and Santa Fe Stage Line to Lew and Thomas Barnum, of Barlow, Sanderson and Company. The transaction included fifty-eight horses, four coaches, three hacks, and all buildings except the Denver stables. Consideration was reported to be $19,000, with the new owners to take possession on July 1.[68] The line's office was moved to the same premises with Wells, Fargo and Company, the U.S. Express Company, and the stage line of John Hughes and Company, which had bought some of Wells, Fargo and Company's staging interests the previous October. All four firms used the same agent.

Southern Overland Mail stages were scheduled to leave Denver for the south every Monday, Wednesday, and Friday at 8 A.M.[69] Acquisition of Jacobs's line by the Barnums brought Barlow, Sanderson and Company directly into Denver for the first time, and their subsidiary company now had a monopoly of the mail, passenger, and express business into Santa Fe from the north and the south. Abraham Jacobs was unable to contend with the expertise and luck of the brothers Barnum, who helped to extend, consolidate, and protect the big Southern Overland Mail system.

Beginning the Third Decade

1870-1872

WHEN THE TERMINUS of the Southern Overland Mail line was shifted in March 1870 from Sheridan, Kansas, to the new Kansas Pacific Railroad town of Kit Carson in Colorado, the main stage line to Santa Fe still dropped south to Fort Lyon on the Arkansas River and then followed the Mountain Branch of the Santa Fe Trail. The Bent's Old Fort stage station, a few miles up the river from the military post, continued to be the point where the branch line to Pueblo started.[1]

Some of the impressions of that peripatetic Denver newsman, W. R. Thomas, of a stagecoach trip from Denver to Trinidad were presented in Chapter 12, pp. 144-45. That journey was the start of a two-month tour of most of the Southern Overland system operated directly by Barlow, Sanderson and Company. After enjoying the overnight comforts of the Sherman House in Trinidad, he left the next night for Santa Fe on a coach driven by Johnny Hull. By dawn they were in Cimarron, the county seat of the recently organized Colfax County, an immense rectangle in northeastern New Mexico just south of the Colorado line between the mountains on the west and Indian Territory and the Texas Panhandle on the east.[2] The following afternoon Thomas was greeted in Santa Fe by Tom McDonald, host of La Fonda.[3]

After nearly three weeks in the New Mexican capital, the *Rocky Mountain News* reporter departed in a storm which cleared after the coach entered the reddish, evergreen-clad mesas and mountains. Station keeper Henderson gave him supper at Tecolote, and at nine that evening he was with his old friend, Charles W. Kitchen, in Las Vegas. He found that town dull and depressed, a condition which he attributed to a big loss of trade

147

when impounded Navajo Indians and six companies of troops were removed from Fort Sumner, on the Pecos River southeast of the town.[4] Thomas spent a day at Las Vegas and then took another Southern Overland Mail coach north to La Junta. In that little community he took lodging at George Gregg's Tavern and then visited the expanding farms of his friends William Kroenig, W. H. Moore, S. B. Watrous, Tipton, Gregg, and other "Americans."

Ed Shoemaker, postmaster at Fort Union, took Thomas in when he arrived at 1 A.M., and the next day the reporter obtained a bed in the rooms of W. H. Moore and Company, the post traders. At the time, the Third Cavalry was being transferred to posts in Arizona and Nevada and was being replaced by units of the Eighth Cavalry.[5] The fort had grown considerably since the first coaches of the old Missouri Stage Company first called there, and in 1870 it was the largest post in New Mexico Territory. It really was a combination of three installations—the Post of Fort Union, the Fort Union Quartermaster Depot, and the Fort Union Ordnance Depot. The new buildings of the fort were built of adobe in the "territorial" style. Commandant at the time of Thomas's visit was Colonel and Brevet Brigadier General Willam N. Grier.[6]

At 10:30 A.M., March 25, Thomas climbed onto the driver's box of a northbound coach at Cimarron; the conductor was an old friend, simply identified as Sandy. At three in the afternoon they stopped at Red River station.[7] Thomas did not describe the place, but it was the well-known Clifton House, built by Tom Stockton over the years 1866 to 1870. The three-story structure, with thick adobe walls, porticoes, and shingle roof, was one of the Southern Overland Mail's major stops. There, Barlow, Sanderson and Company had a home station, corrals, and a blacksmith shop.[8]

Being familiar with the line and many of its employees, Thomas expected that Dan Freeman would be driving from Red River over the Raton Pass to Trinidad. Thomas referred to Freeman as one of the old overland boys, a term which he applied to three other company employees.[9] The stress on "old overland" strongly suggests the Southern Overland Mail and Express Company had hired men who formerly worked for the old central overland route (Ben Holladay and Wells Fargo) before the completion of the transcontinental Union Pacific Railroad put them out of work.

But the driver from Red River turned out to be "Big Nick" (Warlamont).[10] As the coach approached the Raton Pass, Thomas noted that they entered "the mountains through a narrow cañon, [passed] through the 'devil's gate,' and [began] a toilsome ascent for the summit." They reached the crest at sunset, where they caught a brief glimpse of the mesas and the Raton Peak, (resembling "the palisades of the Hudson") and still farther to the north the Spanish Peaks and the Greenhorn Mountain, "its round white summit standing out boldly against the sky."[11]

A rapid descent of two miles brought the coach to "Uncle Dick" Wootton's station, where a fresh team of mules was attached. The famous frontiersman's place was then a rather crude structure of adobes, stones, and timbers. In the public room was a large fireplace, and the walls were decorated with skins, horns, and heads of game animals, along with a variety of firearms mounted on pegs and brackets.[12] Thomas particularly noted that the new team was one of five mules "peculiar to this line," so it may assumed that the old team was of a regular four- or six-mule hitch, which supports other vague references to different hitches being used. Making sure that everything was ready, "Big Nick" mounted the box, took the reins, and shouted to the stock tender to "let 'em go." On the remaining five miles of steep and twisting incline they rolled at nine miles per hour through cuts, over bridges, and around mountainous shoulders while the coach rumbled and the whip cracked. In all, fourteen miles were traversed in an hour and a half. When the coach turned into Trinidad's Main Street, the lights of the Sherman House illuminated the street a short distance away. Thomas was sorry to take leave of a man "of many excellencies as a dashing but careful driver, a safe reinsman, and a good fellow."[13]

At Trinidad, Thomas was impressed by the potential for agriculture, raising stock, lumbering, and coal mining in the area. The Mexican flavor was still there, but the town's prosperity was reflected in substantial new homes and business blocks. He heard talk that Barlow, Sanderson and Company might move the divisional headquarters of their mail line to the town.

Trinidad seemed to him to be the liveliest place between Denver and Santa Fe, but he overestimated the population when he put it at between 600 and 800 people. The census of 1870 gave 562 as the actual number. Of the other places of any significant size served by Southern Overland Mail System, Pueblo had less than a thousand residents and Denver had a population of 4,759, which was slightly exceeded by Santa Fe, the

149

largest town on the line with 4,765 inhabitants in its adobe homes.[14]

Thomas left from the Sherman House at eight o'clock one evening for Fort Lyon in a main line coach conducted by one "Sam" and reined by Burt Ackley. The night was dark and foggy, but they reached Iron Spring station by 6 A.M. for breakfast. Bad weather still threatened as the next driver, Joe "Gimlet" Brannen, (Ackley and Brannen were referred to as "old overland boys")[15] took the coach northward toward the Arkansas, where they stopped for a change of mules at King's Ferry (the site of La Junta, Colorado). The ferry had been replaced by a new toll bridge over the river, built as part of a new freight road south from Kit Carson by the Kit Carson and Fort Union Bridge Company, of which George Mc-Bride was president and in which "Uncle Dick" Wootton was heavily involved.[16]

In less than an hour the coach covered the last seven miles along the north side of river to Bent's Old Fort, where an excellent dinner was provided. The station was run by Messrs. Price and Lander, local cattlemen. From there it was a two-hour drive to Fort Lyon, where Thomas obtained accommodations with Hatch, the sutler, and was entertained that evening in the quarters of Brevet Brigadier General Penrose, the commandant.

Since Thomas's last visit, Fort Lyon had been expanded into a four-company post, and the nearby little settlement of Las Animas had grown from two houses and two under construction to a total of twenty to thirty homes and businesses.[17] He wrote nothing about his trip from Fort Lyon up the Arkansas, but he characterized Pueblo as a very flourishing place of about 800 people, with houses of frame and adobe and a few of stone and brick, but with no brick business blocks as yet. Eminently satisfied with the service he had received during his extended journey over Barlow, Sanderson and Company's system, W. R. Thomas concluded: "What Wells, Fargo & Co. has been, and Hughes & Co. is to Colorado, this company has been and is to New Mexico. For the many favors of the company, as well as for the unceasing attention of their employes [sic], and most of all for the swift, safe and comfortable manner in which they have carried me for so many miles, I now return my thanks, and praise."[18]

Indians were active on the plains of eastern Colorado again in the summer of 1870. Forts Wallace, Lyon, and Reynolds were coordinated under a single command, with particular concern for protecting employees of the Kansas Pacific Railroad as it was built from Kit Carson into Denver, and one cavalry company was stationed near Colorado City for the season.[19] No damages from the Indians were sustained by the Southern Overland Mail and Express Company, but it lost six horses and six harnesses, as well as considerable quantities of hay and grain, when fire destroyed a barn in Colorado City.[20] About a month later the old stage barn on the north side of Pueblo, which was "way out of town" when it was built in 1863, was razed to make way for a two-story, brick building.[21]

"Colonel" Sanderson and Thomas J. Barnum were in Denver in July when Abraham Jacobs sold his Denver and Santa Fe Stage line to Barlow, Sanderson and Company.[22] Other matters besides that transaction probably required their attention. With the Kansas Pacific coming into Denver, the relations of their stage line with the railroad needed careful consideration and decision.

The east-west railroad bisected the plains of eastern Colorado, and Barlow, Sanderson and Company had two terminals—Kit Carson and Denver—for their stage line, which now was mainly a north-south line with two northern branches converging at Trinidad. The probability of more contraction and consolidation in the face of further railroad extensions required planning, and of course Barlow, Sanderson and Company were still the major mail contractors south of Santa Fe.[23] Ownership and operation of the stage line to Mesilla and from there west to Tucson was in the hands of J. F. Bennett and Company.[24]

Barlow, Sanderson and Company's three proprietors were Bradley Barlow, Jared L. Sanderson, and Thomas J. Barnum, while officers of the firm were Sanderson, superintendent; John R. Griffin, secretary-treasurer; and W. S. Stone, paymaster and assistant superintendent. Kansas City was the business address for Sanderson and Griffin, while Denver was listed for Stone.[25] Day-to-day operational management was directed by Thomas J. Barnum's brother, Lewis,[26] with D. D. Ayers (former superintendent of Abraham Jacobs's Denver and Santa Fe Stage and Express Company) in charge of the Denver and Pueblo division, and M. C. (Mac) Frost as a division agent,[27] probably from Pueblo south to New Mexico.

Daily departures with a three-day running time were maintained by 100 men, 600 to 700 horses and mules, and fifty coaches. Fare from Kit Carson to Santa Fe was $90 (fares to points en route not listed), and from the Denver terminus one could go to Colorado City for $9, to Pueblo for $15, to Trinidad for $30, and all the way to Santa Fe for $80.[28] How-

151

ever, express matter consigned to Santa Fe and other New Mexico towns went all the way by rail to Denver and then south by the Southern Overland Mail through Pueblo and Trinidad.[29] The service from Denver to Trinidad and return was only triweekly, while that on the Kit Carson main branch was daily.[30]

In September 1870 Barlow, Sanderson and Company made a couple of agreements with the Maxwell Land Grant and Railway Company. One was a lease of a half acre on Crow Creek, between the Raton Mountains and Cimarron in New Mexico. There the stage company would erect a stage station, which could not be a home station involving the sale of food, whiskey, and merchandise, N. F. Swope, New Mexico agent for Barlow, Sanderson and Company, also agreed to purchase from the Maxwell Land Grant and Railway Company the grain and other food for the livestock at all the stage stations on the grant.[31] On the same day the grant company began to provide stables, grain, and food for eight animals and board for a stocktender at the Cimarron stage station for $2,600 per year.[32]

An important alteration of the Southern Overland Mail system in October was abandonment of the line between Fort Lyon and Trinidad, although service was maintained from Kit Carson south to Fort Lyon and then westward up the Arkansas to Pueblo.[33] The logic of the change was simple. With the terminus of the Kansas Pacific Railroad and a rail connection with the Union Pacific at Cheyenne, Wyoming, Denver and had become the chief transportation center for a large part of the Rocky Mountain West and the Southwest. Strong connections at Denver were of primary importance for Barlow, Sanderson and Company's enterprise, which now had the distinction of being the last major stagecoach system in the country.

Undoubtedly most letter mail directed to the Southwest came by rail into Denver, so relinquishment of the stage line segment between Fort Lyon and Trinidad did not jeopardize service or contractual obligations. There were no significant population centers or even any prospects for such in the foreseeable future along that route. To make the most of a situation while it lasted, Barlow, Sanderson and Company planned a fast freight line between Denver and Santa Fe with stagecoach departures on alternating days, at reduced rates and 100 pounds minimum shipments.[34] And finally in December, they stepped up to daily service in and out of Denver. H. B. Smith, Barlow,

Sanderson and Company's resident agent, operated their new office in Smith's Block, corner of G and Wazee Streets.[35]

About the only cause for complaint in the new arrangement was the removal of the stage line's home station from Trinidad to Captain Foster's station on the Apishapa about twenty miles north for reasons not now known.[36] However, Barlow, Sanderson and Company announced in February 1871 that they would restore the Fort Lyon-Trinidad service,[37] returning Trinidad to its important position as a junction town. But service was not started until April, because the resumption was not a simple return to an old and familiar part of the Mountain Branch of the Santa Fe Trail; a new approach to Trinidad was made by a route much closer to the great canyon of the Purgatoire River.

Duane D. Finch[38] and Mac Frost, Barlow, Sanderson and Company employees, laid out the new section by traversing the proposed route in a buggy drawn by two mules. The new road left the old stage road at Iron Spring station on the Timpas and crossed over the divide to the head of Bent Canyon, a tributary of the Purgatoire. A station was designated in Bent Canyon at its juncture with a side canyon (afterward known as Stage Canyon) on the ranch of pioneer settler Eugene Rourke. Continuing southwestward, the route reached Lockwood Canyon, where another station was planned, and stretched from there to the W. R. Burns ranch on the Purgatoire (later known as the Hog Back stage station). The road workers were then sent back to Kit Carson, while Finch and Frost came into Trinidad, putting up at the Overland Hotel, the town stopping place for the Southern Overland Mail.[39]

The decision to reopen a Kit Carson-Trinidad connection rested on several reasons. Construction of the Kansas Pacific Railroad along the Mountain Branch of the Santa Fe Trail into New Mexico, planned in May of 1870,[40] showed no signs of quickening. So, the big mercantile houses handling the Santa Fe trade, like Otero, Sellar and Company and Chick, Browne and Company, would keep their warehouses at Kit Carson longer than they had at most railhead towns.[41] The little town on the plains retained its commercial importance for some time, and quite a few travelers preferred to make the railroad or stagecoach connection there rather than in Denver. An influx of homesteaders along the lower Purgatoire River and its branches prompted the slight change of route to provide them with outside contact.[42]

Service was resumed into Trinidad from the northeast in the middle part of April, probably April 18 and only one day later than planned. Livestock came from the Kansas City-Fort Scott line which Barlow, Sanderson and Company had recently given up, and new coaches were put into service.[43]

So once again Southern Overland Mail coaches ran on a daily schedule over Route No. 17032 from the railhead to Santa Fe, and the daily mail from Fort Lyon to Pueblo and return was reduced to a tri-weekly run.[44] The most noticeable difference to those people familiar with the old run to Santa Fe was the line's removal from another portion of the Mountain Branch of the Santa Fe Trail—including the well-known stops at Hole-in-the-Rock and Hole-in-the-Prairie—and the new stone stage stations and corrals of stone or of cedar (juniper) posts. It was sixteen miles from the Burns Ranch station into Trinidad, but the new road joined the old far enough out so that the early-day Gray's Ranch station was still on the route.[45] Apparently passenger fares were not changed, but Agent Finch's particular mention of an express and excess baggage rate of 30 cents per pound indicates a change there.[46]

The company enjoyed plaudits from patrons, undoubtedly realizing that praise could quickly disappear in changed circumstances. Pueblo's *Colorado Chieftain* carried an article about the Southern Overland Mail with the headline, "A Model Stage Line," describing the strong, comfortable coaches and magnificent horses. A traveler returning from Santa Fe was quoted in Denver's *Daily Rocky Mountain News* as saying, among other kind things:

. . . The stage line of Barlow, Sanderson & Co. cannot be surpassed in the excellence of its appointments. Everything that can be thought of is done for the comfort of the passengers, and if in crossing the "Divide," or the Raton Pass, they complain of being too warm when the thermometer is below zero, they can lay the blame to Col. Stone, the efficient superintendent, for having his stages fitted up too warm, and for piling in too many buffalo robes and blankets. We were fortunate on our trip to ride with those princes of drivers Big Nick and Jack Timmons, to whose tender care we confide our friends who have occasion to travel over that road in the future.[47]

In addition to its quality of service, the stage contributed to the quality of life of people along its line. On one coach came a $4.50 express package consigned to pioneer Trinidad citizen Riley Dunton, which contained the first horseradish roots imported there.[48] New potatoes sometimes came in by coach from the area around Fort Lyon, and fresh fruit was sent down from Denver in express packages. One Trinidad merchant was irate whenever he thought an express messenger had helped himself too liberally.[49]

On occasion, the stage company's best intentions were nullified by incompetent and indifferent employees. Major General Gordon Granger, commandant of the military district of New Mexico,[50] and party (including ladies) camped near the Red River station, or Clifton House. The ladies went into the stage station dining room for their evening meal, having "what the ranch boys called blue beef and soggy biscuits but no butter and no cream. An officious waiter urged all to help themselves to pepper sauce."[51] There is no indication of the ladies' reaction.

Prolonged heavy rains in September and October slowed the movement of all vehicular traffic between the railheads in Colorado and Santa Fe. The Southern Overland Mail coach from the north, due in Las Vegas on September 11, did not pass through until 6 A.M. the next day, and on the night of September 13 coaches were held over there because of very high water in the Gallinas River. Telegraphic communication was disrupted when the storm washed out a number of poles.[52] The weather did not improve for some time. Early in October the roads were in such bad shape that mule trains, which usually took from eighteen to twenty days from Kit Carson to Santa Fe, had not yet reached the New Mexican capital on the thirty-fifth day.[53]

Bad luck in another form followed the adverse weather. Stage robbers hit the mail and express coach on the branch line from Elizabethtown to Cimarron during a stop at Clear Creek to water the horses. Three men with revolvers stepped out of the brush and took about $500 from the express box, but they did not molest the several passengers. The bandits were alleged to be Tom Taylor, James Buckley (alias Coal Oil Jimmy), and a man named Jones. Employees of the Maxwell Land Grant and Railway Company pursued them for about twenty miles, but the bandits abandoned their horses and escaped on foot into the hills. A reward of $1,500 was posted for Taylor and Buckley, and a cavalry company was sent from Fort Union to help in the search in response to a request from the sheriff of Colfax County. About ten days after the first holdup, the main line coach was stopped near Vermejo Creek, presumably by members of the same gang, with

155

suspicion particularly pointing toward Tom Taylor.[54]

The next day (October 21), it was reported that another Southern Overland Mail coach had been waylaid about two and a half miles northeast of Trinidad by five or six of the same road agents, who knocked the driver from the box. But the spirited stage mules ran away before the gang could examine the express and treasure box.[55] If anyone thought the tale was a bit fishy, their suspicions were confirmed by an item in the *Trinidad Enterprise* asserting that there were no road agents, but that the driver was drunk, fell off the box, and the mules ran away.[56]

In September 1871, Cheyenne and Kiowa Indians harassed settlers in the new southeastern Colorado counties of Bent and Greenwood, created by growing population on the plains.[57] And closer to the mountains, the Ute gathered in the neighborhood of Huerfano Butte in large but not threatening numbers. Buffalo hunting on the plains was an annual event for them.[58]

An army wife made the trip from Kit Carson to Fort Lyon during October "in a funny looking stage coach called a 'jerkey'." Her main complaint was the "wretched ranch and stockade where we got fresh horses and a perfectly uneatable dinner."[59] A jerkey was a light, two-seat conveyance with roll-up canvas sides,[60] which approximates the description given by a traveler from Kit Carson to Trinidad, who said he rode in a two-seated affair drawn by four mules. At Trinidad he transferred to a big, six-horse Concord coach, with a shotgun messenger sitting next to the driver.[61] Apparently horses were supplanting mules on the main line, which had depended almost exclusively on mules for twenty years.

But mules were still the mainstay of the Southern Overland system at that time. In August, the Santa Fe *New Mexican* referred to the magnificent strings of stock to be found every few miles at company stations along the line, and it made particular mention of a notable addition: "a fine, graceful, lively, black mule to be used in the lead on the near side."[62]

On another part of the line, a boy living at Foster's station on the Apishapa River north of Trinidad watched a big Concord coach pulled down the hill at top speed by six black Missouri mules. Even more interesting was the huge driver on that run, an Englishman named John Stokes, who, to the youngster, appeared to be standing up when he

was sitting on the box.[63] The station itself was undergoing a fundamental change during the summer of 1872. The original log cabin (still
standing) had been abandoned for an adobe structure, which in turn
was giving way to a two-story, adobe hotel with a two-story porch on
three sides.[64] The new building was compared with that "wonder of
passers by," Mrs. Miller's place to the north on the Muddy,[65] and with
the Clifton House on Red River in New Mexico.

Basic changes in the region of the Southern Overland Mail system
occurred more slowly than in some parts of the frontier West in the
early 1870s, as is indicated by the survival of a major stage line. In
the wake of the Kansas Pacific Railroad, western Kansas experienced
important population growth[66] as did Colorado along the front range
of the mountains, mainly due to the southward construction of the
Denver and Rio Grande Railway from Denver to Pueblo.[67] But there
was no comparable increase on the plains of southeastern Colorado
and northeastern New Mexico, although the day of the cattleman had
begun.

Vivid aspects of a doomed way of life were highlighted in such reports as the one in January 1872 of thousands of buffalo on the stage
road between Kit Carson and Kiowa Springs, a circumstance described
as a "hunters' paradise."[68] The Grand Duke Alexis of Russia hunted
the big beasts on the plains that summer. But the year 1872 marked a
sharp rise in their slaughter for hides, meat, and bones to be sold on
eastern markets.[69]

The summer of 1872 was not a period of large-scale Indian hostilities,[70] but neither were the tribes quiescent. The Cimarron Ute
(Mohuache Ute from the agency at Cimarron, New Mexico)[71] were
said to have killed three men a few miles north of Trinidad in Colorado.
East of Ocate, New Mexico, a party of forty Kiowa allegedly killed two
herders and stole a large number of horses and mules.[72] There was
some skepticism about the accusations against the Cimarron Ute. It
was suggested that perhaps the deeds were those of a renegade band
of Navajo, Apache, and Ute recently seen near Maxwell's Ranch
(Cimarron), or even those of white raiders disguised as Indians and
known to have been on the Vermejo in New Mexico.[73]

White men were naturally edgy when the Plains tribes came off
their reservations in Indian Territory to their old hunting grounds in
Colorado. Susceptible nerves reacted strongly to a report in Trinidad

157

by Sam Lord, a Southern Overland Mail driver, who told of the killing of Uriel Higbee and his family on the Nine Mile Bottom of the lower Purgatoire by 400 to 500 Sioux and Cheyenne.[74] His story was denied by other employees when a Southern Overland Mail coach reached Kit Carson on September 17.[75]

Some people termed the tales of troubles along the Nine Mile Bottom as "canards," and it was asserted that local ranchers were not worried. The *Rocky Mountain News* told its readers that there were forty peaceful Cheyenne down there, and, to put it all in better perspective, noted that a party of 200 Cheyenne at another point on the Purgatoire had pulled off the road to let a Southern Overland Mail coach pass without threat or molestation.[76]

The Denver editor's Pueblo colleague turned aside the story of slaughter as a "gigantic sell," pointing out that the Cheyenne had done nothing more harmful than look in on Mr. Higbee's watermelon patch. And a dispatch to the *Chieftain* from the Rev. O. P. McMains, a Methodist circuit rider who was there, described the band as forty-three, well-mounted and equipped Kiowa, Cheyenne, and Apache, who were especially interested in scraps of iron for arrowheads.[77]

The railroad continued its slow but inexorable expansion into the domain of the Southern Overland Mail and Express Company. Captain Seymour (no further identification), Southern Overland agent at Santa Fe, announced that government freight would no longer be unloaded at Kit Carson but would go through on the Kansas Pacific to Denver, and from there south to Pueblo on the narrow-gauge Denver and Rio Grande, which would shorten wagon transportation by about seventy miles. The notice became effective in late June upon completion of the narrow-gauge tracks into Pueblo.[78]

The new arrangement meant the end for the town of Kit Carson as an important commercial point, but Barlow, Sanderson and Company did not take its coaches off the run from there to Trinidad. It appears, however, that for the first time in nearly twenty-five years of staging from the Missouri River to Santa Fe, a portion of the Santa Fe Trail became part of a branch line. From Pueblo through Trinidad to Santa Fe was now the main line of the Southern Overland Mail, and the coaches from Kit Carson made connections with it in Trinidad.

In the summer of 1872 the Southern Overland Mail people enjoyed a period of high praise for their tight schedules, skillful drivers, obliging conductors, fine animals, and new nine-passenger coaches on the main line. Preservation of that reputation may have prompted conductor Jake Scarff in early August to blame a delay in reaching Santa Fe on having to wait for the Kit Carson coach at Trinidad, although heavy rains all the way from Pueblo to the Vermejo had damaged the roads. In approval, the *New Mexican* commented: "This 'on time' spirit is characteristic of all the 'boys' on the S.O.M. route, no matter what 'bucks agin' them."[79]

The late summer rains made the country beautifully green. Along the entire line from Santa Fe to Pueblo, the grama grass was reported tall enough to cut with a machine.[80] As was characteristic of the country, however, the weather did not remain moderate. After a brief drying spell in which the roads became hard and dusty, the rains returned and mud clogged the main line. "Colonel" J. L. Sanderson was traveling the route at the time, encountering swollen streams and a six-hour delay at Ocate because of high waters. Another Southern Overland Mail coach was washed several rods below the crossing of an arroyo by the torrent before making it to the other side.[81] Near the northern end of the line a Pueblo-bound coach was stopped by the flooding St. Charles River, and the passengers were taken to the other bank on an impromptu raft.[82]

14

The Stage Line Shortens

1873-1875

RAIN, SNOW, WIND, ROAD AGENTS, even Indians never paralyzed the Southern Overland Mail and Express Company as effectively as did the spread of the "epizootic" early in 1873. The epidemic disease appeared first from Pueblo south, sweeping rapidly into New Mexico, but seeming to slow down as it approached Santa Fe.[1] At the end of the first week in January it was reported that nearly all the animals belonging to the mail company between Pueblo and Cimarron were more or less affected. Several mules trains were delayed at Las Vegas by the disease, and seven dead horses were counted from La Junta to Las Vegas.[2]

Owners of fine teams in Santa Fe were advised to keep their animals well groomed, blanketed, and fed once a day on bran, salt, and ashes, all mixed with warm water. The remedy of a Dr. Falcon, of Bloomington, Illinois, was published: one-half ounce of sectate of potassium dissolved in a half pint of cold water to be given morning and evening.[3] And from San Jose, San Miguel County, New Mexico, came this prescription: upon symptoms—coughing or turning at the nose—work the animal as usual; in the morning and evening give it a strong pinch of snuff by holding it under the animal's nostrils in a burned rag; afterward, put a bit of mashed onion in the nostrils. This source said the affliction was only distemper or "El Mal" and not often fatal.[4] Press reports chronicled the disease as it worked its way toward Santa Fe: first at Sweetwater, then five stage company mules down with it at Pajarito, followed by symptoms of the disease at Atkins station near Glorieta. By late January it appeared at the government corral in Santa Fe.[5]

In Colorado, the epizootic spread westward from Pueblo into the San

Luis Valley around Fort Garland and northward to Denver, where it brought all stagecoach traffic to a standstill. Perhaps the hardest hit, however, were Trinidad, Colorado, and Fort Union, New Mexico.[6] The month of January was the worst, but in New Mexico daily coach service was not fully restored until nearly April 1.[7]

Stoppage of the mails brought problems and public protests. The pile-up was first noted at Pueblo and Foster's station on the Apishapa. Gratuitous advice immediately suggested that buckboards should carry the mails and greater reliance should be placed on mules.[8] The Pueblo-Trinidad run was part of the old Denver and Santa Fe Stage Line on which horses had always been used until its takeover by the Southern Overland Mail and Express Company. Of course, it soon was obvious that mules were far from being immune.

Barlow, Sanderson and Company did what it could to keep the mails moving. Their New Mexico agent, N.F. Swope, started east with the idea of going as far as he could in trying to push the mails through. Conductor Wardwell started with a coach from Santa Fe as far as Pueblo on January 14. The journey took over a week, and it was necessary to use the same team for the whole trip, probably stopping at night to rest the animals. A week later another coach left Santa Fe, and nearly five days of travel took it only as far as Fort Union.[9]

Special Post Office Department agents investigated, hastened by public impatience and the severity of the breakdown. One published story said that Special Agent James McDowell found fifteen sacks of Cimarron mail piled up at Kit Carson. When Southern Overland Mail's Mac Frost blamed it on the epizootic, McDowell told him that another contractor could easily be found. The mail began to move immediately afterward.[10] In view of the abundance of evidence supporting Frost's contention, the story is open to strong doubt. A distant reverberation appeared in the Tucson *Arizona Citizen,* which commented that other stage lines kept going and private expresses had no special difficulty getting healthy horses.[11] That other stage lines and private express lines operated was irrelevant, simply signifying their escape from the disease.

In a relatively short time, a disruption of long-distance transportation by epizootic would be impossible. The iron horse was immune. Temporary end for the Atchison, Topeka and Santa Fe Railroad was at Sargent, Kansas, formerly a tent town known as State Line City, sixty miles east of Fort Lyon, Colorado.[12] From the little town of Las Animas (close to

161

Fort Lyon), the Southern Overland Mail line made daily connection with the Kansas railhead. Daily Southern Overland coaches also plying between Las Animas and Kit Carson on the Kansas Pacific Railroad, as well as a triweekly connection up the Arkansas to Pueblo, made Las Animas an important hub.[13]

By early July the Santa Fe Railroad had built a short distance into Colorado, and the new railhead town of Granada sprouted on the plains. Of course the Southern Overland Mail line met the trains there, announcing its Granada-Las Animas fare at $10.[14] The future of Las Animas looked bright. It could hardly avoid being on the main line of the Santa Fe Railroad, and that summer the Kansas Pacific built a branch line south from Kit Carson in a bid to keep a share of the freighting trade with New Mexico.

During construction of the Kansas Pacific branch, Southern Overland Mail coaches met successive ends of track. At one time when the railhead was ten miles north of Las Animas, it was noted that mail arrived in town five hours sooner than it used to, and prospective passengers were informed that they could buy a combination stage-railroad ticket to Kit Carson.[15]

Preoccupation with prospects of economic well-being drew some public attention away from the annual visits of Plains Indians to the area. About 170 Cheyenne from Indian Territory came to the vicinity of Boggsville in September, and other bands of that tribe remained in the region until mid-October, committing the usual thefts and destruction of settlers' livestock. Fort Lyon was on the alert, and cavalry units were sent out. There was no loss of human life, however, and the Indians managed to stay ahead of settlers' posses and troopers as they moved eastward toward Granada and eventually back to their reservation.[16]

As the Indian scare receded, residents of Las Animas were shocked when the Kansas Pacific spur was shunted away from the town to a point about five miles up the Arkansas River. The location was a derivation from the Vigil and St. Vrain (Las Animas) Grant. The land was deeded to David H. Moffat, Jr. (of the Kansas Pacific Railroad), and others, and it became obvious that a new town would spring up there. The matter is too complicated to be fully treated here. However, Charles W. Bowman, editor of the local *Leader,* on November 1, 1873, began a series of slashing editorials against the allegedly fraudulent land transaction, but his efforts were futile.[17]

The Barlow and Sanderson Company,[18] expecting the Kansas Pacific branch to come into Las Animas, had moved its receiving and supply agent, A. L. Carpenter, from Kit Carson to Las Animas in the early part of July.[19] Then facing the irreversible, the Southern Overland Mail people abandoned "Old Town" for the "New Town" of West Las Animas,[20] erecting there new stables and a corral designed by Mac Frost. A new stage and express office was planned amid signs of unbeatable competition—a water tank, the frame of an engine house, and new material for a railroad depot.

Train connections allowed a stagecoach to leave for Santa Fe every morning at six o'clock.[21] Schedules at the New Mexican capital were changed to meet the new arrangement, coaches arriving at 6 P.M. and departing at 6 A.M. The departure time was approved by the editor of the *New Mexican* with the comment that it would be difficult to get up before dawn on a cold morning to jolt and shiver for two to three hours before breakfast, but the passengers would be on the road only two nights instead of three and most of the journey would be in daylight.[22]

Those were minor seasonal and physical discomforts, but once in a while the hazards of travel brought injuries of a painful and serious nature. A rare example of the risk occurred on January 2, 1874, when the southbound coach out of Trinidad was hit by a freak squall, blowing the vehicle over, breaking the driver's leg, and severely injuring a passenger.[23]

Atrophy of the Southern Overland Mail system was slowed down when the Panic of 1873, set off by the failure of Jay Cooke and Company (promoters of the Northern Pacific Railroad) seized the country. In the West, railroad construction stopped,[24] and pressures against the Southern Overland Mail and Express Company were allayed for almost two years. The Santa Fe was held back at Granada; the Kansas Pacific stopped with its branch to West Las Animas; and the southern extension of the Denver and Rio Grande stopped with thirty-six and a half miles of grade, with no tracks or ties, projecting from Pueblo.[25]

This impermanent stablization of the stagecoach line sent passengers from West Las Animas over the 320 miles to Santa Fe for a fare of $60, and for those going to Trinidad, a major stop, it took $20 and 18 hours. But Barlow and Sanderson officials knew that the railroads were simply in a somnolent state from which they would be aroused as the general economy recovered. Looking to a future change of scene, they planned to put stage lines west of the front range of the Rockies in south-central Colorado, where major railroad takeovers were not expected for some time.

Around June 1, 1874, a shipment of eight new coaches (by Coan and Ten Broeke of Chicago) for the Southern Overland Mail and Express Company arrived at West Las Animas, and thirty-eight head of fine American horses were received for Barlow and Sanderson's extension of service westward across the San Luis Valley to Del Norte, heart of the big mining boom in the San Juan Mountains.[26] The daily run from Pueblo to Del Norte was made under the name of the Pueblo and Del Norte Stage Line Company, and, of course, Barlow and Sanderson coaches made connections to and from Trinidad and Santa Fe with the daily Denver and Rio Grande trains in and out of Pueblo.[27]

Southwest of Granada and West Las Animas a traveler could see the flourishing state of wagon-freighting as that form of commerce entered its last days. Granada was facetiously characterized as a lively place with —in a two-day span—a horse race, a shooting match, a murder, and a horse thief hanging. On the other hand, Kit Carson had slumped to one whiskey shop, one restaurant, and the post office.[28]

But in 1874 West Las Animas was the place of real commercial prosperity in southeastern Colorado because of its concentration of rival commission houses. In one week in July, 182,863 pounds of wool were shipped from there, and the average weekly shipments of hides were given as 87,000 pounds.[29] Sometimes enough teams were not available, and freighters had to advertise for them, while merchants along the way fretted because their goods were piling up in West Las Animas and Granada warehouses.[30] Increasing numbers of emigrants got off Kansas Pacific trains at West Las Animas and dispersed from there into the Southwest.[31] That railroad and the Santa Fe both enticed fastidious travelers by advertising "Pullman Palace Cars" and an "elegant sleeping car,"[32] attractions never possible for a stagecoach line.

Indian troubles flared again in the months of July and August, causing considerable patrol activity by Fort Lyon cavalry especially along the Purgatoire. Herders were attacked in Bent Canyon, a bridge on the Santa Fe railroad was burned, and settlers were reportedly killed near Granada. The incidents were heightened by the sensational assertion that white men had accompanied the Indians in recent raids.[33] But the worst disturbances were in New Mexico and east. There, a military campaign against the Plains tribes culminated during the fall and early winter of 1874 in the Texas Panhandle and Oklahoma. The campaign was known as the Red River War, a series of curiously indecisive engagements which, nevertheless, effectively put an end to Indian hostilities on the southern plains.[34]

News of happenings along the stage line started off sensationally in 1874 with reports of the killing of Chunk Colbert, a well-known rough, by rancher-gunman Clay Allison in the dining room of the Clifton House on the night of January 6.[35] In the middle of February people were saddened by news of the death from natural causes of Alexander Hicklin, pioneer settler (since 1860), at his ranch on the Greenhorn.[36] His ranch had been the location of a swing station on the Denver-Trinidad run from the days of the Denver and Santa Fe Stage Line.

That summer a correspondent of the Pueblo *Chieftain* in the Trinidad area was astonished to find wedge-shaped pieces of wood tipped with iron (secured by a thong) being used as plows pulled by oxen.[37] Oats had to be shipped in from the States for the stations of the Southern Overland Mail and Express Company in Colorado and New Mexico.[38] One of its coaches was robbed of its express box at Rayado, but the box was recovered and the robber caught at Cimarron.[39]

The winter of 1874-1875 was severe for employees and clients of the Southern Overland Mail Line. In mid-December drivers told of having to contend with six to eight inches of snow all the way from Santa Fe to Red River.[40] On one occasion no mail came into Trinidad from the north because trains on both the Denver and Rio Grande and the Kansas Pacific railroads were snowed in. One Kansas Pacific train took eleven days to get across the plains to Denver, and its eighty-five passengers ate all the food products carried in the express cars.[41] Stage messenger Charles Dudrow spent two extremely cold nights in early January 1875 on a coach from Santa Fe to West Las Animas. The night before he reached West Las Animas, the thermometer at Fort Lyon fell to 28 below zero, the coldest temperature there since the post was established in June 1867.[42]

Unmistakable signs of deterioration in the quality of service performed by the Southern Overland Mail and Express Company were evident. As early as October 1874, complaints were heard in Trinidad that the company was not adhering to the terms of its new contract, which called for mail delivery there at noon instead of midnight.[43] From New Mexico in

February 1875, came criticism that running time from West Las Animas to Santa Fe was slowed down from sixty to seventy-two hours. The company replied that the contract allowed ninety-six hours,[44] an answer that was hardly satisfactory. Some people thought the lag was caused by a change in locomotive power from four mules to two horses per coach (undoubtedly a jerkey).[45] However, four mules appear to have been used on some parts of the line and two horses on others, particularly in that section between West Las Animas and Trinidad.[46]

Superintendent Lew Barnum and Jared L. Sanderson, Jr., agent at West Las Animas, devoted much of their energy to stocking the new Colorado route from Canon City to Del Norte. The new route was managed by Colonel Ayers, who had been with the Southern Overland Mail since its absorption of the old Denver and Santa Fe Line, of which he was superintendent. Six new four-horse Concord coaches came on the Kansas Pacific into West Las Animas in March, and early the next month a shipment of fifty-two horses arrived from St. Louis. Forty-two of the animals were iron-greys for the Canon City-Del Norte run, and the remaining twelve were sorrels for the Santa Fe line. Over a month later, Lew Barnum returned from St. Louis in charge of a carload of chestnut sorrels to be used in four-horse teams from Trinidad south.[47]

For people along the route, those indications of retrenchment on the stage line to Santa Fe were countered by signs of revival of railroad construction as part of the general recovery of the nation's economy. The commissioners of Bent County, Colorado, set a bond election in March to aid construction of the Atchison, Topeka and Santa Fe Railroad from Granada to West Las Animas, and Otero, Sellar and Company announced it would set up a commission house in Trinidad as soon as the railroad began building toward the town.[48] And if the Santa Fe built into Pueblo instead of up the Purgatoire, extension of the narrow-guage Denver and Rio Grande to Trinidad seemed almost inevitable.[49] Trinidad's location at the north entrance of the Raton Pass made it practically unavoidable that either railroad building to New Mexico should go through the town, just as it had long been a point of convergence of stage lines south.

Fire destroyed the Hog Back stage station and nearby hay stacks northeast of Trinidad at an estimated loss of $500 to the Southern Overland Mail and Express Company.[50] That was shortly before an unidentified traveler set down his impressions of the stage line that was soon to be extinct. From them comes information about the changes that were transforming southeastern Colorado as railroads began their ascendancy.

The four-mule Southern Overland Mail coach left West Las Animas on a pleasant August morning. Along the lower Purgatoire near Boggsville agriculture was flourishing because of the big new irrigation ditch. Shocks of grain and long rows of green corn were plentiful, and so were sheep and cattle. The first stage station was at Alkali, twenty miles out and kept by "Boss" Perry, a former company employee.[51] There, two horses were hitched in place of the four mules. About a quarter of a mile beyond, a road branched to the left to the extensively cultivated Nine Mile Bottom, already well known for its melons and vegetables. The stage road was always several miles from the Purgatoire Canyon's rim.

Eleven miles from Alkali the coach came to the station in Vogel Canyon at the sheep ranch of Fagin and Brown. Fifteen miles farther it stopped at the Bent Canyon (Benson's)[52] home station, where the passengers ate and acquired a new driver. At twelve miles was the Lockwood Canyon station. Darkness set in there, and the curtains of the stage were pulled down. The chronicler of the trip said little more than that the driver told him when they reached the Hog Back station after seventeen miles. After fifteen more miles, they reached M. G. Frost's station near Hoehne. Another thirteen miles brought the coach to Trinidad at 3 A.M.[53]

The many brick buildings with their stone fronts along Main Street and the numerous new residences throughout Trinidad were observed as signs of progress. The favorable contiguity of good farm land, rich veins of coal, abundant water power, and fine climate pointed to the town "as the coming place of Southern Colorado."

Unexpectedly, the unknown writer made a quick trip north to Pueblo and back. Foster's two-story, adobe station on the Apishapa was reached a bit ahead of time, allegedly because the driver had a sweetheart there. The passengers ate an excellent supper prepared by Mrs. Foster, while rain and hail pelted down outside.

Twenty miles up the line was the Denver and Rio Grande Railway town of Cucharas, with two or three stores and about twenty houses all built of lumber. Only the railway grading had been completed there. Breakfast was eaten at Miller's Muddy Creek station at 7 A.M., and just before noon the stage reached the new town of South Pueblo[54]—good buildings, tree-lined streets, and a ditch of water along each thoroughfare. The narrow-gauge train was ready for its daily trip to Denver as soon as passengers transferred from the Barlow and Sanderson coach.

Heading south again, the newspaper correspondent passed through Trinidad in a Southern Overland coach for Santa Fe. Heavy rains had made the road in the Raton Pass extremely difficult. All of "Uncle Dick" Wootton's bridges had been washed out, and he had men working almost constantly to keep them passable. After a brief nighttime halt at Wootton's place,[55] the coach arrived at Tom Stockton's Clifton House for nine o'clock breakfast. From the Raton Mountains south the grama grass was knee-high, which made the stockmen happy, and about five miles from Cimarron a vestige of earlier days—a Ute encampment of seventy-five or eighty lodges—could be seen. The next day 600 to 700 Ute came into Cimarron, many of them wrapped in bright red and green, government-issue blankets, to receive their rations of flour and meat at the agency.

Cimarron looked interesting enough for a stopover, and the journey to Santa Fe was resumed the next evening in a stage that slogged through a dark and rainy night. Horses were changed at an unidentified station about midnight, and the driver advised his passengers to hold onto their seats because the road would be rough and he had to let the horses take their own head for a while. For about an hour the coach plunged down a long hill, and when it came to an upgrade and an even rougher stretch of road, the gooseneck at the end of the pole straightened, letting the lead bars hit the heels of the lead horses. Those animals then galloped off into the darkness, leaving the driver with the brake hard down and the wheel horses dancing but well in hand. The driver listened intently to the fading sound of the lead horses to determine the direction in which they went. Then he drove as fast as he could to the next station, turned the reins over to the messenger and got off to await daylight, when he would start a search for his lost animals.

With the team restored to full strength the stage passed through Fort Union, and the passengers took breakfast at La Junta at 7 A.M. On the tavern there (probably Gregg's) hung an American flag bearing the words "Hurray for S. B. Elkins!"[56] Between there and Las Vegas the travelers met three companies of the Fifth Cavalry, returning from campaigning under Major General George Crook against the Apache in Arizona.[57]

The matter-of-fact descriptions by the *Leader's* reporter suggest that he was an experienced hand. A little over a month later a novice recorded his reactions in his diary. He was Ernst Kohlberg, a Jewish immigrant on his way from Hamburg, Germany, to El Paso, Texas. He came to Las

Animas, Colorado, on the Santa Fe Railroad and took the stage from there.

We left Las Animas at 6 A.M. September 27 in a fairly comfortable stage-coach whose motive power was four mules. The coaches are as light and strong as they can be built. The sides are gray canvas and the body of the coach is carried by heavy leather straps as regular iron and steel springs would snap on the rough roads. [The vehicle was undoubtedly a Concord mud wagon.] Our first day's journey in the coach was over the prairie and the road being fair the trip was quite comfortable. We reached the Raton Mts. that night and our way led through these mountains clear to Santa Fe. I am sure that I will never forget this ride. We stopped three times daily for twenty minutes for our meals. We also had to stop at intervals for five minutes to change mules. We traveled day and night and always at a gallop whether the road was good and level or rough, over rocks, up hill and down always the same gait. You people cannot conceive of such a road through wild and trackless mountains. . . . Several times I was hurled from my seat and bumped the ceiling of the coach when we hit a bump real hard or went through an arroyo. Some ride! It was very hot during the day while at night it turned real cold. It did not seem to bother the stage-driver if he upset the coach which happened several times. Mr. and Mrs. Schutz and I were turned up side down, but no one was hurt for the coach proper remained lying on its side while the mules went off with the front end. We finally arrived in Santa Fe at 7 A.M. October 1st and I was more happy to get there than I was to arrive in New York, just a month before.[58]

Another contemporary account received much wider circulation, and it appears to be both sloppily written and factitious.[59] William H. Rideing was the only passenger on a Southern Overland Mail stage that left Chapman's hotel and ranch, Las Vegas, at 5 A.M. From then on he complained and made statements that are open to question because they have no substantial support from other sources. He attributed the small volume of passenger traffic to abuses by the Southern Overland Mail and Express Company, and then went on to say he had to bribe conductor, driver, and station master for little services that would make the trip more pleasant. What apparently was a mud wagon, Rideing described as a coach about the size of a coupé, with two crossbenches only six inches wide. He saw Trinidad simply as a thriving little town with "rude wooden buildings," where he changed to an even smaller coach for West Las Animas.[60]

Rideing commented, inaccurately, that the Southern Overland Mail Company had a mail contract for $30,000.[61] At the time Barlow and

Sanderson had their smallest subsidy since they had taken over the Southern Overland Mail; it amounted to $800 for New Mexico Route No. 39113 in the name of J. L. Sanderson.[62] Two years before, Barlow and Sanderson held contracts for close to a half million dollars from Missouri to California.[63]

The advance of railroads, which automatically became mail routes, and the success of other bidders had reduced Barlow and Sanderson's service to the line between Pueblo and Santa Fe and the branch from Trinidad to West Las Animas. And more miles were lopped off the branch, shortly after Rideing traveled over it, when the Santa Fe Railroad resumed construction and put its rails into the new town of La Junta, Colorado, about twenty miles west of West Las Animas, in December 1875.[64] The rival Kansas Pacific also laid tracks from West Las Animas to La Junta, announcing that it soon would be delivering freight for Trinidad at La Junta and would ticket passengers to Trinidad, running a special hack from La Junta at reduced rates for passengers and express. Those plans were capped by the promise to build into Trinidad by spring.[65] Almost simultaneously, it became common knowledge that the engineering corps of the Denver and Rio Grande had located its line to a point on the Purgatoire River about four miles below Trinidad.[66] Small wonder, then, that the Barlow and Sanderson Company devoted much attention to developing stage lines in the mountainous mining districts of central and western Colorado and on the California-Oregon coast. With railroad companies stirred by the general economic recovery of the country, there would be at most several years of constantly shrinking mail stage service from the railheads to Santa Fe.

End of the Santa Fe Trail

1876-1880

ONE OF THE FIRST DECISIONS made in 1876 by Barlow and Sanderson management was not to move the Southern Overland Mail terminus from West Las Animas to La Junta.[1] There was no point in moving it. Both the Santa Fe and the Kansas Pacific railroads had depots in West Las Animas, where stage passengers could make connections, and it appeared more than likely that one (perhaps both) of the railroads soon would lay tracks southwestward along the Santa Fe Trail from King's Ferry (La Junta) to Trinidad. Some recent talk suggested a Kansas Pacific depot at the site of the old Iron Spring stage station on the Mountain Branch of the Trail.[2] There was no sense in making changes in a stage line which before long would be completely defunct.

Track-laying went on with little hindrance. By February 22 Denver and Rio Grande rails reached the new town of Cucharas, and a few days later the Santa Fe had completed its line up the Arkansas valley to Pueblo.[3] Then by April 6 the narrow-gauge Denver and Rio Grande was at El Moro, its new and associated town on the Purgatoire below Trinidad, much to the anger and consternation of the people of Trinidad. The town's consolation was in the probability of a broad-gauge railroad coming to it, the odds then favoring the Kansas Pacific.[4]

In anticipation of the rapid phasing out of the Southern Overland Mail lines into Trinidad from the north, Lewis Barnum and Harley Sanderson, J. L.'s brother, were directly involved in arrangements for a new line of stages between Cucharas—the Denver and Rio Grande town northeast of Walsenburg (the Huerfano County seat)—and Lake City in the San Juan Mountains, a fast-growing town in a developing gold-silver

171

mining district.[5] A contemporary mail-cover corner-card says that Harley Sanderson was general superintendent of the Southern Overland Mail and Express Company, with its principal office in Pueblo. Lewis Barnum was listed as assistant superintendent.[6] The new route evidently went from Cucharas to Badito (the old county seat on the Huerfano River) and then over Sangre de Cristo Pass into the San Luis Valley. It was at the Summit House, atop Sangre de Cristo Pass, that Lewis Barnum suddenly died from pneumonia on January 13, 1876 at the age of forty-six.[7] Loss of Barnum's expertise must have been strongly felt in that critical period of transition.

In the spring "Colonel" Sanderson appeared in West Las Animas to confer with his brother Harley, Division Superintendent Mac Frost, and others.[8] In addition to the problems of closing out their old services, making the new mountain lines operational still required much attention. A published report said that three carloads of horses and ten coaches were on the way from the States for Barlow and Sanderson's stage line from Cucharas to Lake City. On the evening of Monday, March 20, thirty horses arrived in West Las Animas via the Kansas Pacific for the run into the San Juan Mountains.[9] Their intentions were further revealed in April with the announcement that as soon as the line westward from Cucharas was ready, their livestock in use from West Las Animas to Trinidad and from Pueblo to Trinidad would be transferred to the new route.[10] A few days later they inaugurated a daily stage service between Canon City and Rosita,[11] a booming silver camp on the west slope of the Greenhorn (Wet) Mountains.[12]

The last Barlow and Sanderson coach to run south out of Pueblo left on the morning of Wednesday, May 3, 1876. Trinidad was now the northern terminus of the stage line to Santa Fe, although some sort of connection would be maintained to West Las Animas for the time being. That left two Barlow and Sanderson stage lines in Colorado detached from the former main lines that used the Mountain Branch of the Santa Fe Trail (or ran close to it) and the Denver and Fort Union Road: the line from Cucharas via the Sangre de Cristo Pass to Del Norte (which crossed the old Denver and Fort Union Road) and from Canon City up the Arkansas, through Poncha Pass to Saguache, and over Cochetopa Pass to the San Juan country.

From the moment of its inception, the line over the Sangre de Cristo Pass existed in the shadow of the Denver and Rio Grande's plan to build

172

west from Cucharas, through Walsenburg, and over the adjacent La Veta Pass to Fort Garland and the San Luis Valley. That rail route would tap the San Juan region and also provide a new connection with the northern New Mexico trade. The branch line westward reached the new railhead town of La Veta by July 4, 1876, shortly before the frightening news of General Custer's annihilation by the Sioux on the Little Big Horn, far to the north.[13]

There were probably expressions of thankfulness that the local Indians were pretty well secured on their reservations, but the shocking information about Custer was a temporary distraction from the exciting political developments culminating in Colorado. A constitution for the new state had been ratified, and on August 1, 1876, President Ulysses S. Grant proclaimed Colorado (the Centennial State) a member of the Union. The new state's three electoral votes proved crucial in keeping the Republicans in control in Washington by giving Rutherford B. Hayes his extremely narrow margin over Democrat Samuel J. Tilden in the presidential election of that year.[14]

Barlow and Sanderson decided to continue operating their coaches between West Las Animas and Trinidad during the summer of 1876, leaving the former place at 9 P.M. and reaching Trinidad at 3 A.M. the second morning to make an inconvenient connection with a Denver and Rio Grande train at El Moro.[15] Business dwindled rapidly that summer, however, as most passengers and mail came into the Denver and Rio Grande railhead town of El Moro.

The Southern Overland Mail stage station remained at Trinidad. But the Barlow and Sanderson Company, as mail contractors, picked up the mail and transfer passengers at El Moro and brought them to Trinidad in a four-mule stage with iron axles and heavy leather straps for springs.[16]

There is uncertainty about the abandonment of stagecoach service between West Las Animas and Trinidad. The Santa Fe *New Mexican*, quoting the Las Vegas *Gazette*, complained about the undependable mail deliveries by the Denver and Rio Grande (allegedly because of washouts) and suggested that Barlow and Sanderson should have their coaches operating on the West Las Animas-Trinidad run at least for the rainy season.[17] The item suggests that by midsummer that stage service had become very irregular (perhaps in response only to demand), so that notice of its abandonment on September 1 was simply official notification of what was practically a *fait accompli*. A week later the buckboard mail, which had taken its place, was discontinued.[18]

With Barlow and Sanderson's Southern Overland Mail system restricted to the two hundred miles between Trinidad and Santa Fe, the final phases of truncation set in. On the same September 1 that brought an end to stage line connections from Trinidad to points northeast, daily coaches between Trinidad and Santa Fe were scheduled on a thirty-six-hour running time, leaving Trinidad at noon and Santa Fe at 6 A.M.

South from Santa Fe a much reduced service (not by Barlow and Sanderson as mail contractors) was in operation. There were only two passenger coaches per week on that line, the mail being carried by buckboard on the other seven days.[19] The new Barlow and Sanderson schedule was published over the name of E. P. Black, agent for the Overland Stage Company in Santa Fe, who had recently taken over from Frank Ford.[20] A tendency to use the shortened version of the firm's name reflected the growing unsuitability of "Southern Overland" as applied to Barlow and Sanderson's line. The older name continued to be used also, along with an understandable trend toward using "Southern Overland Mail" (or the common abbreviation, SOM) in reference to the mail stage service south of Santa Fe.[21]

The Barlow and Sanderson line was still an important link in communication and transportation, subject, of course, to the vicissitude that had always beset stage lines. From Silver City, in the southwestern part of New Mexico, for example, six bars of silver, totaling 320 pounds, and 105 ounces of gold were brought to Santa Fe and then sent northward to the railhead in Colorado on the Barlow and Sanderson "eastern coach," a persistent term from the days when the stage line extended to the Missouri River.[22]

Bad weather was a major problem, especially in winter. Coaches were put off schedule in February 1877 by deep snow along most of the line. One of them was forced to remain at Tecolote for several hours because of the storm.[23] The evidence shows, however, that the early railroads were not as weatherproof as was commonly thought. For employees and patrons of the Barlow and Sanderson Company, the chief change was the welcome lack of Indian raids.

A few people were more than aware of the fundamental economic changes being wrought in the Southwest by the advance of the railroads. They were sensitive to the end of another phase of the American scene, and occasionally there was a hint of nostalgia. Barlow and Sanderson and the firm of Kerens and Mitchell, who together dominated much of the staging between El Moro, Colorado, and Fort Yuma, Arizona, were urged by the editor of the Las Vegas (New Mexico) *Gazette* to cater to those on their way to California who would be interested in the romance of staging and a close look at New Mexico and Arizona, implying that those relatively unspoiled territories would soon be altered beyond recognition. The firm of Kerens and Mitchell had obtained the mail contract from Mesilla, New Mexico, to San Diego, California, in 1874.[24]

A predictable new element of competition developed in the spring and summer of 1877 for the Barlow and Sanderson Company. By the middle of June the Denver and Rio Grande tracks had been laid over La Veta Pass, and on the western slope the railroad used the same egress to the San Luis Valley—Sangre de Cristo Creek—that was followed by Barlow and Sanderson's stage line from Cucharas to Del Norte. The distance to Santa Fe by stagecoach from the railroad across the San Luis Valley was considerably shorter than that by stagecoach from Trinidad—ninety miles shorter according to one estimate. That meant competition for Barlow and Sanderson's Southern Overland Mail and Express on the old route over the Raton Pass to Santa Fe.[25] The Barlow and Sanderson Company, of course, already was established in the San Luis Valley, but it was not able to stifle some fast-developing competition there. F. M. Prescott and Company's Santa Fe and Garland (City) Line, also advertised as the Santa Fe and Northern Express Line, began weekly trips by four-horse passenger and express wagons, going through in four days on a $15 passenger fare and an express rate of 5 cents per pound.[26] By the first of the year the route was taken over by the Southern Stage and Express Company, operating four-horse Concords (coaches or mud-wagons) between Santa Fe and Garland City, which was six miles east of Fort Garland, three times a week in thirty hours for $30. That firm was probably the same as the one referred to as the Southern Express—also dubbed "S.O.M." by the *New Mexican*—a line running south from Santa Fe also, whose proprietor, Numa Raymond, had had to pay to the U.S. collector the $510 lost in a stage holdup in May.[27]

With the railhead on the east edge of the San Luis Valley, Barlow and Sanderson's operation (formerly east of the mountains between Fort Lyon and Trinidad), extended across the valley to Del Norte and then into the San Juan Mountains as far as Lake City, where the stage station was located in the American House. Mac Frost was superintendent. Barlow and Sanderson coaches also ran from Del Norte westward along the Rio Grande to South Fork. One of the drivers on that section was G. W. Stout, a veteran from the defunct Western Stage Company, which used to operate between Fort Kearney, Nebraska, and Denver. On the route from Del Norte into the mountains two former drivers for Ben Holladay —L. M. Hill and James Billingsbee—drove between that town and Jackson's. From Del Norte to Lake City passengers and mail were carried in a jerky, and on the line from Saguache to Lake City the Barlow and Sanderson Company used two-horse, double-seated buckboards, taking two days for the trip. The company agent at Lake City was identified by the Pueblo *Chieftain* as "J. L. Sanderson, No. 2, nephew of 'the old man.' "

After the railroad reached the new town of Alamosa (July 4, 1878), the shortened stage line ran through Riverside and Venable to Del Norte and on to Lake City. Other well-known drivers were Jim Madison, "Three Finger" Jack Hayes, and a fellow from Kansas City identified only as "K. C." Big John Stokes, a former stage driver for Barlow and Sanderson east of the mountains, had become so huge that he was given the job of hauling grain to stations from Alamosa to Lake City, and he was a familiar figure on the road with his wagon and trailer drawn by eight large horses.[28]

After an unpublicized decision by the Atchison, Topeka and Santa Fe Railroad Company to build south into New Mexico from La Junta, Colorado, its swift seizure of control of the Raton Pass ruined the plans of the Denver and Rio Grande narrow-gauge to build through it. The Santa Fe's decision was taken in late February 1878, and by early April it was public information that the railroad would closely follow the route of the Barlow and Sanderson stage line from Trinidad to Clifton House. Most of the distance was through the defile of the Raton Pass, the only feasible route. From Clifton House south, however, the railroad line would be several miles east of the stage road as far as Las Vegas.[29]

The Barlow and Sanderson Company was not indifferent to the changing circumstances and new competition, but its reaction was slow and deliberate. Harley Sanderson and Division Superintendent Swope were registered in February at the Exchange Hotel, Santa Fe, the hostelry generally used by SOM people.[30] It is a reasonable guess that they were in town on stage line business. When Harley Sanderson returned in April with his brother, Jared, and David C. Dodge, general freight and passenger agent for the Denver and Rio Grande Railway,[31] there could have been little doubt that communication and transportation matters were uppermost in their minds.

The *New Mexican* reported that the trio was discussing a new coach and mail route from Santa Fe to Alamosa, the new Denver and Rio Grande town in the San Luis Valley of Colorado. The basic details of a weekly mail service and a daily coach service (through in twenty-four hours for a passenger fare of $20) were soon revealed. After about a week in the New Mexican capital, the two Sandersons and Dodge returned to Alamosa, leaving the *New Mexican* to publicize the information that hopefully, the line to Alamosa would be ready by June 1, and the 140-mile route would be the best in the Barlow and Sanderson Overland Stage and Express Company's system.

The route was described as going from the railhead at Alamosa south along the west bank of the Rio Grande via Conejos, Santa Cruz, and Ojo Caliente to San Juan (Pueblo). There, it crossed to the east bank of the river and followed it toward Santa Fe. Once again a target date was postponed as Superintendent Swope and his men were busy digging wells, building stations, and improving the road for a July 1 opening.[32]

Over on the old line between Trinidad and Santa Fe, coaches performed their scheduled runs, with occasional disruptions of one sort or another. Rather notable was a holdup of the Southern Overland Mail about four miles north of Las Vegas on an April night. Charles Dudrow was the driver, taking the coach from San Jose to Sapello, and there was no conductor that trip.[33] Several unidentified men stopped the stage and took three leather mailbags from the boot, cutting them open and strewing letters and packages on the ground. The robbers were obviously looking for money but were disappointed. There was some mail from Old Mexico, but no registered packages or letters with money with one exception—a letter with 25 cents to pay for two dime novels and one 5 center. At least, that was the story carried on the telegraph wire.[34] And a different kind of interference was the destruction by fire (caused by a nearby camp fire) of the stage station, out buildings, and haystack at the Rock Corral, not far out of Santa Fe.[35]

Occupation of the Raton Pass by Santa Fe Railroad men early in 1878 did not mean immediate laying of track over it. The seizure was a defensive action against the Denver and Rio Grande and was far in advance of actual construction. Miles of iron were put down that summer southwestward from La Junta, but at the end of August the track was fourteen and a half miles short of Trinidad. A train with one passenger coach left La Junta each morning at six for the run to the end of track, leaving for the return trip about 2 P.M. Presumably, the Barlow and Sanderson Company reached out the few miles from Trinidad to make the connection. Their coaches for New Mexico departed regularly from the United States Hotel in Trinidad, where popular agent Duane D. Finch managed the business from his office in a corner room of the hotel block. The Pueblo *Chieftain*, in a contemporary item, remarked about the stage line's "fine horses," and a little later the Santa Fe *New Mexican* in an article about an incident on the line spoke only of horses.[36] Other evidence substantiates the inference that mules had been entirely replaced by horses in the last several years of Barlow and Sanderson's service to Santa Fe, and it does not appear that mules were used on their Colorado mountain routes.

Another change in the last days of the Southern Overland Mail and Express Company was the withdrawal of Bradley Barlow from the partnership of Barlow and Sanderson, proprietors of the stage line to Santa Fe. Ownership was transferred to the new firm of J. L. Sanderson and Company. Conclusive evidence of this is a photograph taken on Trinidad's Main Street, showing a mud-wagon bearing the name of the new owner along with the old designation of Southern Overland Mail and Express Company. The familiar "Barlow and Sanderson" still remained in common use until the end.

Completion of the Santa Fe Railroad into Trinidad in the fall of 1878 was celebrated by about 2,000 people from the community and the surrounding area. The imminent economic changes for a town and region getting a direct railroad connection were eagerly welcomed. Someone with a sense of history helped plan the occasion by having Alexander Hatch, an old resident and a participant in the 1849 gold rush to California, drive a golden spike to mark the event.[37] Soon the railroad advertised its train leaving Trinidad at 10:50 A.M. and arriving at La Junta at 4:40, and leaving La Junta at 12:40 P.M. and arriving at Trinidad by 6:15. Patrons were advised that railroad time was fifty-five minutes faster than local time.[38]

By December Raton Pass was surmounted by switchbacks, and railroad trains made their entry into New Mexico, past the abandoned stage station at Willow Spring formerly kept by S. A. Sayre[39] and on toward the well-known Clifton House station. In February the railroad dropped the name of Clifton for its new town, calling the settlement Otero in honor of Miguel A. Otero of the big commission house of Otero, Sellar and Company. The office of Barlow and Sanderson was transferred to Otero for connection with the daily Santa Fe mail and passenger train that came over the pass from Trinidad in the morning. With the U.S. mail at last reaching New Mexico by rail, hope was expressed in Santa Fe that the Post Office Department would send all the mail to the Otero railhead rather than to Alamosa, the Denver and Rio Grande town in the San Luis Valley of Colorado, because "the Alamosa mail continues to arrive [in Santa Fe] very regularly behind time."[40]

During the summer of 1878 the bulk of the U.S. mail for Santa Fe had gone over the Denver and Rio Grande tracks to Alamosa, Colorado, and from there south. Probably most of the passenger traffic had followed the same route. Barlow and Sanderson's main service was temporarily on the Alamosa-Santa Fe run, but a skeletal operation was maintained from Trinidad over the Raton Pass, which resumed its importance as the Santa Fe Railroad steadily advanced toward the town.

When that literary-military figure, General Lew Wallace, came out to be New Mexico's governor, he reached Trinidad by rail in September soon after the Santa Fe had been completed that far. For the rest of the journey Wallace was in a Barlow and Sanderson buckboard (probably with three or four seats), which he described with painful recollection as "a low wheeled affair, floored with slats; the springs are under the seats and so weak that with the least jolt they smite together with a horrible blow, which is all the worse if overloaded, as was the case when I rode on them."[41]

There appears to have been a few months in which the Alamosa line deteriorated, while the Raton Pass route was not restored as the main line. When the railroad reached New Mexico there was little reason to keep the other line.

Operational circumstances for the Barlow and Sanderson Company were also changing elsewhere. Their stage line from Canon City up the Arkansas had a station at Bale's Tavern. It took a day's travel time between the two places. Andy Woodruff and John Hock handled the ribbons on that part of the line in 1877.

Several miles upstream from the tavern was the little settlement of South Arkansas, where the coaches for Saguache and the San Juan country crossed the main Arkansas River and went up the South Arkansas as far as Poncha Pass, and from there southward through it into the San Luis Valley. Business in the valley and in the San Juan mining region seems to have improved in 1878. The Post Office Department ordered that Barlow and Sanderson's service be increased, as of October 1, 1878, from triweekly to daily between South Arkansas and Del Norte and between Saguache and Lake City.[42]

The miners' rush to Leadville, near the headwaters of the Arkansas, caused the Barlow and Sanderson Company to extend its service and take advantage of the business which the town offered. The opportunities were brief for the stage line, however: the business potential of the bonanza area was so great that only a railroad could handle it, and that was just a few miles away. The Denver and Rio Grande Railway was victorious in its rivalry with the Atchison, Topeka and Santa Fe for use of the Royal Gorge of the Arkansas, and when the jubilant Denver and Rio Grande people built into Leadville in the summer of 1880, the stagecoach and freight wagon were displaced again. Barlow and Sanderson sold out goods that had not been claimed and took their livestock to South Arkansas, now a railroad town soon to be renamed Salida, from which point their stages maintained their scheduled runs into the San Juan country. Service to the new mining camp of Gunnison had been inaugurated on July 24, 1880.

Some miles to the south, Barlow and Sanderson's stage and mail line from Alamosa to Santa Fe had such a reduced volume of business that by August of 1879 the mail was being carried over it in a one-horse buckboard,[43] and it appears that passenger traffic never met expectations. Part of the trouble, of course, was that mail trains on the Santa Fe Railroad had started regular service to Las Vegas, New Mexico, the previous month.[44] Duane D. Finch, former Southern Overland Mail agent at Trinidad, drove the last stagecoach out of Otero on one July day, and the first Santa Fe train rolled into Las Vegas on the next. For a few months passengers and mail transferred from the new to the old mode of transportation, or vice versa, at Las Vegas.[45] At one time more than 800 miles long, the stage line to Santa Fe now was a sixty-five mile stub through Tecolote, San Jose, Pajarito Springs, Pigeon's Ranch, Johnson's Ranch, and Rock Corral to the territorial capital.

South and west of Santa Fe the stagecoach era had a longer claim on life, but it was obvious that its time would be short. The Southern Pacific Railroad, building eastward from California, was already at Yuma, Arizona Territory, and showed every sign of continuing its race to cross Arizona before its westward building rival, the Texas Pacific, could get there.[46]

In early 1879 the National Mail and Transportation Company was organized to control the stage line from Santa Fe to Tucson by way of Mesilla and Silver City. Fare to Tucson was $98.98, and to Mesilla, $46.50. The company offered connections to Texas, California, and Mexico. Especially indicative of the trend of events was the firm's advertisement as "carriers of the Great Southern Overland Mail."[47] Southern now meant south of Santa Fe, but the old staging connotation of overland— to California—had been destroyed by the Southern Pacific Railroad. Barlow and Sanderson's nearly fifteen years of association with the term had ended for all practical purposes.

Almost the last news story about Barlow and Sanderson's stage line was about a holdup on August 18 about two miles north of Tecolote. A man sat on a log with a gun across his knee, and when the coach came down the hill, he pointed "his fowling piece" at the driver and called upon him to halt the vehicle. When the driver complied, "the gentlemanly road agent then politely invited" the driver and the two passengers to step down, "which order was cheerfully obeyed." One of the passengers was a New Yorker by the name of J. H. Strahn, and the other was the distinguished New Mexico Republican, Governor W. F. M. Arny [the title was a courtesy one—while Secretary of the Territory, Arny had served as acting governor on occasions during the administrations of Governors Henry Connelly (1861-1866) and Robert B. Mitchell (1866-1869)].[48] Two accomplices appeared and helped the road agent search through the mail. Strahn was relieved of a gold watch and about $500, but Arny, for some reason, appears not to have been molested. The stage robbers, taking the coach horses, departed with a warning to driver and passengers not to leave the coach for twenty minutes. Two days later the trio was arrested in Santa Fe by Santa Fe Railroad Detective Cole.[49]

The governor of New Mexico Territory at the coming of the railroad age was Lew Wallace (1878-1881). While residing at the Palace of the Governors, Wallace worked when he could on his novel *Ben-Hur* and dealt with the aftermath of the classic of frontier violence, the Lincoln County War—and particularly with William H. Bonney, alias Billy the Kid. Such preoccupations, along with the mounting public excitement as the railroad approached Santa Fe, dulled recollection of his arrival in a

181

Barlow and Sanderson Company, four-spring buckboard. In times that were geared to speed and progress, hardly anyone looked back more than briefly.

The end came on January 24, 1880, when the Barlow and Sanderson Company drew off all its stock from what the *New Mexican* chose to call "the eastern branch of the famous Southern Overland Mail." About fifteen miles south of Santa Fe the railroad had reached the point (later called Lamy) from which a spur track would be built into the capital, while the main line of the Santa Fe Railroad continued south toward Albuquerque.

For less than a month travelers changed from railroad coach to a "modern omnibus seating the passengers along the sides and having a place for the baggage on the top." In a kind of epitaph the newspaper noted that the old stage line had operated with surprising regularity, usually within its contract time—that is, in spite of Indians, road agents, and sometimes irritated passengers.[50] Those remarks were hardly adequate as a summary of the past thirty years, but a little over a fortnight later that newspaper reached an impersonal, laconic high with a subheadline: "And the Old Santa Fe Trail Passes into Oblivion."[51]

Epilogue

THE SANTA FE AND SOUTHERN PACIFIC RAILROADS destroyed the last long-distance stage line in the nation within five years after the editor of the Las Vegas (New Mexico) *Gazette* suggested its possibilities as a tourist attraction. Under the circumstances the end was inevitable, but it took the Industrial Revolution thirty years to connect the Missouri River with the Pacific Coast by way of Kansas, Colorado, New Mexico, and Arizona, which was ten years more than were required to make the railroad link along the central route.

Eighteenth-century modes of transportation survived longer on a significant scale in the great Southwest than anywhere else in the nation. The Pacific railroad surveys of the 1850s favored the central routes, and eradication of the southern, ox-bow route of the Butterfield Overland Mail stage line by the Civil War fastened the attention of both stage and rail promoters on possibilities between the 38th and 39th parallels. And while public adulation was being lavished on William H. Russell's Pony Express and the staging activities of Ben Holladay and the directors of Wells Fargo, successive owners of the stage line to Santa Fe continued the operation, only indirectly affected by the rivalries for control of the central route. When completion of the Union Pacific Railroad stifled Wells, Fargo and Company's stage system to California, the line to Santa Fe and its extensions to San Diego and Los Angeles had the distinction of being the last and only through connection by stagecoach to the Pacific Coast.

Between 1850 and 1880 management of the Santa Fe stage line evolved from simply an adjunct to a successful firm of Santa Fe traders to a large enterprise called the Overland Mail and Express. The transition of control was accomplished amid conditions of remarkable constancy. In comparison with other areas, homesteaders and miners did not surge into the Southwest, yet demand grew enough to gradually increase mail and passenger service from monthly to daily. Patterns of ancient culture remained prominent because they were not swamped by those of outsiders. The different lifestyle of the Southwest was tough and resistant, imposing its will in ways that ranged from the more widespread use of mules to the big grants of land from republican Mexico or royal Spain.

Successive managers of the line to Santa Fe were apparently capable businessmen with their share of frailties in attitude and action. None emerges in sharp distinction. Perhaps Preston Roberts, Jr., was the most experienced in the world of transportation. Thomas J. Barnum remains a two-dimensional figure based upon vague newspaper comments about his expert ability; the only personal bit found about him tells of his unrealized exposure to smallpox at Santa Fe in 1863 and, after making the trip to Kansas City, coming down with it there.[1] Commonplace data exists concerning Lewis Barnum and Mahlon H. Cottrill, as well as Abraham Jacobs of the Denver and Santa Fe line. Considerable uncertainty about Jared L. Sanderson (who died at Boulder, Colorado, in 1915) results from contradictions in the brief biographical materials, but it is clear that he was a prime factor in management of the line during the final fifteen years. Possibly the most important person during that period was Bradley Barlow, substantial citizen of St. Albans, Vermont, who was elected as a national republican to the Forty-sixth Congress in 1878, close to the end of the great stagecoach era in the Southwest and probably about when he withdrew from his partnership with Sanderson there. Barlow died while staying with relatives in Denver in 1889.[2] There was not one among the owners or managers of the Santa Fe stage line who was a financial plunger like William H. Russell, or a hard-bitten empire builder of the Ben Holladay type, although the Southern Overland Mail and Express Company's ruthless price-cutting to force the Denver and Santa Fe Stage and Express Company to capitulate was certainly in the Holladay tradition. Nor was the parent company ever a joint stock association of the great size and impersonality of Wells, Fargo and Company. From Hockaday and Hall to Barlow and Sanderson, partnership management was on an intimate scale with much direct involvement. About the only attempt to take over the Santa Fe line and its Denver branch, except through the usual channel of contract-bidding, was by David Butterfield's Overland Despatch. The business moved along in its mildly profitable way, its volume never showing spectacular increases that would arouse envy. Perhaps prosaic circumstances attracted only the less daring and imaginative, but the stage lines to Santa Fe served their purpose long and well.

And they all came to the same end. The biggest staging and freighting ventures were not physically or financially strong enough to have transported the last phase of the westward movement that ended the frontier. The speed and strength of the railroads, the money power of their corporate owners, and generous government subsidies were stronger, and they did the job.

Notes

INTRODUCTION

1. John Bach McMaster, *A History of the People of the United States from the Revolution to the Civil War* (New York: D. Appleton and Co., 1921), 7:204-05; Henry Pickering Walker, *The Wagonmasters: High Plains Freighting from the Earliest Days of the Santa Fe Trail to 1880* (Norman: University of Oklahoma Press, 1966), pp. 19-22.

2. Hunter Miller, ed., *Treaties and Other International Acts of the United States of America* (Washington, D.C.: Government Printing Office, 1933), 3:3-31; Le Roy R. Hafen and Carl Coke Rister, *Western America: The Exploration, Settlement, and Development of the Region beyond the Mississippi*, 2d ed. (Englewood Cliffs, N.J.: Prentice-Hall, Inc., 1950), pp. 260-61; Jack Ericson Eblen, *The First and Second United States Empires: Governors and Territorial Government, 1786-1912* (Pittsburgh: University of Pittsburgh Press, 1968), pp. 147-49.

3. Lieutenant Zebulon Pike, after his journey of 1806-1807, used expressions in his report that foreshadowed Long's judgment. W. Eugene Hollon, *The Great American Desert* (New York: Oxford University Press, 1966), pp. 63-64; Hafen and Rister, pp. 187-88.

4. Hafen and Rister, pp. 247-48; David Lavender, *Bent's Fort* (Garden City, N.Y.: Doubleday & Company, 1954), pp. 53-54, 373 n. 3; Walker, pp. 19, 95.

5. Nick Eggenhofer, *Wagons, Mules and Men: How the Frontier Moved West* (New York: Hastings House, Publishers, 1961), pp. 58, 66; Walker, pp. 102-03.

6. Donald J. Berthrong, *The Southern Cheyennes* (Norman: University of Oklahoma Press, 1963), pp. 17-23.

7. Ernest Wallace and E. Adamson Hoebel, *The Comanches, Lords of the South Plains* (Norman: University of Oklahoma Press, 1952), pp. 285-86.

8. Morris F. Taylor, "Ka-ni-ache," Part 1, *The Colorado Magazine*, 43 (fall 1966): 276.

9. Walker, pp. 19-22; Hafen and Rister, pp. 248-49; Blanche C. Grant, *One Hundred Years Ago in Old Taos* (Taos, 1925), p. 11.

10. Hafen and Rister, p. 249; Grant, p. 11. On p. 18, Grant notes that the shortened name of Taos did not come into official use until the 1880s. Taos will be used hereafter, however.

11. Walker, p. 27; Grant, pp. 13-16.

12. Hafen and Rister, p. 249; Josiah Gregg, *Commerce of the Prairies*, ed. Max L. Moorhead (Norman: University of Oklahoma Press, 1954), pp. 20-21, 24-25.

13. Gregg, pp. 24-25; Walker, p. 106. Grant, p. 16, says that Charles Bent brought

186

NOTES

the first ox-drawn caravan across the plains in 1831. Perhaps she meant that his was the first private wagon train to use oxen.

14. Hafen and Rister, pp. 249-50.

15. F. F. Stephens, "Missouri and The Santa Fe Trade," *Missouri Historical Review,* 11 (July 1917) : 303-04.

16. Hafen and Rister pp. 218-20.

17. Ibid., p. 224.

18. Stephens, pp. 305-10; Gregg, pp. 213-14.

19. Gregg, p. 80.

20. Walker, p. 148.

21. Ralph Emerson Twitchell, *The Leading Facts of New Mexican History* (Albuquerque: Horn & Wallace, Publishers, 1963), 2:107, 118; Gregg, p. 17 n. 16; Howard Roberts Lamar, *The Far Southwest, 1846-1912: A Territorial History* (New Haven: Yale University Press, 1966), p. 48.

22. Although the towns of San Miguel del Vado and Taos were supposed to have customs houses, tariffs were maily collected at Santa Fe. Gregg, pp. 75, n. 13, 264-68, 344 n. 18, 19; Hafen and Rister, pp. 252-55; Walker, pp. 137-38.

23. Walker p. 32.

24. Ray Allen Billington, *The Far Western Frontier, 1830-1860* (New York: Harper & Row, 1956), p. 22; Nelson Klose, *A Concise Study Guide to the American Frontier* (Lincoln: University of Nebraska Press, 1964), p. 78.

25. Hafen and Rister, pp. 263-65.

26. Lavender, p. 81.

27. Gregg, pp. 266-67.

28. Darrell Garwood, *Crossroads of America: The Story of Kansas City* (New York: W. W. Norton & Company, 1948), p. 19; Susan Shelby Magoffin, *Down the Santa Fe Trail and into New Mexico,* ed., Stella M. Drumm, foreword by Howard W. Lamar (New Haven: Yale University Press, 1962), p. 1 n. 1.

29. Gregg, pp. 26, 29, 33-34, 41.

30. Ross Calvin, ed., *Lieutenant Emory Reports: A Reprint of Lieutenant W. H. Emory's Notes of a Military Reconnoissance* (Albuquerque: University of New Mexico Press, 1951), p. 27; Klose, p. 50.

31. Gregg, pp. 49-50, 442.

32. Gregg, pp. 50-51, 54-55.

33. Hollon, p. 18.

34. Charles L. Kenner, *A History of New Mexican-Plains Indian Relations* (Norman: University of Oklahoma Press, 1969), p. 75.

35. Herbert O. Brayer, *William Blackmore: The Spanish-Mexican Land Grants of New Mexico and Colorado, 1863-1878* (Denver: Bradford-Robinson, 1949), p. 163.

36. The Texas-Santa Fe Expedition of 1841, although a failure, and the attacks in 1843 by Texan filibusters John McDaniel, Jacob Snively, and Charles A. Warfield—whose freebooters penetrated as far as Mora—in 1843 had pointed out the vulnerability of the provincial frontiers at a time when war with the United States seemed possible. Lavender, pp. 198-203, 204, 218-25.

37. For a good summary of those northern grants see Lamar, pp. 49-52. Gervacio Nolan received a grant on the Arkansas west of the Vigil and St. Vrain in 1843, and there were several other smaller grants on the approaches to Santa Fe.

38. Lavender, pp. 131, 386 n. 12.

39. Gregg, pp. 63-64; Eggenhofer, pp. 72-75. See also Kenner, Chaps. 4 and 5.

40. J. B. Salpointe, *Soldiers of the Cross: Notes on the Ecclesiastical History of New Mexico, Arizona and Colorado* (Albuquerque: Calvin Horn, Publisher, 1967), pp. 127-28, 164-65.

41. Calvin, pp. 32-49.

42. LeRoy R. Hafen, *The Overland Mail, 1849-1869: Promoter of Settlement, Precursor of Railroads* (Cleveland: Arthur H. Clark Company, 1926), p. 54. Carson's route to

Santa Fe and Taos was over the Old Spanish Trail, and from there north and east by way of the Platte River to Fort Leavenworth. Carson's latest biographer is not certain that this distinction belongs to him. Harvey Lewis Carter, *'Dear Old Kit,' The Historical Kit Carson* (Norman: University of Oklahoma Press, 1968), pp. 119-21.

43. Hafen and Rister, p. 312.

44. The Mormon migrations into the vicinity of the Great Salt Lake were within the confines of the Mexican Cession, but there was no real contact between the Mormon settlements and the Mexican ones far to the south. Also, the religious peculiarities of the Mormons set them apart from the Roman Catholics along the Rio Grande and parts of California, as well as from the Protestants who dominated religious life in the Oregon country.

45. Salpointe, pp. 194-96, 206.

46. Calvin Horn, *New Mexico's Troubled Years: The Story of the Early Territorial Governors* (Albuquerque: Horn & Wallace, Publishers, 1963), p. 45.

47. See early issues of the Santa Fe *Weekly Gazette* and *Weekly New Mexican*.

48. Horn, pp. 43-45; Salpointe, pp. 200-201.

49. For examples, see Lewis H. Garrard, *Wah-To-Yah and the Taos Trail* intro. by Carl I. Wheat (Palo Alto, Calif.: American West Publishing Company, 1968), originally published in 1850, and William W. H. Davis, *El Gringo: Or New Mexico and Her People* (New York: Harper and Brothers, 1857).

50. U.S., *Statutes at Large*, 5:733.

51. Clyde Kelly, *United States Postal Policy* (New York: D. Appleton & Company, 1932), pp. 56-58.

52. U.S., *Statutes at Large*, 9:194.

53. J. Christopher Schnell, "William Gilpin and the Destruction of the Desert Myth," *The Colorado Magazine*, 46 (spring 1969) : 134-35; Charles N. Glaab, *Kansas City and the Railroads: Community Policy in the Growth of a Regional Metropolis* (Madison: State Historical Society of Wisconsin, 1962), pp. 26-27; Garwood, pp. 13-16.

54. U.S., Congress, Senate, *Report of the Secretary of War, 1849*, 31st Cong. 1st sess., Senate Ex. Doc. no. 26, serial no. 554, pp. 23, 26, 30.

55. Edwin C. Bearss and Arrell M. Gibson, *Fort Smith: Little Gibraltar on the Arkansas* (Norman: University of Oklahoma Press, 1969), pp. 199-207; Randolph B. Marcy, *The Prairie Traveler. A Hand-book for Overland Expeditions* (New York: Harper & Brothers, 1859), pp. 18-19, 257-60, 307-15.

56. *Report of the Secretary of War*, pp. 23, 26, 30.

57. Walker, pp. 142-43.

58. See extant copies in Library of the Museum of New Mexico, Santa Fe.

59. Sheldon H. Dike, *The Territorial Post Offices of New Mexico* (Albuquerque: By the author, 1958). This work has no page numbers but is arranged alphabetically.

60. There was a post office on the west side of the plaza during the Mexican period, which took care of the mail to and from the south. The location may have been maintained by the U.S. government. Ralph Emerson Twitchell, *Old Santa Fe: The Story of New Mexico's Ancient Capital* (Chicago: Rio Grande Press, 1963), p. 237.

61. Martin Hardwick Hall, *Sibley's New Mexico Campaign* (Austin: University of Texas Press, 1960), p. 6.

62. Ibid.

63. Eblen, p. 7.

64. Lamar, pp. 70-73; Odie B. Faulk, *Land of Many Frontiers: A History of the American Southwest* (New York: Oxford University Press, 1968), pp. 138-42.

65. Lamar, pp. 73-81.

66. Route No. 4888, Star Route Register, Missouri Section, p. 190, Record Group 28, National Archives, Washington, D.C. Hereafter, all mail routes will be cited by number, section, and page.

67. Howard L. Conard, ed., *Encyclopedia of the History of Missouri: A Compendium of History and Biography for Ready Reference* (New York: The Southern History Com-

pany, 1901), 4:246-47; *Missouri Historical Review*, 23 (October 1928-July 1929) : 335-36; Route No. 4888, Missouri Section, p. 191; Brief for Complainants, Hall vs. Huffaker, Circuit Court of the United States for the District of Kansas; copy in the Kansas State Historical Society Library, Topeka.

68. Gregg, pp. 16, 229; Eggenhofer, p. 130; Louise Barry, "Kansas Before 1854: A Revised Annals," *Kansas Historical Quarterly* 33 (winter 1966) : (hereafter cited as Barry, KHQ), quoting the *New York Daily Tribune*, May 31, 1852 and February 4, 1853; Mitford M. Mathews, ed., *A Dictionary of Americanisms on Historical Principles* (Chicago: University of Chicago Press, 1951), p. 469; James Brice, *Reminiscences of Ten Years Experience on the Western Plains: How the United States Mails Were Carried before Railroads Reached the Santa Fe Trail* (Kansas City, Mo.: n.n., n.d.), pp. 1-3; Davis, pp. 14-15.

69. H. B. Möllhausen. "Over the Santa Fe Trail through Kansas in 1858," trans. John A. Burzle, ed. Robert Taft, *Kansas Historical Quarterly*, 16 (November 1948) : 363.

70. Walker, pp. 101-06, 148.

71. Ralph Moody, *Stagecoach West* (New York: Thomas Y. Crowell Company, 1967), pp. 46, 68-69.

72. Clipping from the *Missouri Republican* (St. Louis), March 22, 1852 in the State Records and Archives Center, Santa Fe, New Mexico; Way Bill of the U.S. Mail from Santa Fe, N.M., to El Paso, Tex., Route No. 12851, in the same collection.

73. Oscar Osburn Winther, *Via Western Express & Stagecoach* (Stanford, Calif.: Stanford University Press, 1945), pp. 4-25.

74. Eggenhofer, pp. 172, 175.

75. *Daily Chieftain* (Pueblo, Colo.), May 11, 1876, p. 4; William H. Ryus, *The Second William Penn: A True Account of Incidents that Happened Along the Old Santa Fe Trail in the Sixties* (Kansas City, Mo.: Frank T. Riley Publishing Company, 1913), p. 13; recollections of John Jackson, who worked as a whipper on the Santa Fe mail stage line (information obtained from Julia Harris, Grand Junction, Colo.).

76. Barry, KHQ, 32 (summer 1966) : 249; Way Bill, Route No. 12851, *passim*.

77. Milton W. Callon, "The Merchant-Colonists of New Mexico," *Brand Book of the Denver Westerners (1965)*, ed. Arthur L. Campa (Boulder, Colo.: Johnson Publishing Co., 1966), pp. 9-14; U.S., Department of the Interior, *Register of Officers and Agents, Civil, Military, and Naval, in the Service of the United States on the Thirtieth September, 1861*, p. 558; ibid., *1863*, p. 798; ibid., *1865*, p. 525; ibid., *1867*, p. 842; Biographical Sketch of A. H. Taylor, Samuel W. DeBusk Papers, Trinidad State Junior College Library; *Daily Rocky Mountain News* (Denver), April 3, 1867, p. 1; William J. Parish, "The German Jew and the Commercial Revolution in Territorial New Mexico, 1850-1900," *New Mexico Historical Review* 35 (January 1960) : 1-29.

78. Fort Atkinson was temporarily reoccupied during the summer of 1854. Robert W. Frazer, *Forts of the West: Military Forts and Presidios and Posts Commonly Called Forts West of the Mississippi River to 1898* (Norman: University of Oklahoma Press, 1965), pp. 50-51, 55, 56. Mileages given here are based on distances recorded by a traveler on the Trail in 1848; the list is more detailed that that given by Josiah Gregg, but the mileages generally agree. Nicholas P. Hardeman, ed., "Camp Sites on the Santa Fe Trail in 1848 as Reported by John A. Bingham," *Arizona and the West*, 6 (winter 1964) : 317-18. Davis, pp. 26-29; Way Bill, Route 12851, *passim*.

79. Route No. 4888, Missouri Section, p. 191; Route No. 8912, Missouri Section, p. 288; Route No. 10532, Missouri Section, pp. 352, 356; *Junction City* (Kans.) *Union*, June 30, 1866, p. 2.

80. Barry, KHQ, 32 (winter 1966) : 465-66; Davis, p. 13; Carrie Westlake Whitney, *Kansas City, Missouri: Its History and its People, 1808-1898* (Chicago: S. J. Clarke Publishing Company, 1908), 1:166; *Daily Kansas City* (Mo.) *Western Journal of Commerce*, April 30, 1862, p. 2; *Daily Rocky Mountain News*, July 4, 1864, p. 3.

81. Kelly, pp. 30, 126-27, 262.

82. Glaab, pp. 38, 40; Kelly, pp. 127-28.

83. Kelly, pp. 127-28; U.S., *Statutes at Large*, 9:587.

84. Hafen and Rister, pp. 371-72, 517-19.

85. Ibid., p. 518; Percy Stanley Fritz, *Colorado, the Centennial State* (New York: Prentice-Hall, Inc., 1941), p. 83.

86. *Kansas City Daily Western Journal of Commerce*, February 20, 1859, p. 2.

87. LeRoy R. Hafen, ed., *Colorado and its People: A Narrative and Topical History of the Centennial State* (New York: Lewis Historical Publishing Company, 1948) 1:1888; Moody, pp. 156-64.

88. Morris F. Taylor, "Fort Wise," *The Colorado Magazine*, 46 (spring 1969) : 93-119.

89. Route No. 10532, Missouri Section, p. 356.

90. Lamar, pp. 90-91, 107-08; Hall, pp. 6-7.

91. Letter from Jacob Hall to Colonel E. V. Sumner, September 3, 1859, and from Captain George N. Steuart to Captain D. R. Jones, October 30, 1859, Letters Received by the Office of the Adjutant General, Main Series (1859), microfilm no. 567, roll no. 603, National Archives Microfilm Publications, Washington, D.C.; clipping from the *Kansas City Star*, September 23, 1906, in T.S. Dawson Scrapbooks, 14:141, Library of the State Historical Society of Colorado, Denver.

92. William Frank Zornow, *Kansas: A History of the Jayhawk State* (Norman: University of Oklahoma Press, 1957), pp. 70, 87; Hafen, *Colorado and its People*, 1:283.

93. *Canon City* (Colo.) *Times*, May 16, 1861, p. 3; Route No. 10532, Missouri Section, p. 427; Route No. 14465, New Mexico Section, pp. 367-68.

94. Glaab, pp. 117, 121.

95. Hollon, pp. 11-12.

96. Barlow and Sanderson had a controlling interest in the Santa Fe Stage Company, successor to M. Cottrill and Company. In 1872 the firm's name was changed from Barlow, Sanderson and Company to Barlow and Sanderson Company, because a reorganization left Bradley Barlow and Jared L. Sanderson as sole partners rather than the principal ones. *Kansas City Daily Journal of Commerce*, January 21, 1865, p. 1; *Daily Colorado Chieftain*, May 11, 1876, p. 4.

97. The predecessor Santa Fe Stage Company had made Pacific coast connections since 1866. John and Lillian Theobald, *Arizona Territory Post Offices & Postmasters* (Phoenix: Arizona Historical Foundation, 1961), pp. 38-39, 69; *Weekly New Mexican*, December 9, 1969, p. 1; Letter from Barlow, Sanderson and Company to Postmaster General Cresswell, May 1869, State Historical Society of Colorado Library, Denver.

98. Fritz, p. 217.

99. Morris F. Taylor, *Trinidad, Colorado Territory* (Trinidad: Trinidad State Junior College, 1966), p. 185.

100. L. L. Waters, *Steel Trails to Santa Fe* (Lawrence: University of Kansas Press, 1950), pp. 51, 55-56, 97-100; Faulk, pp. 218-21.

101. *Weekly New Mexican*, January 11, 1876, p. 1; Alamosa, Conejos and Costilla Counties (Civil Works Administration Interviews), p. 26, State Historical Society of Colorado Library, Denver; *Colorado Chieftain*, September 2, 1880, p. 4; Moody, pp. 299-300; William S. Wallace, "Stagecoaching in Territorial New Mexico," *New Mexico Historical Review*, 32 (April 1957).

102. A. Jay Hertz, "Barlow, Sanderson and Company: Corruption Enters the Express," *Western Express* (July 1963), pp. 29-31.

103. Lamar, p. 170.

CHAPTER 1

1. U.S., *Statutes at Large*, 9:194. The wording of the statute anticipated territorial status for Oregon, which was not confirmed by Congress until 1848.

2. E. J. Dallas, "Kansas Postal History," *Transactions of the Kansas State Historical Society*, 2 (1879-1880) : 255.

3. Sheldon H. Dike, "The Postal History of New Mexico Territory," *Western Express*, 9 (January 1959), appended alphabetical list of territorial post offices.

4. Louise Barry, "Kansas Before 1854: A Revised Annals," *Kansas Historical Quarterly*, 30 (autumn 1964) : 402 (hereafter cited as Barry, *KHQ*).

5. Barry, *KHQ*, 30 (winter 1964) : 493, 497; Lewis H. Garrard, *Wah-To-Yah and the Taos Trail*, intro. by Carl I. Wheat (Palo Alto, Calif.: American West Publishing Company, 1968), pp. 97-98.

6. Barry, *KHQ*, 30 (winter 1964) : 492, 503.

7. Ibid., p. 498.

8. Leo E. Oliva, *Soldiers on the Santa Fe Trail* (Norman: University of Oklahoma Press, 1967), pp. 9-10.

9. Garrard, pp. 246-47.

10. Barry, *KHQ*, 30 (winter 1964) : 501.

11. Ibid., pp. 505, 515, 542, 555, 556.

12. *Santa Fe Republican*, February 12, 1848, p. 2.

13. Ibid., November 13, 1847, p. 2.

14. T. D. Bonner, *The Life and Adventures of James P. Beckwourth, Mountaineer, Scout, Pioneer, and Chief of the Crow Nation of Indians* (Minneapolis: Ross & Haines, Inc., 1965), pp. 476-83.

15. One Hundred and Ten Mile Creek, so called because it was 110 miles from Fort Osage, Missouri (est. 1808), which was abandoned in 1827 when Fort Leavenworth was established. Oliva, p. 14; Robert W. Frazer, *Forts of the West; Military Forts and Presidios and Posts Commonly Called Forts West of the Mississippi River to 1898* (Norman: University of Oklahoma Press, 1965), pp. 75-76.

16. *Santa Fe Republican*, February 12, 1848, p. 2; April 4, 1848, p. 2.

17. U.S., Congress, Senate, *Report of the Secretary of War*, 31st Cong., 1st sess., Sen. Ex. Doc. no. 26, serial no. 554, p. 23.

18. *Santa Fe Republican*, June 9, 1848, p. 2.

19. Ibid., July 14, 1848, quoted by Sheldon H. Dike in "Early Mail Contracts on the Santa Fe Trail," *American Philatelist*, 72 (August 1959) : 811.

20. Dike, "Postal History" part 2, *Western Express*, 8 (April 1958) : 8.

21. *Report of the Secretary of War*, p. 23.

22. Ibid.; Barry, *KHQ*, 31 (autumn 1965) : 266.

23. Grant Foreman, *Marcy and the Gold Seekers: The Journal of Captain R. B. Marcy, With an Account of the Gold Rush Over the Southern Route* (Norman: University of Oklahoma Press, 1939), pp. 88, 211, 246; Barry, *KHQ*, 31 (autumn 1965) : 320, There is mention of meeting this mail party along the Pecos River in Lansing B. Bloom, ed., "From Lewisburg (Pa.) to California in 1849: Notes from the Diary of William H. Chamberlin," *New Mexico Historical Review*, 20 (January 1945) : 53.

24. Captain L. Evans left the Cherokee Nation on April 20, 1849 with forty wagons and 130 people, emigrants to California. Grant Foreman, "Early Trails Through Oklahoma," *Chronicles of Oklahoma*, 3 (June 1925) : 110-11.

25. Foreman, *Marcy and the Gold Seekers*, pp. 88, 211, 246; Barry, *KHQ*, 31 (autumn 1965) : 320.

26. *Report of the Secretary of War*, p. 23.

27. Barry, *KHQ*, 31 (autumn 1965) : 325-26.

28. David Lavender, *Bent's Fort* (Garden City, N.Y.: Doubleday & Co., Inc., 1954), pp. 315-18.

29. Barry, *KHQ*, 31 (autumn 1965) : 328; Calvin Horn, *New Mexico's Troubled Years: The Story of the Early Territorial Governors* (Albuquerque: Horn & Wallace, Publishers, 1963), pp. 23-24, 34.

30. Barry, *KHQ*, 31 (autumn 1965) : 337.

31. Ibid., 32 (spring 1966) : 34, 37.

32. Ibid., pp. 39, 40.

33. A Spanish word meaning journey, perhaps in this case a contraction of *Jornada del Muerto*, or journey of death, applied to a difficult, dry stretch of about fifty miles from the Arkansas River south to the Lower Spring of the Dry Cimarron.

34. It was an adobe structure, described as nearly square with walls four feet thick and about eighteen feet high. There was a watchtower over the south gate. Early Far West Notebook 1, Cragin Collection, Pioneers' Museum, Colorado Springs, Colo., 1: 4; Herbert M. Hart, *Old Forts of the Southwest* (Seattle: Superior Publishing Company, 1964), p. 80.

35. Barry, *KHQ*, 32 (spring 1966) : 52, 82; Annie Heloise Abel, *The Official Correspondence of James S. Calhoun While Indian Agent at Santa Fe and Superintendent of Indian Affairs in New Mexico* (Washington, D.C.: Government Printing Office, 1915), pp. 198-99.

36. Barry, *KHQ*, 32 (spring 1966) : 82; Abel, pp. 199-200. Burnside later became a prominent Union general in the Civil War.

CHAPTER 2

1. Sheldon H. Dike "The Postal History of New Mexico Territory," *Western Express*, 8 (April 1958) : 7; John Bach McMaster, *A History of the People of the United States From the Revolution to the Civil War* (New York: D. Appleton and Company, 1921), 8: 113.

2. Dr. David Waldo graduated from Transylvania College, Lexington, Kentucky, in 1822. He practiced in Missouri and New Mexico before leaving his profession to participate in the Santa Fe trade. In 1846 he helped recruit Company A, First Regiment of Missouri Volunteers, serving as captain during the war with Mexico. His familiarity with New Mexico put him close to General Kearny and Governor Bent. Waldo Douglas Sloan, "Dr. David Waldo," *Journal of the Jackson County* (Missouri), *Historical Society*, 11 (spring 1968) : 6; Stella M. Drumm, "David Waldo," *Dictionary of American Biography*, ed. Dumas Malone (New York: Charles Scribner's Sons, 1936), 19: 332-33.

3. Route No. 4888, Star Route Register, Missouri Section, p. 190, Record Group 28, National Archives, Washington, D.C. Hereafter, all mail routes will be cited by number, section, and page.

4. Ralph P. Bieber, "Some Aspects of the Santa Fe Trail," *Chronicles of Oklahoma*, 2 (March 1924) : 7; Ralph Emerson Twitchell, *Old Santa Fe: The Story of New Mexico's Ancient Capital* (Chicago: Rio Grande Press, 1963), p. 242. Samuel H. Woodson received a contract to carry the mail from Independence to Salt Lake City, but his service was irregular, generally unsuccessful, and apparently did not use vehicles. Ralph Moody, *Stagecoach West* (New York: Thomas Y. Crowell Company, 1967), pp. 46, 68-70.

5. Route No. 4888, Missouri Section, p. 190; Route No. 8912, Missouri Section, p. 288.

6. Eleanor and Grace Minor, "William McCoy," *Journal of the Jackson County* (Missouri) *Historical Society*, 7 (March 1964) : 10; Howard L. Conard, ed., *Encyclopedia of the History of Missouri: A Compendium of History and Biography for Ready Reference* (New York: The Southern History Company, 1901), 4: 246-47.

7. Louise Barry, "Kansas Before 1854: A Revised Annals," *Kansas Historical Quarterly*, 32 (spring 1966) : 86 (hereafter cited as Barry, KHQ) ; Robert W. Frazer, *Forts of the West; Military Forts and Presidios and Posts Commonly Called Forts West of the Mississippi River to 1898* (Norman: University of Oklahoma Press, 1965), pp. 181-82.

8. Barry, *KHQ*, 32 (spring 1966) : 90.

9. Raymond W. and Mary Lund Settle, *War Drums and Wagon Wheels: The Story of Russell, Majors and Waddell* (Lincoln: University of Nebraska Press, 1966), p. 33.

10. Sloan, p. 6; Barry, *KHQ*, 32 (spring 1966) :249.

11. Captain William Banning and George Hugh Banning, *Six Horses* (New York: The Century Company, 1930), p. 399.

12. *Missouri Historical Review*, 23 (October, 1928-July, 1929) : 335-36, which copied an item from the *St. Louis Western Journal* (September 1850), which in turn quoted from the Independence *Missouri Commonwealth*. The *Missouri Commonwealth* article is quoted in part in Moody, p. 63.

13. This is a regional (New Jersey) term to describe a small wagon. Mitford M. Mathews, ed., *A Dictionary of Americanisms on Historical Principles* (Chicago: University of Chicago Press, 1951), p. 904. A Jersey wagon was a straight-sided wagon with four supports for the canvas roof; it had roll-up side curtains and, for the driver, an outside, open seat with a footboard. Nick Eggenhofer, *Wagons, Mules and Men: How the Frontier Moved West* (New York: Hastings House Publishers, 1961), p. 130.

14. Barry, *KHQ*, 32 (winter 1966): 465-66, quoting from the *New York Daily Tribune*, May 31, 1852, and February 4, 1853.

15. Ibid., 32 (spring 1966) : 92.

16. *Missouri Historical Review*, p. 335.

17. Brief for Complainants, Hall vs. Huffaker, Circuit Court of the United States for the District of Kansas, p. 9-10; copy in the Kansas State Historical Society Library, Topeka, (hereafter cited as Brief for Complainants).

18. Ibid.

19. Frazer, p. 50; Herbert M. Hart, *Old Forts of the Southwest* (Seattle: Superior Publishing Co., 1964), pp. 75-76.

20. Leo E. Oliva, *Soldiers on the Santa Fe Trail* (Norman: University of Oklahoma Press, 1967), p. 102.

21. Brief for Complainants, p. 10.

22. *Missouri Historical Review*, p. 335.

23. Barry, *KHQ*, 32 (spring 1966) : 96.

24. Moody, pp. 46, 68-70.

25. Route No. 4888, Missouri Section, p. 190.

26. Barry, *KHQ*, 32 (spring, 1966) : 105.

27. Route No. 4888, Missouri Section, p. 190; Dike, "Postal History," *Western Express*, 8 (July 1958), appended alphabetical list of territorial post offices.

28. Barry, *KHQ*, (spring 1966) :111.

29. Oliva, p. 96.

30. Barry, *KHQ*, 32 (summer 1966) : 211.

31. Ibid., p. 239.

32. Today known as Corrumpa Creek, it is an upper tributary of the North Fork of the Canadian River. It was called McNees Creek because a young Santa Fe trader of that name was killed there by Indians in 1828. Ralph Emerson Twitchell, *The Leading Facts of New Mexican History* (Albuquerque: Horn & Wallace, Publishers, 1963), 2: 127.

33. Barry, *KHQ*, 32 (summer 1966) : 280-81.

34. Ibid., p. 250.

35. Ibid., p. 215. This comment was published in the *New York Daily Tribune* for May 7, 1851.

36. Ibid., 32 (winter 1966) : 439.

37. Sheldon H. Dike, "Early Mail Contracts on the Santa Fe Trail," *American Philatelist*, 72, (August 1959) : 811-12.

38. Clippings from the *Missouri Republican* (St. Louis), March 27, 1852, New Mexico State Records and Archives Center, Santa Fe.

39. U.S. *Statutes at Large*, 9: 587-88; McMaster, pp. 113-14; Clyde Kelly, *United States Postal Policy* (New York: D. Appleton and Company, 1932), pp. 62-65.

40. Robert M. Utley, *Fort Union National Monument, New Mexico* (Washington, D.C.: Government Printing Office, 1962), pp. 9-10; Early Far West Notebook 1, Cragin Collection, Pioneers' Museum, Colorado Springs, Colo., 1:4; Barry, *KHQ*, 32 (winter 1966) ; 465; Dike, "Postal History," *Western Express*, 8 (July 1968), appended list.

41. Robert M. Utley, "Fort Union and the Santa Fe Trail," *New Mexico Historical Review*, 36 (January 1961) : 39-40; James Brice, *Reminiscences of Ten Years Experience on the Western Plains: How the United States Mails Were Carried Before the Railroads Reached the Santa Fe Trail* (Kansas City, Mo.: n.n., n.d.,), p. 9.

42. Barry, *KHQ*, 32 (winter 1966) : 465-66, 480-81.

43. Ibid., p. 487. Francis X. Aubry is credited with having laid out this route in 1851-1852 to shorten the Cimarron Cutoff and avoid the Cimarron *Jornada*. From Cold Creek, the route crossed the Dry Cimarron to Bear Creek, following the creek to a point on the Arkansas about seventy miles west of the Cimarron Crossing. It was never heavily used. Eugene Bandel, *Frontier Life in the Army, 1854-1861*, Southwest Historical Series, ed. Ralph P. Bieber (Glendale: The Arthur H. Clarke Company, 1932), 2:189.

44. Calvin Horn, *New Mexico's Troubled Years: The Story of the Early Territorial Governors* (Albuquerque: Horn & Wallace, Publishers, 1963), pp. 37-51.

45. Barry, *KHQ*, 33 (winter 1967) : 59.

46. The official route record says the post office at Fort Atkinson was established November 11, 1851, and it erroneously lists the location as Fort Atchison. Route No. 4888, Missouri Section, p. 190; "Early Military Posts, Missions, and Camps," *Transactions of the Kansas State Historical Society*, 2 (1879-1880) : 265; Oliva, p. 102.

47. Barry, *KHQ* 33 (spring 1967) : 52. The *Isabel* was a Missouri River steamboat.

48. Ibid., p. 61.

49. Susan Magoffin said the tree was standing when she passed there in June of 1846. She also gave the distance from Independence as thirty-five miles. Susan Shelby Magoffin, *Down the Santa Fe Trail and into New Mexico*, ed., Stella M. Drumm, foreword by Howard W. Lamar (New Haven: Yale University Press, 1962), pp. 4-5. Davis's distances seem to be reasonably accurate. Whenever possible they were checked against other more or less contemporary sources; sometimes discrepancies of several miles were found. The sources in addition to Magoffin's diary are: Josiah Gregg, *Commerce of the Prairies*, ed. Max L. Moorhead (Norman: University of Oklahoma Press, 1954), p. 217; Randolph B. Marcy, *The Prairie Traveler. A Hand-book for Overland Expeditions* (New York: Harper & Brothers, 1859), pp. 260-63, 295-301; Surveyor Berry's distances prepared for Jacob Hall and published in the *Kansas City* (Mo.) *Daily Western Journal of Commerce*, February 20, 1859, p. 2.

50. George P. Moorehouse, "Diamond Springs, 'The Diamond of the Plains,'" *Collections of the Kansas State Historical Society*, 14 (1915-1918) : 797.

51. Gregg, p. 217 n. 4.

52. This may have been the place where, in 1844, wagons belonging to Dr. Henry Connelly and Albert Speyer were caught in a blizzard and most of their mules were lost. David Lavender, *Bent's Fort* (Garden City, N.Y.: Doubleday & Co., Inc., 1954), p. 235; Twitchell *Leading Facts*, 2:126. Twitchell refers to Speyer as M. Speyer.

53. Some people believed that the same Jicarilla band, under Chief Lobo, destroyed the Clay-Hendrickson mail party in 1850. See Lieutenant Bell's Report, March 7, 1854, and Cooke to Nichols, March 8, 1854, Records of the Adjutant General's Office, Selected Letters Received, 1853-55, Record Group 94, National Archives, Washington, D.C.

54. The name appears in Albert Pike's *Prose Sketches and Poems Written in the Western Country*, ed. David J. Weber (Albuquerque: Calvin Horn, Publisher, 1967), p. 6. First published in 1834.

55. Utley, "Fort Union," pp. 38-40; Utley, *Fort Union National Monument*, pp. 10-11, 12.

56. Tecolote had a post office established August 16, 1851, and so did San Miguel, at the southern extremity of the Trail. The one at San Miguel was discontinued June 7, 1852. The postal route record erroneously refers to Barclay's Fork.

57. William W. H. Davis, *El Gringo: Or New Mexico and Her People* (New York: Harper and Brothers, 1857), pp. 13-15, 17-22, 25-34, 37-40, 44-48, 51-56.

58. Oliva, p. 108.

59. Barry, *KHQ*, 33 (spring 1967) : 62-63, 196; clipping from the *New York Daily Times*, May 31, 1854, p. 3, New Mexico State Records and Archives Center, Santa Fe.

60. U.S., Congress, House, *Memorial of the New Mexico Legislature*, 33rd Cong., 1st sess., Misc. Doc. no. 47, serial no. 741.

61. Barry, *KHQ*, 33 (spring 1967) : 196-98; Oliva, pp. 102-03; Frazer, p. 51. On p. 57, Frazer states that Fort Riley was established on the north bank of the Kansas River, at

the junction of the Republican and Smoky Hill rivers. It became a cavalry post in 1855.

62. Barry, *KHQ*, 33 (spring 1967) : 192.

63. David Meriwether, *My Life in the Mountains and on the Plains,* ed. and with an introduction by Robert A. Griffen (Norman: University of Oklaoma Press, 1965), pp. 144, 190-93.

CHAPTER 3

1. Route No. 8912, Star Route Register, Missouri Section, pp. 288-90, Record Group 28, National Archives, Washington, D.C. (hereafter, all mail routes will be cited by number, section, and page) ; U.S., Congress, House, *Letter from the Postmaster General,* 33rd Cong., 2d sess., Ex. Doc. no. 86, serial no. 789, pp. 318-19.

2. Brief for Complainants, Hall vs. Huffaker, Circuit Court of the United States for the District of Kansas, pp. 9-10; copy in the Kansas Historical Society Library, Topeka (hereafter cited as Brief for Complainants).

3. Susan Shelby Magoffin, *Down the Santa Fe Trail and into New Mexico,* ed., Stella M. Drumm, foreword by Howard W. Lamar (New Haven: Yale University Press, 1962), pp. 4, 15.

4. Louise Barry, "Kansas Before 1854; A Revised Annals," *Kansas Historical Quarterly,* 30 (autumn 1964) : 399 (hereafter cited as Barry, KHQ) ; Brief for Complainants, p. 9. Miss Barry's comprehensive survey, based on contemporary sources, says nine wagons; Hall in his testimony given in Brief for Complainants (taken in 1862) says fourteen or fifteen wagons.

5. Route No. 8912, Missouri Section, p. 288.

6. *Santa Fe Weekly Gazette,* March 3, 1855, p. 1. Similar advertisements appeared through the spring of 1858. Hockaday later operated J. M. Hockaday and Company, which carried the U.S. mail from St. Joseph, Missouri, to Salt Lake City, Utah Territory. Raymond W. and Mary Lund Settle, *War Drums and Wagon Wheels: The Story of Russell, Majors and Waddell* (Lincoln: University of Nebraska Press, 1966), p. 98. The W. H. Davis listed as agent for Hockaday and Hall probably was William W. H. Davis, the author of *El Gringo: Or New Mexico and Her People* (New York: Harper and Brothers, 1857).

7. Route No. 8912, Missouri Section, p. 288.

8. Barry, *KHQ,* 33 (summer 1967) : 188.

9. Davis, *El Gringo,* p. 272.

10. U.S., *Statutes at Large,* 10:684.

11. LeRoy R. Hafen and Carl Coke Rister, *Western America: The Exploration, Settlement, and Development of the Region Beyond the Mississippi* (Englewood Cliffs, N.J.: Prentice-Hall, Inc., 1950), p. 157.

12. *Santa Fe Weekly Gazette,* March 10, 1855, p. 2.

13. Route No. 8912, Missouri Section, p. 288.

14. Ibid., pp. 288, 291. This source shows that the post office at the site of Fort Atkinson was a reestablished one and was in existence from November 8, 1855 to June 1, 1857.

15. U.S., Congress, House, Report No. 299 (Jacob Hall, August 2, 1856), 34th Cong., 1st sess., found in Pamphlet V, Kansas State Historical Society Library, Topeka, and cited hereafter as Report No. 299.

16. Route No. 8912, Missouri Section, p. 289; U.S., *Statutes at Large,* 10:684. The same act allowed George H. Giddings an additional $33,500 on the Santa Fe-San Antonio route for one year, effective the same date.

17. Letter from John W. Whitfield to A. Cumming, August 15, 1855, Letters Received by the Office of Indian Affairs, 1824-1881, Upper Arkansas Agency, 1855-1864, microcopy no. 234, roll no. 878, National Archives Microfilm Publications, Washington, D.C. (hereafter cited as Upper Arkansas Agency Letters).

18. Route No. 8912, Missouri Section, p. 289; U.S., *Statutes at Large,* 11:95. George H. Giddings' extra $33,500 was similarly extended.

19. Letter from Hiram Kelly to H. E. Crain, March 22, 1915, in *Letters from Old*

Friends and Members of the Wyoming Stock Growers Association (Cheyenne: S. A. Bristol Company, 1923), pp. 14-21.

20. Route No. 8912, Missouri Section, p. 190; *Kansas City* (Mo.) *Enterprise*, February 28, 1857, p. 2; *Santa Fe Weekly Gazette*, February 7, 1857, p. 2 which said that Messrs. Bowler and Green were the special contractors.

21. *Santa Fe Weekly Gazette*, February 21, 1857, p. 2.

22. LeRoy R. and Ann W. Hafen, eds., *Relations with the Plains Indians, 1857-1861*, The Far West and the Rockies Historical Series (Glendale, Calif.: The Arthur H. Clark Company, 1959), 9:103 n. 8.

23. Barry, *KHQ*, 32 (spring 1966 and winter 1966), and 33 (spring 1967 and summer 1967), *passim*.

24. Route No. 8912, Missouri Section, p. 291.

25. Ibid.

26. Alvin F. Harlow, *Old Waybills* (New York: D. Appleton-Century Company, 1934), p. 196, says that Hockaday and Hall put on "real coaches" in 1857. This is an ambiguous term and should not be taken to mean the introduction of Concord coaches on the line.

27. Route No. 8912, Missouri Section, pp. 288, 290; Carrie Westlake Whitney, *Kansas City, Missouri: Its History and its People, 1808-1898* (Chicago: S. J. Clarke Publishing Company, 1908), 1:166.

28. Colonel Sumner's reports in Hafen and Hafen, pp. 21-22, 26-28.

29. Agent Miller's report, ibid., p. 39.

30. Letter from Robert C. Miller to A. Cumming, July 20, 1857, Upper Arkansas Agency Letters.

31. Letter from Miller to Cumming, August 15, 1857, ibid.

32. Letter from Colonel Sumner to Miller, August 19, 1857, ibid.; Hafen and Hafen, pp. 31-32.

33. Agent Miller's report, October 14, 1857, Hafen and Hafen, p. 38.

34. Letter from four Cheyenne chiefs to Colonel Hafferty, October 28, 1857, Upper Arkansas Agency Letters.

35. Nyle H. Miller (ed.), "Surveying the Southern Boundary Line of Kansas: From the Private Journal of Colonel Joseph E. Johnston," *KHQ*, 1 (1931-1932) : 129.

36. Robert M. Utley, "Fort Union and the Santa Fe Trail," *New Mexico Historical Review*, 36 (January 1961) : 41.

37. Leo E. Oliva, *Soldiers on the Santa Fe Trail* (Norman: University of Oklahoma Press, 1967), p. 109.

38. Ibid., pp. 108-09; Utley, pp. 41-42.

39. H. B. Möllhausen, "Over the Santa Fe Trail through Kansas in 1858," trans. John A. Burzle, ed. Robert Taft, *KHQ*, 16 (November 1948) : 363-64.

CHAPTER 4

1. Ralph Moody, *Stagecoach West*, (New York: Thomas Y. Crowell Company, 1967), pp. 72-73; Frank L. Owsley, "Aaron V. Brown," *Dictionary of American Biography*, ed. Allen Johnson (New York: Charles Scribner's Sons, 1957), 3:98-99.

2. Moody, p. 74.

3. W. Turrentine Jackson, "A New Look at Wells Fargo, Stagecoaches and the Pony Express," *California Historical Society Quarterly* (December 1966), a reprint by the Wells Fargo Bank, San Francisco.

4. Moody, p. 73.

5. The data do not give particular names in describing the vehicles used on the Independence-Santa Fe line, with the one exception of Jersey wagon (see p. 29). The vehicles were possibly Concord spring wagons or Troy coaches. See Mitford M. Mathews, ed., *A Dictionary of Americanisms on Historical Principles* (Chicago: University of Chicago Press, 1951), pp. 289, 372, 1772. Both mules and horses were used to pull the "celerity wagon" on the first westbound Butterfield Overland Mail. Moody, pp. 118-23.

6. Route No. 10532, Star Route Register, Missouri Section, p. 353, Record Group 28,

National Archives, Washington, D.C. Hereafter all mail routes will be cited by number, section, and page.

7. LeRoy R. Hafen and Carl Coke Rister, *Western America: The Exploration, Settlement, and Development of the Region Beyond the Mississippi* (Englewood Cliffs, N.J.: Prentice-Hall, Inc., 1950), pp. 457-59.

8. Moody, pp. 90, 125-30.

9. San Miguel had had an office briefly in 1851-1852. Route No. 10532, Missouri Section, pp. 252-53; Sheldon H. Dike, "The Postal History of New Mexico Territory," *Western Express*, 9 (January 1959), appended alphabetical list of territorial post offices.

10. The letter was written for Bent by his clerk, John W. Prowers, and therefore does not contain Bent's highly original spelling. Prowers' few errors have been corrected. Letters Received by the Office of Indian Affairs, 1824-1881, Upper Arkansas Agency, 1855-1864, Microcopy no. 234, roll no. 878, National Archives Microfilm Publications, Washington, D.C. (hereafter cited as Upper Arkansas Agency Letters).

11. Henry Pickering Walker, *The Wagonmasters: High Plains Freighting from the Earliest Days of the Santa Fe Trail to 1880* (Norman: University of Oklahoma Press, 1966), pp. 148-49.

12. Letter from Robert C. Miller to Charles E. Mix, April 30, 1858, Upper Arkansas Agency Letters.

13. Letter from John W. Whitfield to A. Cumming, August 15, 1855, and from William Bent to A. M. Robinson, December 17, 1858, ibid.

14. Like most accounts, Brice's does not mention all the points of call along the way.

15. James Brice, *Reminiscences of Ten Years Experience on the Western Plains: How the United States Mails Were Carried Before the Railroads Reached the Santa Fe Trail* (Kansas City, Mo.: n.n., n.d.), pp. 1-3.

16. Brice, pp. 2-3.

17. Darrell Garwood, *Crossroads of America: The Story of Kansas City* (New York: W. W. Norton and Company, 1948), pp. 28-31. The masthead of the *Kansas City* (Mo.) *Daily Western Journal of Commerce* in 1858 used City of Kansas.

18. *Kansas City Daily Western Journal of Commerce*, December 17, 1858, p. 3; December 18, 1858, p. 1.

19. Ibid., December 18, 1858, p. 2; Moody, pp. 126-27.

20. *Kansas City Daily Western Journal of Commerce*, December 29, 1858, p. 3.

21. Raymond W. and Mary Lund Settle, *War Drums and Wagon Wheels: The Story of Russell, Majors and Waddell* (Lincoln: University of Nebraska Press, 1966), pp. 100-101; Moody, pp. 155-64.

22. *Kansas City Daily Western Journal of Commerce*, January 12, 1859, p. 2; January 16, 1859, p. 2.

23. Ibid., January 12, 1859, p. 2; February 2, 1859, p. 2; February 15, 1859, p. 2.

24. Ibid., February 27, 1859, p. 2.

25. Ibid., February 20, 1859, p. 2; Brief for Complainants, Hall vs. Huffaker, Circuit Court of the United States for the District of Kansas, p. 10; copy in the Kansas State Historical Society Library, Topeka (hereafter cited as Brief for Complainants).

26. Brief for Complainants, pp. 2-11.

27. The mail station at Pawnee Fork may have been listed in the hope that Hall would have it ready when spring traffic began on the Trail. Actually, the station was not set up until autumn because of hostilities by the Kiowa Indians. Letter from Postmaster General Joseph Holt to Secretary of the Interior Jacob Thompson, August 1, 1859, Letters Received by the Office of the Adjutant General (Main Series), 1822-1860 (1859), microcopy no. 567, roll no. 603, National Archives Microfilm Publications, Washington, D.C. (hereafter cited as Letters Received by the Office of the Adjutant General).

28. *Kansas City Daily Western Journal of Commerce*, February 20, 1859, p. 2.

29. Ibid., March 11, 1859, p. 2.

30. Ibid., June 2, 1859, p. 3; Settle and Settle, pp. 100-101.

31. U.S., *Statutes at Large*, 10:714.

32. Route No. 15050, Kansas Section, p. 108.

33. Ibid.

34. Route No. 10615, Missouri Section, p. 96.

35. U.S., *Statutes at Large*, 10:532.

36. Ibid., 11:353.

37. Randolph B. Marcy, *The Prairie Traveler: A Hand-book for Overland Expeditions* (New York: Harper & Brothers, 1859), pp. 18-19, 257-60. Captain Marcy specially noted that he was the originator of that road and suggested that, for unknown reasons, his name was excluded from that distinction.

38. Route No. 10615, Missouri Section, p. 96.

39. LeRoy R. Hafen, *The Overland Mail, 1849-1869: Promoter of Settlement, Precursor of Railroads* (Cleveland: The Arthur H. Clark Company, 1926), p. 118.

40. Route No. 15050, Kansas Section, p. 109.

41. Hafen, pp. 115-17; Moody, p. 91.

42. *Kansas City Daily Western Journal of Commerce*, March 1, 1859, p. 2.

43. Ibid., February 1, 1859, p. 2; July 23, 1859, p. 2.

44. *Border Star* (Westport, Mo.), May 27, 1859, p. 2.

45. *Kansas City Daily Western Journal of Commerce*, July 23, 1859, p. 2.

46. Ibid.

47. Route No. 15050, Kansas Section, p. 109. There is evidence that claims for losses were being pressed as late as 1868.

48. Route No. 10615, Missouri Section, pp. 96-97; *Kansas City Daily Western Journal of Commerce*, January 18, 1859, p. 2, which says that Green's party started first from Kansas City; Hafen, pp. 117-18, quoting the *San Francisco Bulletin*, November 19, 1858. Lieutenant Beal, USN, was preparing to leave Fort Smith for Albuquerque to survey a road from there to the Colorado River. W. J. Ghent, "Edward Fitzgerald Beale," *Dictionary of American Biography*, ed. Allen Johnson (New York: Charles Scribner's Sons, 1957), 2:89.

49. W. Turrentine Jackson, *Wagon Roads West: A Study of Federal Road Surveys and Construction in the Trans-Mississippi West, 1846-1869* (Berkeley: University of California Press, 1952), p. 252.

50. *Border Star*, December 31, 1858, p. 1; *Kansas City Daily Western Journal of Commerce*, January 11, 1859, p. 2.

51. *Kansas City Daily Western Journal of Commerce*, January 11, 1859, p. 2; February 1, 1859, p. 2.

52. Route No. 10615, Missouri Section, p. 96.

53. *Kansas City Daily Western Journal of Commerce*, March 20, 1859, p. 2.

54. Route No. 10532, Missouri Section, p. 355.

55. Clyde Kelly, *United States Postal Policy* (New York: D. Appleton and Company, 1932), p. 67.

56. Kelly, pp. 67-68; Moody, pp. 133-34; Hafen, pp. 136-37.

57. Route No. 10615, Missouri Section, p. 97; Route No. 15050, Kansas Section, p. 109.

58. Ibid.

59. *Kansas City Daily Western Journal of Commerce*, May 14, 1859, p. 3.

60. Hafen, p. 150 n. 314; Moody, p. 136.

61. Route No. 10532, Missouri Section, p. 355.

62. Letter from Jacob Hall to Colonel E. V. Sumner, September 3, 1859, Letters Received by the Office of the Adjutant General.

63. Route No. 10532, Missouri Section, pp. 354-56. Formal departmental approval was given on January 31, 1860.

CHAPTER 5

1. *Kansas City* (Mo.) *Daily Western Journal of Commerce*, June 7, 1859, p. 2.

2. Ralph Moody, *Stagecoach West* (New York: Thomas Y. Crowell Company, 1967), pp. 165-70; LeRoy R. Hafen, ed., *Colorado and its People: A Narrative and Topical His-

tory of the Centennial State (New York: Lewis Historical Publishing Company, 1948), 1:189.

3. *Kansas City Daily Western Journal of Commerce,* June 8, 1859, p. 2.

4. Hafen, pp. 176-78.

5. *Kansas City Daily Western Journal of Commerce,* July 26, 1859, p. 2; September 6, 1859, p. 2.

6. Ibid., June 7, 1859, p. 2; Henry Pickering Walker, *The Wagonmasters: High Plains Freighting from the Earliest Days of the Santa Fe Trail to 1880* (Norman: University of Oklahoma Press, 1966), p. 149.

7. This was Thomas Hart Benton, longtime senator from Missouri (1820-1850) and promoter of the central route to the Pacific, who had died in 1858. He had been a colonel since the War of 1812. Francis B. Heitman, *Historical Register and Dictionary of the United States Army, from its Organization, September 29, 1789, to March 2, 1903* (Washington, D.C.: Government Printing Office, 1903), 1:213.

8. *Border Star* (Westport, Mo.), April 8, 1859, p. 2.

9. *Kansas City Daily Western Journal of Commerce,* April 10, 1859, p. 3.

10. Route No. 10532, Star Route Register, Missouri Section, p. 352, Record Group 28, National Archives, Washington, D.C. Hereafter all mail routes will be cited by number, section, and page.

11. Clara M. Fengel Shields, "The Lyon Creek Settlement," ed. William E. Connelley, *Collections of the Kansas State Historical Society,* 14 (1915-1918) : 143.

12. The Kansas City paper also said that antelope and prairie dogs would first be seen near the Big Bend of the Arkansas around Walnut Creek. The listing of "firsts" along the route, of course, referred only to approximate locations and did not allow for seasonal or other variations. A traveler that summer reported the first buffalo at Cottonwood Creek, about eighteen miles west of Lost Spring, and prairie dogs at the Little Arkansas, thirty-five miles east of the Big Bend. LeRoy R. and Ann W. Hafen, eds., *Relations with the Plains Indians, 1857-1861,* The Far West and the Rockies Historical Series (Glendale, Calif.: The Arthur H. Clark Company, 1959), 9:100.

13. Leo E. Oliva, *Soldiers on the Santa Fe Trail* (Norman: University of Oklahoma Press, 1967), pp. 113-14; *Kansas City Daily Western Journal of Commerce,* February 20, 1859, p. 2; Letter from Jacob Hall to Colonel E. V. Sumner, September 3, 1859, Letters Received by the Office of the Adjutant General (Main Series), 1822-1860 (1859), microcopy no. 567, roll no. 603, National Archives Microfilm Publications, Washington, D.C. (hereafter cited as Letters Received by the Office of the Adjutant General).

14. *Kansas City Daily Western Journal of Commerce,* June 21, 1859, p. 2.

15. U.S., Department of the Interior, *Annual Report of the Commissioner of Indian Affairs, 1859* (Washington, D.C.: George W. Bowman, Printer, 1860), pp. 137-38.

16. *Kansas City Daily Western Journal of Commerce,* June 21, 1859, p. 2.

17. Letter from Joseph Holt to Jacob Thompson, August 1, 1859, Letters Received by the Office of the Adjutant General.

18. Letter from Joseph Holt to William R. Drinkard, August 4, 1859; Letter from Drinkard to Holt, August 4, 1859; Letter from Colonel Sumner to the adjutant general, August 10, 1859; Letter from Captain De Saussure to Captain D. R. Jones, September 26, 1859; ibid.

19. Letter from Jacob Hall to Colonel Sumner, September 3, 1859; Report from William Butze to Jacob Hall, September 30, 1859; ibid.

20. Letter from Hall to Sumner, September 3, 1859, ibid.

21. Letter from Major Donaldson to Captain De Saussure, September 21, 1859; Letter from Captain Walker to Captain De Saussure, September 23, 1859; Letter from Captain De Saussure to Captain Jones, September 26, 1859; ibid. The Westport, Missouri, *Weekly Border Star* reported on October 8, 1859, p. 2, that the original altercation at Allison's Ranche between the two Kiowa and the white men had grown out of a horse trading incident.

22. Affidavit of William Cole, October 8, 1859; Report from William Butze to Jacob

Hall, September 30, 1859, ibid. Several other accounts of the disaster exist, some of them differing in details from Cole's version. Cole's affidavit is the most substantial and probably the most reliable. The Beach Valley post office, west of Big Turkey Creek, was established February 10, 1859. Route No. 10532, Missouri Section, p. 352; Route No. 10547, Missouri Section, p. 425.

23. Reports from William Butze to Jacob Hall, September 30 and October 1, 1859, Letters Received by the Office of the Adjutant General.

24. Affidavit of William Cole, ibid.

25. Letter from Joseph Holt to Jacob Thompson, October 7, 1859, ibid.

26. Letter from Jacob Hall to Colonel Sumner, October 9, 1859, ibid.; Letter from Joseph Holt to Jacob Thompson, October 7, 1859, Letters Received by the Office of Indian Affairs, 1824-1881, Upper Arkansas Agency, 1855-1864, Microcopy no. 234, roll no. 878, National Archives Microfilm Publications, Washington, D.C. (hereafter cited as Upper Arkansas Agency Letters).

27. One of several names used by the firm of Russell, Majors, and Waddell. Raymond W. and Mary Lund Settle, *War Drums and Wagon Wheels: The Story of Russell, Majors, and Waddell* (Lincoln: University of Nebraska Press, 1966), pp. 44, 46, 47; Walker, p. 68.

28. Letter from Jacob Hall to Colonel Sumner, October 9, 1859, Letters Received by the Office of the Adjutant General.

29. James Brice, *Reminiscences of Ten Years Experience on the Western Plains: How the United States Mails were Carried Before the Railroads Reached the Santa Fe Trail* (Kansas City, Mo.: n.n., n.d.), p. 5. It is not known whether Matthew and Peter Kelly were related.

30. Letter from William Bent to A. B. Greenwood, March 17, 1860, Upper Arkansas Agency Letters.

31. Letter from Joseph Holt to Jacob Thompson, October 7, 1859, ibid.; Letter from Jacob Hall to Colonel Sumner, October 9, 1859, Letters Received by the Office of the Adjutant General.

32. Letter from S. H. Woodson to J. B. Floyd, October 10, 1859, Letters Received by the Office of the Adjutant General. This was the same Woodson who held the Independence-Salt Lake City contract in 1850. See Moody, pp. 46, 68-70.

33. Letter from Colonel Sumner to Jacob Hall, October 4, 1859, Department of the Missouri, Letters Sent, August 1859-March 1860, United States Continental Commands, Record Group 393, National Archives, Washington, D.C. Hereafter cited as Department of the Missouri, Letters Sent.

34. Letter from Captain D. R. Jones to Captain De Saussure, October 4, 1859, ibid.

35. Letter from Colonel Sumner to Captain De Saussure, October 6, 1859, ibid.

36. Letter from Colonel Bonneville to Lieutenant Colonel Thomas, October 17, 1859; Letter from Lieutenant J. D. Williams to Captain R. M. Morris, October 15, 1859 and October 17, 1859; Letter from Lieutenant Wilkins to Lieutenant Jackson, October 17, 1859, Letters Received by the Office of the Adjutant General.

37. *Weekly Border Star*, November 12, 1859, p. 3; Robert M. Utley, "Fort Union and the Santa Fe Trail," *New Mexico Historical Review*, 36 (January 1961): 42-43.

38. The *Weekly Border Star*, November 12, 1859, p. 3, says Cottonwood Holes, but its place in the listed sequence of points on the Trail indicates Cottonwood Spring or Creek on the Cimarron Cutoff. There was a point known as Cottonwood Holes east of Big Turkey Creek in Kansas. See Randolph B. Marcy, *The Prairie Traveler: A Hand-book for Overland Expeditions* (New York: Harper & Brothers, 1859), p. 261.

39. *Weekly Border Star*, November 12, 1859, p. 3; *Kansas Press* (Council Grove), October 10, 1859, p. 4. McCutchen and another passenger named Tipton, in the Westport paper, erroneously referred to Fauntleroy as major, while the Council Grove paper referred to Colonel Font LeRoy. For information on the two captains, see Heitman, 1:511, 674.

NOTES

40. Letter from Colonel Fauntleroy to Colonel Samuel Cooper, October 25, 1859, Letters Received by the Office of the Adjutant General.
41. The young man's name was Patrick Cahill. *Weekly Border Star,* November 12, 1859, p. 3. The *Kansas Press,* November 7, 1859, p. 3, said Cahill was the conductor. Fauntleroy spoke only of the boy accompanying the mail. It is doubtful that Cahill was conductor; an experienced man would hardly have been so rash.
42. Letter from Colonel Fauntleroy to Colonel Cooper, October 25, 1859, Letters Received by the Office of the Adjutant General.
43. Letter from Captain Steuart to Captain Jones, October 30, 1859, ibid.; *Weekly Border Star,* November 12, 1859, p. 3.
44. *Weekly Border Star,* November 12, 1859, p. 3.
45. Letter from Jacob Hall to Colonel Sumner, October 9, 1859, Letters Received by the Office of the Adjutant General.
46. *Kansas Press,* October 17, 1859, p. 2.
47. Route No. 10532, Missouri Section, p. 354.
48. *Kansas Press,* October 31, 1859, p. 2; *Weekly Border Star,* November 19, 1859, p. 3.
49. W. Turrentine Jackson, *Wagon Roads West: A Study of Federal Road Surveys and Construction in the Trans-Mississippi West, 1846-1869* (Berkeley: University of California Press, 1952), p. 253.
50. *Weekly Border Star,* November 26, 1859, p. 2.
51. Letter from Captain Steuart to Captain Jones, October 30, 1859, Letters Received by the Office of the Adjutant General.
52. *Weekly Border Star,* November 19, 1859, p. 3; November 26, 1859, p. 2.
53. Brice, pp. 7-9.
54. Letter from Captain Steuart to Captain Jones, October 30, 1859; Letter from Lieutenant Bell to Captain Jones, November 25, 1859, Letters Received by the Office of the Adjutant General.
55. Brice, pp. 7-9.
56. *Kansas City Daily Western Journal of Commerce,* February 20, 1859, p. 2.
57. Although William Bent abandoned the Old Fort in 1849, it was occupied to some degree in 1859; travelers were informed that everything necessary for men and animals could be obtained there. Ibid.
58. Brice, p. 9.
59. *Weekly Border Star,* December 10, 1859, p. 1.
60. Letter from Lieutenant Bell to Captain Jones, November 25, 1859; Letter from Captain Steuart to Captain Jones, October 30, 1859, Letters Received by the Office of the Adjutant General.
61. Letter from Lieutenant Bell to Captain Jones, November 25, 1859, ibid. Bell was no frontier novice, having served with distinction under Lieutenant Colonel Philip St. George Cooke against the Jicarilla Apache in 1854. Otis E. Young, *The West of Philip St. George Cooke, 1809-1895* (Glendale, Calif.: The Arthur H. Clark Company, 1955), pp. 254-60.
62. Letter from Colonel Sumner to Colonel Cooper, November 15, 1859, Letters Received by the Office of the Adjutant General.
63. Letter from Lieutenant Bell to Captain Jones, January 4, 1860, ibid.
64. Ibid., November 25, 1859.
65. Letters from Captain Jones to Lieutenant Bell and to Major Sedgwick, December 6, 1859, Department of Missouri, Letters Sent.
66. Letter from Lieutenant Bell to Captain Jones, January 4, 1860, Letters Received by the Office of the Adjutant General; *Weekly Border Star,* January 21, 1860, p. 2; Utley, p. 43.
67. *Weekly Border Star,* January 21, 1860, p. 2.
68. Article by George H. Lake in *The Morning Light* (Trinidad, Colo.), August 18, 1939, pp. 4, 8.

CHAPTER 6

1. Robert W. Frazer, *Forts of the West: Military Forts and Presidios and Posts Commonly Called Forts West of the Mississippi River to 1898* (Norman: University of Oklahoma Press, 1965) p. 55.
2. *Weekly Border Star* (Westport, Mo.), April 7, 1860, p. 2.
3. *Border Star*, May 12, 1860, p. 2.
4. *Weekly Border Star*, December 24, 1859, p. 2.
5. *Border Star*, May 26, 1860, p. 2.
6. Route No. 10532, Star Route Register, Missouri Section, p. 356, Record Group 28, National Archives, Washington, D.C. Hereafter, all mail routes will be cited by number, section and page.
7. *Border Star*, June 16, 1860, p. 1.
8. Named for Colonel Benjamin F. Larned, paymaster general. Frazer, p. 55.
9. Named for Auguste P. Chouteau, Indian trader, whose party fended off a Pawnee attack in 1816 by taking refuge on the island. Josiah Gregg, *Commerce of the Prairies*, ed. Max L. Moorhead (Norman: University of Oklahoma Press, 1954), pp. 19-20.
10. LeRoy R. and Ann W. Hafen, eds., *Relations with the Plains Indians, 1857-1861*, The Far West and the Rockies Historical Series (Glendale, Calif.: The Arthur H. Clark Company, 1959), 9:202-04.
11. Ibid., pp. 208-12; *Daily Kansas City* (Mo.) *Journal of Commerce*, July 31, 1860, p. 2. The word *Western* had been dropped from the name of the paper.
12. Hafen and Hafen, pp. 259-60; *Daily Kansas City Journal of Commerce*, June 28, 1860, p. 3; August 2, 1860, p. 3; August 24, 1860, p. 3.
13. Morris F. Taylor, "Fort Wise," *Colorado Magazine*, 46 (spring 1969): 97.
14. U.S., Congress, House, *Letter from the Postmaster General*, 37th Cong., 2d sess., Ex. Doc. no. 37, serial no. 1139, p. 258.
15. *Daily Kansas City Journal of Commerce*, July 12, 1860, p. 3.
16. *Daily Kansas City Western Journal of Commerce*, September 4, 1860, p. 3. The name of the paper was changed again on August 3, 1860.
17. Ibid., September 13, 1860, p. 3.
18. Leroy R. Hafen, ed., *Colorado and its People: A Narrative and Topical History of the Centennial State* (New York: Lewis Historical Publishing Company, 1948), 1:182.
19. Raymond W. and Mary Lund Settle, *War Drums and Wagon Wheels: The Story of Russell, Majors and Waddell* (Lincoln: University of Nebraska Press, 1966), pp. 101-02, 197-202; Ralph Moody, *Stagecoach West* (New York: Thomas Y. Crowell Company, 1967), pp. 175-77, 189-90.
20. Settle and Settle, pp. 126-27.
21. *Letter from the Postmaster General*, p. 197.
22. *Council Grove* (Kans.) *Press*, August 25, 1860, p. 2.
23. Route No. 10532, Missouri Section, p. 356.
24. *Santa Fe Weekly Gazette*, December 15, 1860, p. 2.
25. *Kansas City Daily Western Journal of Commerce*, September 26, 1860, p. 3.
26. *Santa Fe Weekly Gazette*, September 29, 1860, p. 2. In 1859, Bill Allison died suddenly at Wayne City, where he was loading a train of wagons. A man named Peacock, from Independence, took over management. James Brice, *Reminiscences of Ten Years Experience on the Plains: How the United States Mails Were Carried Before the Railroads Reached the Santa Fe Trail* (Kansas City, Mo.: n.n., n.d.), p. 4.
27. *Kansas City* (Mo.) *Enquirer and Star*, December 22, 1860, p. 4.
28. *Daily Kansas City Western Journal of Commerce*, December 23, 1860, p. 2.
29. Brief for Complainants, Hall vs. Huffaker, Circuit Court of the United States for the District of Kansas, p. 1; copy in the Kansas State Historical Society Library, Topeka.
30. Howard L. Conard, ed., *Encyclopedia of the History of Missouri: A compendium of History and Biography for Ready Reference* (New York: The Southern History Company, 1901), 5:372; *Letter from the Postmaster General*, p. 426.
31. *Daily Kansas City Journal of Commerce*, September 21 and 23, 1859, p. 3; Henry

Tisdale, "Travel by Stage in the Early Days," *Transactions of the Kansas State Historical Society,* 7 (1901-1902) : 460.

32. Tisdale, p. 460.

33. *Daily Kansas City Western Journal of Commerce,* September 4, 1860, p. 3.

34. Ibid., December 23, 1860, p. 2; January 10, 1861, p. 2. The December 23 edition noted that there was only one express currently operating to the mines, which carried letters at 25 cents each. That was on the Platte route, and a revenue of $125,000 was expected for the coming year. An express line from Kansas City to the mines could expect $40,000. The Platte route express referred to the Central Overland California and Pike's Peak Express. However, since September the Western Stage Company had been carrying the U.S. mail over much the same line, thus ruining the Central Overland's lucrative monopoly. Apparently, neither the Kansas City editor nor Preston Roberts, Jr., were aware of the Western Stage Company's operations.

W. G. Barkley was also the Kansas City agent for the *Canon City Times* (Kans. Terr.). See that paper, July 15, 1861, p. 2.

35. Robert M. Utley, *Fort Union National Monument, New Mexico* (Washington, D.C.: Government Printing Office, 1962), pp. 64, 66.

36. *Daily Kansas City Western Journal of Commerce,* January 24, 1861, p. 2. *Western* had been restored to the paper's name; *Daily* now preceded *Kansas City.*

37. Robert M. Utley, "Fort Union and the Santa Fe Trail," *New Mexico Historical Review,* 36 (January 1961) : 43-44; Leo E. Oliva, *Soldiers on the Santa Fe Trail* (Norman: University of Oklahoma Press, 1967), p. 110. The list of military engagements in Francis B. Heitman's *Historical Register and Dictionary of the United States Army from Its Organization, September 29, 1789, to March 2, 1903* (Washington, D.C.: Government Printing Office, 1903), 2: 405 gives the location as Cold Spring on the Cimarron River.

38. Utley, "Fort Union and the Santa Fe Trail," pp. 43-44; Oliva, p. 110.

39. *Canon City Times* (Kans. Terr.), February 2, 1861, p. 2; *Daily Kansas City Western Journal of Commerce,* February 26, 1861, p. 2.

40. Post Returns of Fort Wise, December, 1860; January, February, 1861, Microcopy no. 617, roll no. 659, National Archives Microfilm Publications, Washington, D.C.

41. *Daily Kansas City Western Journal of Commerce,* December 27, 1860, p. 2.

42. He sometimes sent mail east via Denver City. Hafen and Hafen, pp. 263-64, 277-81.

43. *Daily Kansas City Western Journal of Commerce,* February 16, 1861, p. 2.

44. Route No. 10532, Missouri Section, pp. 354, 356; *Weekly Rocky Mountain News* (Denver), March 6, 1861, p. 2; Letter from A. G. Boone to A. B. Greenwood, February 23, 1861, Letters Received by the Office of Indian Affairs, 1824-1881, Upper Arkansas Agency, 1855-1864, microcopy no. 234, roll no. 878, National Archives Microfilm Publications, Washington, D.C.; Taylor, pp. 105-07.

45. William Bent had resigned as agent in September, 1860. David Lavender, *Bent's Fort* (Garden City, N.Y.: Doubleday & Co., Inc., 1954), p. 346.

46. Charles J. Kappler, *Indian Affairs: Laws and Treaties* (Washington, D.C.: Government Printing Office, 1904), 1: 807-11.

47. Oliva, p. 142.

48. For a critical summary of Boone's treaty see Lavender, p. 346.

49. Percy Stanley Fritz, *Colorado, The Centennial State* (New York: Prentice-Hall, Inc., 1941), pp. 194-97; Hafen, pp. 220-21.

50. *Canon City Times,* February 9, 1861, p. 5.

51. Obituary of James S. Gray, December, 1884; clipping in the State Historical Society of Colorado Library, Denver.

52. Kenyon Riddle, *Records and Maps of the Old Santa Fe Trail* (Raton, N.M.: The Raton Daily Range,* 1949), p. 60; Margaret Long, *The Santa Fe Trail* (Denver: W. H. Kistler Stationery Company, 1954), p. 234.

53. *Canon City Times* (Colo. Terr.), April 20, 1861, p. 6; *Daily Kansas City Western Journal of Commerce,* January 20, 1861, p. 2.

54. *Canon City Times,* April 20, 1861, p. 6.

55. *Canon Times* (Jefferson Terr.), October 27, 1860, p. 2. The provisional government known as Jefferson Territory disappeared with the creation of Colorado Territory in February, 1861.

56. Ibid., September 29, 1860, p. 3.

57. Ibid., October 27, 1860, p. 2.

58. Ibid., November 10, 1860, p. 3; Hafen, p. 190.

59. *Canon Times,* December 1, 1860, p. 3; *Canon City Times,* January 19, 1861, p. 8. Hinkley and Company shipped east out of Denver by means of the Western Stage Company. Moody, p. 189.

60. *Rocky Mountain News* (Denver and Auraria), January 11, 1860, p. 2. Inclusion of Taos must have been in terms of a branch line from Fort Union.

61. *Daily Rocky Mountain News* (Denver), March 20, 1861, p. 2.

62. *Canon City Times,* May 4, 1861, pp. 3, 6.

63. *Canon City Times,* January 26, 1861, p. 2.

64. Ibid., May 4, 1861, p. 6; May 9, 1861, p. 3.

65. Ibid., May 16, 1861, p. 3.

66. *Letter from the Postmaster General,* pp. 101, 104, 105, 109, and 173-96 *passim;* Route No. 10532, Missouri Section, p. 354.

67. *Canon City Times,* May 16, 1861, p. 3.

68. *Daily Western Journal of Commerce* (Kansas City, Mo.), June 7, 1861, p. 2. California Gulch, near the headwaters of the Arkansas River, was the site of the richest placer deposit of gold ever found in Colorado. Hafen, p. 195.

69. Slemmons, Roberts and Company, as successors to the Missouri Stage Company, undoubtedly maintained the Kansas City-Independence service.

70. *Daily Western Journal of Commerce,* May 28, 1861, p. 2.

71. Ibid., May 18, 1861, p. 2.

72. Ibid., June 7, 1861, p. 2.

73. *Kansas City Daily Western Journal of Commerce,* June 10, 1859, p. 2.

74. Ibid., and June 7, 1861, p. 2.

75. *Canon City Times,* July 1, 1861, p. 3.

76. Ibid., September 12, 1861, p. 3.

77. Ibid., July 4, 1861, p. 3; July 8, 1861, p. 4.

CHAPTER 7

1. Darrell Garwood, *Crossroads of America: The Story of Kansas City* (New York: W. W. Norton and Company, 1948), pp. 46-49.

2. LeRoy R. Hafen ed., *Colorado and its People: A Narrative and Topical History of the Centennial State* (New York: Lewis Historical Publishing Company, 1948), 1: 279.

3. *Council Grove* (Kans.) *Press,* June 1, 1861, p. 3; Frank Hall, *History of the State of Colorado* (Chicago: The Blakely Printing Company, 1891), 3: 394.

4. Hafen, pp. 279-81.

5. Calvin Horn, *New Mexico's Troubled Years: The Story of the Early Territorial Governors* (Albuquerque: Horn & Wallace, Publishers, 1963), pp. 85-87.

6. Robert M. Utley, *Fort Union National Monument, New Mexico* (Washington, D.C.: Government Printing Office, 1962), p. 23; Morris F. Taylor, "Fort Wise" *Colorado Magazine,* 46 (spring 1969) : 108-09.

7. *Daily Western Journal of Commerce* (Kansas City, Mo.), June 7, 1861, p. 2; *Canon City* (Kans. Terr.) *Times,* June 13, 1861, p. 4.

8. Route No. 10532, Star Route Register, Missouri Section, pp. 353, 356, Record Group 28, National Archives, Washington, D.C. (hereafter all mail routes will be cited by number, section, and page) ; U.S., Congress, House, *Letter From the Postmaster General,* 37th Cong., 2d sess., Ex. Doc. no. 37, serial no. 1139, p. 579. Pueblo had a post office briefly (established Dec. 13, 1860) while in Kansas Territory, but as Pueblo, Colorado

NOTES

Territory, its post office dated from October 14, 1861. Article by Mrs. T. R. Malone, McClelland Public Library, Pueblo, Colo.

9. *Daily Rocky Mountain News* (Denver), June 10, 1861, p. 3.

10. *Canon City Times,* June 13, 1861, p. 4.

11. Ibid., July 8, 1861, p. 3. This may have been the Andrew Stuart listed as having bid for the mail contract on Route No. 10532 in 1858. Route No. 10532, Missouri Section, p. 3554. The Canon City paper described him as one of the proprietors of the stage line.

12. *Canon City Times,* July 11, 1861, p. 3.

13. Ibid., July 15, 1861, p. 2.

14. Ibid., July 25, 1861, p. 3; *Council Grove Press,* July 20, 1861, p. 3.

15. *Canon City Times,* September 5, 1861, p. 3. Canon City continued to have difficulty in maintaining contacts with the rest of the world. In September 1861, no one was carrying the U.S. mail over the forty-mile stretch north to Colorado City, so there was no connection with Denver. It was expected that the gap would be closed before long. Ibid., September 5, 1861, p. 2; September 19, 1861, p. 3.

16. *Daily Kansas City* (Mo.) *Western Journal of Commerce,* March 3, 1861, p. 3.

17. Oscar Osburn Winther, *Via Western Express & Stagecoach* (Stanford, Calif.: Stanford University Press, 1945), p. 138.

18. *Daily Kansas City Western Journal of Commerce,* August 20, 1861, p. 2. The figures given by the paper were approximately correct. See Major James Cooper McKee, *Narrative of the Surrender of a Command of U.S. Forces at Fort Fillmore, New Mexico, in July, A.D. 1861* (Houston: Stagecoach Press, 1960), and Herbert M. Hart, *Old Forts of the Southwest* (Seattle: Superior Publishing Company, 1964), pp. 82-83.

19. U.S., Department of the Interior, *Annual Report of the Commissioner of Indian Affairs, 1861* (Washington, D.C.: George W. Bowman, Printer, 1861), pp. 105-06; Albert Pike, *Prose Sketches and Poems Written in the Western Country,* ed. David J. Weber (Albuquerque: Calvin Horn, Publisher, 1967), p. xxiii.

20. Henry Inman, *The Old Santa Fe Trail: The Story of a Great Highway* (Topeka: Crane & Company, 1916), pp. 154-55.

21. *Daily Kansas City Western Journal of Commerce,* March 18, 1862, p. 2.

22. Arthur M. Wright, "Colonel John P. Slough and the New Mexico Campaign, 1862," *Colorado Magazine,* 39 (April 1962) : 89-105; William Clarke Whitford, *Colorado Volunteers in the Civil War : The New Mexico Campaign of 1862* (Denver: The State Historical and Natural History Society, 1906), p. 77.

23. *Daily Kansas City Western Journal of Commerce,* March 25, 1862, p. 2.

24. Hafen, 1 : 301-04; Whitford, pp. 77-78; Utley, pp. 64, 66.

25. Horn, p. 102.

26. *Daily Kansas City Western Journal of Commerce,* March 25, 1862, p. 2; April 1, 1862, p. 2.

27. Ibid., March 25, 1862, p. 2.

28. Horn, pp. 102-03.

29. *Daily Kansas City Western Journal of Commerce,* April 29, 1862, p. 3.

30. Ibid., April 30, 1862, p. 2. During the troubled times in New Mexico, the weekly express coaches of the Kansas City, Santa Fe and Canon City Express reached Buckskin Joe with full loads of packages. *Daily Rocky Mountain News,* March 10, 1862, p. 3, quoting the Buckskin Joe *Mountaineer.*

31. Henry Pickering Walker, *The Wagonmasters: High Plains Freighting from the Earliest Days of the Santa Fe Trail to 1880* (Norman: University of Oklahoma Press, 1966), p. 152.

32. Garwood, p. 33.

33. Slemmons, Roberts and Company did not become defunct because of loss of the Santa Fe contract. They were awarded a contract to carry the mail from Sedalia to Independence, Missouri. *Daily Kansas City Western Journal of Commerce,* May 6, 1862, p. 2. And in 1864, the company was running daily mail coaches to St. Louis and making connection with the Pacific Railroad at Dresden, Missouri. They also operated from

205

Sedalia through Warsaw, Quincey, and Bolivar to Springfield. *Daily Kansas City Journal of Commerce*, February 4, 1864, p. 2.

34. Route No. 10547, Missouri Section, p. 427.

35. U.S., Congress, House, *Letter From the Postmaster General*, 37th Cong., 2d sess., Ex. Doc. no. 37, serial no. 1139, pp. 111-12.

36. *Biographical Sketch of Col. J. L. Sanderson of St. Louis, Mo.* (Kansas City, Mo.: Ramsey, Millett & Hudson, 1880), p. 1. This source is the earliest biographical data on Sanderson and probably the most accurate. Later items are very dubious. One of them says that the government bestowed the title of colonel in gratitude for his protection of U.S. property in 1861. Civil Works Administration Interviews, Pam. 348/21, pp. 1-2, quoting *Boulder* (Colo.) *Daily Camera*, May 10, 1915, State Historical Society of Colorado Library, Denver. No contemporary data support this.

37. Abby Maria Hemenway, ed., *Vermont Historical Gazetteer* (Montpelier: Vermont Watchman and State Journal Press, 1882), 4: 520; Hamilton Child, *Gazetteer and Business Directory of Franklin and Grand Isle Counties, Vermont, 1882-1883* (Syracuse, N.Y.: Journal Office Printers, 1883). By 1862, Barlow had become a prominent businessman of St. Albans, Vermont. *St. Albans Daily Messenger and Advertiser*, November 4, 1889.

38. U.S., Congress, House, *Letter from the Postmaster General*, 32nd Cong., 1st sess., Ex. Doc. no. 101, serial no. 644, p. 68.

39. *Biographical Sketch of Col. J. L. Sanderson*, p. 1.

40. Letter from Barlow, Sanderson and Company to Postmaster General J. A. J. Cresswell, May 1869, State Historical Society of Colorado Library, Denver. *The Rocky Mountain Directory and Colorado Gazetteer for 1871* (Denver: S. S. Wallihan & Company, n.d.), p. 124, also indicates that Barlow and Sanderson controlled the company in 1862. William H. Ryus in *The Second William Penn: A True Account of Incidents That Happened Along the Old Santa Fe Trail in the Sixties* (Kansas City, Mo.: Frank T. Riley Publishing Company, 1913), p. 33, says that he drove Messrs. Barnum, Vaile, Vickroy, Barlow, and Sanderson over the line when they were thinking of buying it.

41. James Brice, *Reminiscences of Ten Years Experience on the Western Plains: How the United States Mails Were Carried Before the Railroads Reached the Santa Fe Trail* (Kansas City, Mo.: n.n., n.d.), p. 14.

42. *Kansas City Daily Journal of Commerce*, August 8, 1863, p. 2.

43. Route No. 14313, Colorado Section, pp. 468-69.

44. Ralph Moody, *Stagecoach West* (New York: Thomas Y. Crowell Company, 1967), p. 218.

45. *Daily Rocky Mountain News*, March 28, 1862, p. 2; Moody, p. 212.

46. *Daily Kansas City Western Journal of Commerce*, November 25, 1862, p. 2.

47. Ibid., June 6, 1862, p. 2; *Daily Rocky Mountain News*, July 9, 1862, p. 3.

48. Letter from Jane F. Smith, director of the Social and Economic Records Division, National Archives, Washington, D.C., to Morris F. Taylor, August 15, 1969.

49. Frank A. Root and William E. Connelley, *The Overland Stage to California* (Topeka, 1901), p. 50.

50. *Daily Rocky Mountain News*, March 6, 1862, p. 3; April 1, 1862, p. 3; April 3, 1862, p. 3.

51. Ibid., July 9, 1862, p. 3. It is not certain that Colorado City was dropped from the route, but, if so, it was also temporary. And if Colorado City was bypassed, the route probably followed a segment of the Cherokee Trail, passing such points as Fagan's Grave and the controversial Jimmy's Camp. Dorothy Price Shaw, "Jimmy's Camp on the Cherokee Trail," *The Colorado Magazine*, 27 (January 1950): 63-72.

52. *Daily Kansas City Western Journal of Commerce*, June 6, 1862, p. 2.

53. For descriptions and illustrations of these vehicles, see Mitford M. Mathews, ed., *A Dictionary of Americanisms on Historical Principles* (Chicago: University of Chicago Press, 1951), pp. 289, 372, 1097, 1772; Nick Eggenhofer, *Wagons, Mules and Men: How the Frontier Moved West* (New York: Hastings House Publishers, 1961), pp. 158,

159, 162, 163, 167; Jack D. Rittenhouse, *American Horse-Drawn Vehicles* (Los Angeles: Dillon Lithograph Company, 1948), pp. 46-48; Ramon F. Adams, *Western Words: A Dictionary of the American West* (Norman: University of Oklahoma Press, 1968), pp. 59, 72, 203.

54. *Daily Kansas City Western Journal of Commerce*, June 29, 1862, p. 2.

55. Ibid., July 6, 1862, p. 2.

56. Ibid., July 20, 1862, p. 2.

57. Ibid., June 6, 1862, p. 2; July 12, 1862, p. 2.

58. Hemenway, p. 520.

59. *Daily Rocky Mountain News*, July 17, 1862, p. 3; *Weekly Rocky Mountain News*, October 2, 1862, p. 2.

60. *Daily Rocky Mountain News*, August 18, 1862, p. 2; August 19, 1862, p. 3; August 22, 1862, p. 2.

61. Leo E. Oliva, *Soldiers on the Santa Fe Trail* (Norman: University of Oklahoma Press, 1967), pp. 143-45; Taylor, p. 119.

62. *Weekly Rocky Mountain News*, October 2, 1862, p. 2; November 27, 1862, p. 3.

63. *Daily Kansas City Western Journal of Commerce*, November 26, 1862, p. 3; December 2, 1862, p. 2; December 28, 1862, p. 2.

64. *Weekly Rocky Mountain News*, January 15, 1863, p. 3.

65. William A. Keleher, *Turmoil in New Mexico, 1846-1868* (Santa Fe: The Rydal Press, 1962), pp. 226, 257; Ralph Emerson Twitchell, *The Leading Facts of New Mexican History* (Albuquerque: Horn & Wallace, Publishers, 1963), 2: 390. Carleton was promoted to the rank of brigadier general of volunteers on April 28, 1862. Francis B. Heitman, *Historical Register and Dictionary of the United States Army, from its Organization, September 29, 1789 to March 2, 1903* (Washington, D.C.: Government Printing Office, 1903), 1: 282.

66. *Daily Kansas City Western Journal of Commerce*, December 13, 1862, p. 2. The southern portion of New Mexico Territory was known as Arizona. Horn, p. 88. In August 1862, Brigadier General Carleton made Mesilla the headquarters of the military District of Arizona. Lee Myers, "Military Establishments in Southwestern New Mexico: Stepping Stones to Settlement," *New Mexico Historical Review*, 43 (January 1968): 19. Arizona Territory was created February 24, 1863.

67. *Daily Kansas City Western Journal of Commerce*, April 19, 1863, p. 2.

CHAPTER 8

1. Route No. 14465, Star Route Register New Mexico Section, p. 368; Route No. 14313, Star Route Register Colorado Section, p. 469, Record Group 28, National Archives, Washington, D.C. Hereafter, all mail routes will be cited by number, section and page.

2. Ibid.; Hamilton Child, *Gazetteer and Business Directory, of Franklin and Grande Isle Counties, Vermont, 1882-1883* (Syracuse, N.Y.: Journal Office Printers, 1883).

3. *Daily Kansas City* (Mo.) *Western Journal of Commerce*, March 31, 1863, p. 4.

4. Ibid. and November 25, 1862, p. 2.

5. Ibid., March 6, 1863, p. 3; April 1, 1863, p. 2.

6. Ibid., January 14, 1863, p. 3; June 14, 1863, p. 3.

7. Route No. 14465, New Mexico Section, pp. 367-368.

8. *Daily Rocky Mountain News* (Denver), July 29, 1863, p. 2.

9. *Kansas City Daily Journal of Commerce*, July 24, 1863, p. 3; July 28, 1863, p. 3; August 15, 1863, p. 3.

10. Occasionally, the company was referred to as Cottrill, Barlow and Barnum's line. *Daily Rocky Mountain News*, March 22, 1864, p. 3.

11. *Daily Kansas City Western Journal of Commerce*, March 31, 1863, p. 4.

12. Ibid., April 3, 1863, p. 2; May 2, 1863, p. 2; June 14, 1863, p. 3; June 27, 1863, p. 3.

13. Ibid., June 14, 1863, p. 3.

14. Everett Dick, *The Sod-House Frontier, 1854-1890* (Lincoln, Nebraska: Johnson Publishing Company, 1954), p. 185.

15. Route No. 14465, New Mexico Section, p. 366. The Lost Spring post office was discontinued May 23, 1864, as was the one at Walton, Kansas, on June 9, 1864.

16. William H. Ryus, *The Second William Penn: A True Account of Incidents That Happened Along the Old Santa Fe Trail in the Sixties* (Kansas City, Mo.: Frank T. Riley Publishing Company, 1913), pp. 12-13; Henry Inman, *The Old Santa Fe Trail: The Story of a Great Highway* (Topeka: Crane & Company, 1916), pp. 154-55.

17. *Daily Kansas City Western Journal of Commerce*, April 3, 1863, p. 2.

18. Julia S. Lambert, "Plain Tales of the Plains," *The Trail*, 8 (April 1916) : 9.

19. Route No. 14465, New Mexico Section, p. 366; Mrs. Fred Bullen, comp., "Early History of Pueblo" Scrapbook, 1: p. 9, 2: 79, and article by Mrs. T. R. Malone, McClelland Public Library, Pueblo, Colo. *Daily Chieftain* (Pueblo, Colo.), January 15, 1876, p. 4.

20. Ibid. It was said that the stage company was dissatisfied with James H. Haynes' treatment of its livestock and asked Colonel Boone to take the stage station to his place. Ryus, p. 43; Inman, p. 157.

21. Interview with Granville (Gus) Withers, Civil Works Administration Interviews, Pueblo County, Pam. 344, p. 286, State Historical Society of Colorado Library, Denver.

22. Morris F. Taylor, *Trinidad, Colorado Territory* (Trinidad: Trinidad State Junior College, 1966), pp. 30-31, 36, 42.

23. Route No. 10532, Missouri Section, p. 353.

24. Henry Pickering Walker, *The Wagonmasters: High Plains Freighting from the Earliest Days of the Santa Fe Trail to 1880* (Norman: University of Oklahoma Press, 1966), pp. 257-58; Inman, pp. 158-59; Ryus, p. 16; R. L. Duffus, *The Santa Fe Trail* (New York: Longmans, Green and Company, 1930), p. 248.

25. James Brice, *Reminiscences of Ten Years Experience on the Plains: How the United States Mails Were Carried Before the Railroads Reached the Santa Fe Trail* (Kansas City, Mo.: n.n., n.d.), pp. 14-15.

26. *Daily Kansas City Western Journal of Commerce*, June 27, 1863, p. 3.

27. Ibid., June 14, 1863, p. 3; June 27, 1863, p. 3; June 28, 1863, p. 3; July 12, 1863, p. 3.

28. Ibid., July 12, 1863, p. 3.

29. Brice, p. 20.

30. Darrell Garwood, *Crossroads of America: The Story of Kansas City* (New York: W. W. Norton and Company, 1948), pp. 50-51.

31. Duffus, p. 248.

32. *Kansas City Daily Journal of Commerce*, August 8, 1863, pp. 2, 3.

33. Garwood, pp. 54, 56-57.

34. Ibid., p. 55.

35. *Kansas City Daily Journal of Commerce*, August 11, 1863, p. 3.

36. Ibid., September 13, 1863, p. 3.

37. Ibid., October 10, 1863, p. 3.

38. Ibid., October 18, 1863, p. 2.

39. Ibid., December 1, 1863, p. 3; December 6, 1863, p. 3. Watts, of course, was returning to Washington to attend the lame-duck session of the Thirty-seventh Congress to which he was the Territory's delegate. Perea's term as delegate commenced with the first session of the Thirty-eighth Congress, which convened in March 1864.

40. Ibid., January 1, 1864, p. 2.

41. Ibid., January 7, 1864, p. 2.

42. Ibid., February 24, 1864, p. 3.

43. Ibid., December 8, 1863, p. 3; February 12, 1864, p. 3.

44. Ibid., February 4, 1864, p. 2.

45. Ibid., February 7, 1864, p. 2.

46. Ibid., April 5, 1864, p. 2.

47. Ibid., March 26, 1864, p. 3.

48. *Daily Rocky Mountain News*, March 15, 1864, p. 3; August 2, 1864, p. 3.

49. Ibid, March 8, 1864, p. 2.

50. Ibid., March 15, 1864, p. 3.

51. Ibid., July 5, 1864, p. 3.

52. Ibid., March 22, 1864, p. 3.

53. Ibid., March 15, 1864, p. 3; July 12, 1864, p. 3; August 2, 1864, p. 3.

54. *Kansas City Daily Journal of Commerce*, September 20, 1863, p. 3; Robert W. Frazer, *Forts of the West: Military Forts and Presidios and Posts Commonly Called Forts West of the Mississippi River to 1898* (Norman: University of Oklahoma Press, 1965), p. 100.

55. Leo E. Oliva, *Soldiers on the Santa Fe Trail* (Norman: University of Oklahoma Press, 1967), p. 149.

56. Ibid., p. 151; Paper by Mrs. Daniel Hayden read to the Southern Colorado Pioneers Association, June 28, 1918, "Early History of Pueblo" Scrapbook, 2: 91-92, McClelland Public Library, Pueblo.

57. Hayden Paper pp. 91-92.

58. *Council Grove* (Kans.) *Press*, June 4, 1864, p. 3.

59. Oliva, pp. 151-52.

60. Hayden Paper, pp. 91-92.

61. Oliva, pp. 151-56.

62. *Kansas City Daily Journal of Commerce*, June 28, 1864, p. 2.

63. Withers Interview, p. 288.

64. *Kansas City Daily Journal of Commerce*, July 29, 1864, p. 3; August 6, 1864, p. 2.

65. Hayden Paper, pp. 91-92; Route No. 14465, New Mexico Section, p. 366.

66. Oliva, pp. 152-53.

67. *Kansas City Daily Journal of Commerce*, June 29, 1864, p. 2; *Daily Rocky Mountain News*, August 23, 1864, p. 3; August 26, 1864, p. 3; September 5, 1864, p. 3; September 9, 1864, p. 2.

68. *Kansas City Daily Journal of Commerce*, June 18, 1864, p. 3.

69. Garwood, pp. 61-70.

70. *Kansas City Daily Journal of Commerce*, August 26, 1864, p. 2.

71. LeRoy R. Hafen, ed., *Colorado and its People: A Narrative and Topical History of the Centennial State* (New York: Lewis Historical Publishing Company, 1948), 1: 312; *Daily Rocky Mountain News*, September 5, 1864, p. 3.

72. *Kansas City Daily Journal of Commerce*, July 28, 1864, p. 2; September 4, 1864, p. 2. Lambert (p. 8), undoubtedly describing the same incident, says there were only two men and one woman, and she places the locale of the killings as closer to Fort Lyon.

73. *Kansas City Daily Journal of Commerce*, September 4, 1864, p. 2. The two men were on their way to testify in the case of James H. Haynes, who, as a government contractor, was charged with stealing horses at Fort Lyon. U.S., Department of the Interior, *Annual Report of the Commissioner of Indian Affairs, 1864* (Washington, D.C.: Government Printing Office, 1865), p. 375.

74. *Kansas City Daily Journal of Commerce*, September 4, 1864, p. 2.

75. *Daily Rocky Mountain News*, August 1, 1864, p. 3; August 26, 1864, p. 3; August 27, 1864, p. 3.

76. Letter from Barlow, Sanderson and Company to Postmaster General J.A.J. Cresswell, May 1869, State Historical Society of Colorado Library, Denver.

77. *Kansas City Daily Journal of Commerce*, June 25, 1864, p. 3; *Daily Rocky Mountain News*, August 2, 1864, p. 3.

78. *Daily Rocky Mountain News*, August 2, 1864, p. 3.

79. *Kansas City Daily Journal of Commerce*, October 12, 1864, p. 3; October 19, 1864, p. 2.

80. Ibid., October 20, 1864, p. 3; Abby Maria Hemenway, ed., *Vermont Historical*

Gazetteer (Montpelier: Vermont Watchman and State Journal Press, 1882), 4: 520. Former Santa Fe mail contractor Jacob Hall also died in 1864. Brief for Complainants, Hall vs. Huffaker, Circuit Court of the United States for the District of Kansas, p. 1; copy in the Kansas State Historical Library, Topeka.

81. These names are found scattered in numerous references in the *Kansas City Daily Journal of Commerce*. Kelly was an employee of the stage line at least since 1859, and he stayed with the line until well along in the railroad era. He retired to a farm in Jackson County, Missouri, where he died shortly after the turn of the century. T. F. Dawson Scrapbook, 14: 147, State Historical Society of Colorado Library, Denver.

82. *Daily Rocky Mountain News*, November 7, 1864, p. 1; November 19, 1864, p. 3.

83. Ibid., December 6, 1864, p. 3.

84. Stan Hoig, *The Sand Creek Massacre* (Norman: University of Oklahoma Press, 1961), pp. 136-62.

CHAPTER 9

1. *Kansas City* (Mo.) *Daily Journal of Commerce*, January 21, 1865, p. 1.

2. Ibid., February 1, 1865, pp. 2 and 3. Sanderson retained his interest in the Kansas City and Fort Scott line. Notes from Duane D. Finch, Samuel W. DeBusk Papers, Trinidad State Junior College Library, Trinidad, Colo.; *Weekly New Mexican* (Santa Fe), April 11, 1871, p. 1.

3. *Daily Rocky Mountain News* (Denver), April 4, 1865, pp. 2, 3; July 31, 1865, p. 4.

4. The paper mail alone exceeded 2,000 pieces. *Kansas City Daily Journal of Commerce*, February 24, 1865, p. 3.

5. Ibid, March 11, 1865, p. 3.

6. Ibid., March 16, 1865, p. 2.

7. Ibid., June 16, 1865, p. 3.

8. Ibid., May 2, 1865, p. 3. Two Santa Fe coaches reached Kansas City a couple of days later. Ibid., May 4, 1865, p. 3.

9. Ibid., May 2, 1865, p. 3.

10. Robert M. Utley, "Fort Union and the Santa Fe Trail," *New Mexico Historical Review*, 36 (January 1961) : 47.

11. *Kansas City Daily Journal of Commerce*, June 20, 1865, p. 2. The *Daily Rocky Mountain News*, July 24, 1865, p. 2, carried a brief item apparently about the same encounter. It said that seventy-five Indians were engaged with Jenkins's five-man escort, and two civilian passengers were wounded.

12. *Kansas City Daily Journal of Commerce*, June 20, 1865, p. 2.

13. Leo E. Oliva, *Soldiers on the Santa Fe Trail* (Norman: University of Oklahoma Press, 1967), p. 162; Leo E. Oliva, "Fortification on the Plains, Fort Dodge, Kansas 1864-1882," *The 1960 Brand Book of the Denver Posse of the Westerners*, ed. Guy M. Herstrom (Boulder, Colo.: Johnson Publishing Company, 1961), pp. 143-44.

14. Oliva, p. 163.

15. Post Returns from Fort Lyon for July and August, 1865, microcopy no. 617, roll no. 659, National Archives Microfilm Publications, Washington, D.C.

16. *Daily Rocky Mountain News*, July 31, 1865, p. 4.

17. Ibid., July 24, 1865, p. 4: *Daily Denver Gazette*, July 23, 1865, p. 3.

18. Route No. 14465, Star Route Register, New Mexico Section, pp. 366-67, Record Group 28, National Archives, Washington, D.C. Hereafter all mail routes will be cited by number, section, and page.

19. Reminiscences of D. L. Taylor, DeBusk Papers.

20. Colorado, *Session Laws*, 1865, p. 117.

21. Howard Louis Conard, *"Uncle Dick" Wootton, The Pioneer Frontiersman of the Rocky Mountain Region: An Account of the Adventures and Thrilling Experiences of the Most Noted American Hunter, Trapper, Guide, Scout, and Indian Fighter Now Living* (Chicago: W. E. Dibble and Company, 1890), pp. 418-19, 433-48. Conard's volume is really an autobiography of Wootton. Like other old timers recalling the past, Wootton

is unreliable. He claims that his toll road brought the Santa Fe Trail through the Raton Pass—the inference being that wagons and stagecoaches had not used it regularly before he made the improvements. That is simply not true. And his "Stage Coach Stories" (Chapter 28) have no chronological tie-in, and therefore are of little historical value by themselves. He says (pp. 419-20) that he had no trouble doing business with the stage company, but he gives no details. The fragment of a toll book kept by his partner, George McBride (1869-1870) gives no information on that subject. James F. Willard, "A Raton Pass Mountain Road Toll Book," *The Colorado Magazine*, 7 (March 1930) : 78. Willard says there is no record of a charter from New Mexico. See also Bess McKennan, "The Toll Road Over Raton Pass," *New Mexico Historical Review*, 2 (January 1927) : 83-89.

22. Route No. 14465, New Mexico Section, p. 368.

23. Ralph C. Taylor, *Colorado, South of the Border* (Denver: Sage Books, 1963), pp. 304-05; Frank Hall, *History of the State of Colorado* (Chicago: The Blakely Printing Company, 1891), 3:394-95.

24. Route No. 14465, New Mexico Section, pp. 367-68; Kenyon Riddle, *Records and Maps of the Old Santa Fe Trail* (Raton, N.M.: The Raton Daily Range, 1949), pp. 41-42.

25. U.S., Post Office Department, *Annual Report of the Postmaster General For the Fiscal Year 1865* (Washington, D.C.: Government Printing Office, 1865), p. 19.

26. Oliva, pp. 163-64.

27. Aubry was stabbed to death during an encounter with Richard Weightman in a Santa Fe *cantina* in 1854. Ralph Emerson Twitchell, *Old Santa Fe: The Story of New Mexico's Ancient Capital* (Chicago: Rio Grande Press, 1963), pp. 346-48.

28. Robert W. Frazer, *Forts of the West: Military Forts and Presidios and Posts Commonly called Forts West of the Mississippi River to 1898* (Norman: University of Oklahoma Press, 1965), pp. 51-52; Route No. 14465, New Mexico Section, p. 366; Route No. 14020, Kansas Section, p. 68.

29. Franktown, on Cherry Creek, was the seat of Douglas County. Russellville was retained as a stage station, but by 1867 the only building there was the stage station. "Place Names in Colorado," *The Colorado Magazine*, 19 (September 1942) : 184.

30. Margaret Long, *The Santa Fe Trail* (Denver: W. N. Kistler Stationery Company, 1954), p. 190; Riddle, p. 40.

31. *Daily Rocky Mountain News*, January 9, 1866, p. 2.

32. *Harper's New Monthly Magazine* from December 1864 through November 1866 (vols. 30-33) has no article or other communication on the subject by a man named Russell.

33. *Daily Rocky Mountain News*, January 23, 1866, p. 2.

34. *Weekly Denver Gazette*, February 7, 1866, p. 3.

35. *Daily Rocky Mountain News*, February 15, 1866, p. 2.

36. Ibid., February 6, 1866, p. 4.

37. Ibid., February 15, 1866, p. 2.

38. Francis B. Heitman, *Historical Register and Dictionary of the United States Army from its Organization, September 29, 1789, to March 2, 1903* (Washington, D.C.: Government Printing Office, 1903), 1:244.

39. *Daily Rocky Mountain News*, February 15, 1866, p. 1; March 9, 1866, p. 3. David A. Butterfield was a storage, forwarding, and commission merchant at Atchison, Kansas, who went into the freighting business in 1865. He was not related to John Butterfield. Henry Pickering Walker, *The Wagonmasters: High Plains Freighting from the Earliest Days of the Santa Fe Trail to 1880* (Norman: University of Oklahoma Press, 1966), pp. 48, 61; Ralph Moody, *Stagecoach West* (New York: Thomas Y. Crowell Company, 1967), pp. 280-87.

40. Moody, pp. 285-86.

41. *Daily Rocky Mountain News*, March 9, 1866, p. 3.

42. *Junction City* (Kans.) *Union*, December 30, 1865, p. 3.

43. *Kansas City Daily Journal of Commerce*, December 8, 1863, p. 3.

44. Ibid., July 17, 1864, p. 2.

45. Captain Eugene F. Ware, *The Indian War of 1864*, intro. and notes by Clyde C. Walton (Lincoln: University of Nebraska Press, 1960), p. 424.

46. *Kansas City Daily Journal of Commerce*, July 17, 1864, p. 2.

47. *Daily Rocky Mountain News*, February 15, 1866, p. 2.

48. *Junction City Union*, March 17, 1866, p. 2.

49. Colorado, *Session Laws, 1866*, p. 136.

50. Route No. 14020, Kansas Section, pp. 70-71.

51. Ware, p. 421; Moody, p. 281. Eaton was also agent for the Union Pacific Eastern Division Railroad. Hall, 1:416.

52. Moody, p. 281.

53. Ibid., pp. 268-69. The Western Stage Company sold out to Holladay's Overland Mail Company about May 1, 1861. *Daily Rocky Mountain News*, May 8, 1861, p. 3.

54. Route No. 14020, Kansas Section, p. 70.

55. Ibid., pp. 70-71.

56. *Junction City Union*, May 5, 1866, p. 2.

57. Route No. 14020, Kansas Section, p. 70.

58. *Junction City Union*, March 24, 1866, p. 2; Moody, pp. 289-90.

59. *Junction City Union*, March 24, 1866, p. 2; April 7, 1866, p. 2.

60. *Daily Rocky Mountain News*, April 3, 1866, p. 4.

61. Ibid., May 4, 1866, p. 4.

62. Route No. 17001, Colorado Section, pp. 316-17.

63. LeRoy Hafen, ed., *Colorado and its People: A Narrative and Topical History of the Centennial State* (New York: Lewis Historical Publishing Company, 1948), 1:283; Hall, 1:310-11.

64. Eudochia Bell Smith, "Women," *Colorado and its People: A Narrative and Topical History of the Centennial State*, ed. LeRoy R. Hafen (New York: Lewis Historical Publishing Company, 1948), 2:563; Moody, pp. 278-79; William McDonald, "Schuyler Colfax," *Dictionary of American Biography*, ed. Allen Johnson and Dumas Malone (New York: Charles Scribner's Sons, 1930), 4:297-98; Hafen, 1:200.

CHAPTER 10

1. It is more common to see them referred to as Barlow and Sanderson, but contemporary post office records use the other order, because Sanderson was originally awarded the contract.

2. *Weekly Western Journal of Commerce* (Kansas City, Mo.), April 14, 1866, p. 4.

3. Ibid., April 21, 1866, p. 1.

4. Route No. 14020, Star Route Register, Kansas Section, pp. 66-67, 71, Record Group 28, National Archives, Washington, D.C. (hereafter all mail routes will be cited by number, section, and page); *Junction City (Kans.) Union*, June 30, 1866, p. 2; Robert W. Frazer, *Forts of the West: Military Forts and Presidios and Posts Commonly called Forts West of the Mississippi River to 1898* (Norman: University of Oklahoma Press, 1965), pp. 53, 59.

5. *Junction City Union*, July 21, 1866, p. 2.

6. *Daily Rocky Mountain News* (Denver), October 17, 1866, p. 4; *The Rocky Mountain Directory and Colorado Gazetteer for 1871* (Denver: S. S. Wallihan & Company, n.d.), p. 124.

7. Notes from Duane D. Finch, Samuel W. DeBusk Papers, Trinidad State Junior College Library, Trinidad, Colo.; Las Animas County, DeBusk Memorial, State Historical Society of Colorado Library, Denver.

8. Biographical Sketch of A. H. Taylor, ibid.

9. *New Mexican* (Santa Fe), December 8, 1866, p. 2; Robert M. Wright, *Dodge City, The Cowboy Capital and the Great Southwest in the Days of the Wild Indian, the Buffalo, the Cowboy, Dance Halls, Gambling Halls and Bad Men* (n.p., n.n., n.d.), pp. 31-32; T. F. Dawson Scrapbooks, 9: State Historical Society of Colorado Library, Denver.

10. Biographical Sketch of A. H. Taylor, DeBusk Papers and DeBusk Memorial.

11. Lieutenant W. H. Emory in his *Notes* of 1847 refers to "the hole in the rock" on the Timpas as a large hole with stagnant water and "hole in the prairie" as a place with water and grass about fourteen and a half miles farther southwest. Ross Calvin, ed., *Lieutenant Emory Reports: A Reprint of Lieutenant W. H. Emory's Notes of a Military Reconnoissance* (Albuquerque: University of New Mexico Press, 1951), p. 34. These places were listed in a table of distances from Kansas City to Santa Fe published in the *Kansas City Daily Journal of Commerce*, May 28, 1865, p. 2, as 598.63 miles and 613.50 miles, respectively, from Kansas City.

12. U.S., Post Office Department, Record of Appointment of Postmasters, 1:225, Record Group 28 National Archives, Washington, D.C.

13. Las Animas County (Colo.) Deed Record, 1:49.

14. *New Mexican*, July 28, 1866, p. 2.

15. Route No. 14020, Kansas Section, p. 69.

16. Route No. 17001, Colorado Section, p. 317.

17. *Daily Rocky Mountain News*, June 28, 1866, p. 4; August 31, 1866, p. 1; *Daily Chieftain* (Pueblo, Colo.), May 11, 1876, p. 4.

18. Route No. 17001, Colorado Section, p. 317.

19. *Daily Rocky Mountain News*, August 1, 1866, p. 1; July 27, 1866, p. 4.

20. Ibid., July 5, 1866. Santa Fe Stage Company advertisements stopped with this issue.

21. Ibid., August 31, 1866, p. 1. It is not clear whether reference was made to Thomas or Lewis Barnum. The former was setting up stage stations between Mesilla and Tucson toward the end of July (*New Mexican*, July 28, 1866, p. 2) but may have returned. Lewis Barnum became western division manager for Barlow and Sanderson, but perhaps at a later time. Daisy Roberts Malone, "Creeks East of Pueblo Bear Names of Pioneers Settling Along Their Banks," "Early History of Pueblo" Scrapbook (unnumbered), McClelland Public Library, Pueblo, Colo.; Charles W. Hurd, "A History of Southeastern Colorado," no. 77 of a series in the *Arkansas Valley Journal*, Local History Collection, Carnegie Public Library, Trinidad, Colo.

22. *Daily Rocky Mountain News*, August 31, 1866, p. 1.

23. Route No. 14020, Kansas Section, pp. 69-71; *New Mexican*, August 4, 1866, p. 2.

24. Leo E. Oliva, *Soldiers on the Santa Fe Trail* (Norman: University of Oklahoma Press, 1967), pp. 180-81.

25. *Daily Rocky Mountain News*, June 27, 1866, p. 1.

26. Ibid., July 26, 1866, p. 2.

27. Morris F. Taylor, "Ka-ni-ache," part 1, *Colorado Magazine*, 43 (fall 1966): 296-300.

28. *Daily Rocky Mountain News*, October 17, 1866, p. 4. The telegram had to be sent over the branch wire from Denver to Julesburg and then east on the transcontinental line (completed in 1861) to a point where it could be sent down to Junction City. Le Roy R. Hafen, ed., *Colorado and its People: A Narrative and Topical History of the Centennial State* (New York: Lewis Historical Publishing Company, 1948), 1:297.

29. *New Mexican*, November 3, 1866, p. 1.

30. W. Turrentine Jackson, "A New Look at Wells Fargo, Stagecoaches and the Pony Express," *California Historical Society Quarterly* (December 1966), a reprint by the Wells Fargo Bank, San Francisco; pp. 306-07; *Daily Rocky Mountain News*, November 2, 1866, p. 1.

31. Frank A. Root and William E. Connelley, *The Overland Stage to California* (Topeka, 1901), pp. 166-67; *Daily Rocky Mountain News*, February 1, 1867, p. 4; February 2, 1867, p. 1.

32. Abby Maria Hemenway, ed., *Vermont Historical Gazetteer* (Montpelier: Vermont Watchman and State Journal Press, 1882), 4:520.

33. *Daily Rocky Mountain News*, February 23, 1867, p. 4.

34. Calvin Horn, *New Mexico's Troubled Years: The Story of the Early Territorial Governors* (Albuquerque: Horn & Wallace, Publishers, 1963), pp. 118-19.

35. *Junction City Weekly Union,* January 12, 1867, p. 2; *New Mexican,* January 19, 1867, p. 1.

36. *Junction City Weekly Union,* December 1, 1866, p. 3; February 2, 1867, p. 1; Frazer, p. 53.

37. Route No. 14020, Kansas Section, pp. 70-71.

38. *Junction City Weekly Union,* June 8, 1867, p. 3.

39. Route No. 14020, Kansas Section, p. 72.

40. Ibid.

41. *Weekly Colorado Tribune* (Denver), September 25, 1867, p. 1; Joseph Thomas, *Universal Pronouncing Dictionary of Biography and Mythology* (Philadelphia: J. B. Lippincott Company, 1930), p. 831.

42. *Daily Colorado Tribune,* September 7, 1867, p. 4.

43. *Weekly Denver Gazette,* August 21, 1867, p. 1.

44. *Junction City Weekly Union,* October 5, 1867, p. 2.

45. Oliva, pp. 187-88.

46. U.S., Congress, Senate, *Message of the President of the United States,* 40th Cong., 2d sess., Ex. Doc. no. 1, pp. 5-6.

47. Frazer, p. 54; Margaret Long, *The Smoky Hill Trail* (Denver: W. H. Kistler Stationery Company, 1943), pp. 69-70.

48. Route No. 14020, Kansas Section, p. 72.

49. Ibid.

50. *New Mexican,* November 26, 1867, p. 2; December 17, 1867, p. 2.

51. Route No. 14020, Kansas Section, p. 69.

52. Hamilton Child, *Gazetteer and Business Directory, of Franklin and Grand Isle Counties, Vermont 1882-1883,* (Syracuse, N.Y.: Journal Office Printers, 1883), pp. 93, 96; *St. Albans* (Vt.) *Daily Messenger and Advertiser,* November 4, 1889. The newspaper item is Barlow's obituary.

53. *Kansas City Daily Journal of Commerce,* January 21, 1865, p. 1.

54. Early Far West Notebook 28:5-8; Cragin Collection, Pioneers' Museum, Colorado Springs, Colo.; Arthur Woodward, "Sidelights on Bent's Old Fort," *Colorado Magazine,* 33 (October 1956) : 279.

55. Newspaper clippings of 1911 and 1915 in T. S. Dawson Scrapbook, 14:141; *Kansas City* (Mo.) *Times,* May 11, 1915, p. 3.

56. *Kansas City* (Mo.) *Times,* May 11, 1915, p. 3.

57. Civil Works Administration Interviews, Pam. 348/21, pp. 1-2, State Historical Society of Colorado Library, Denver; T. F. Dawson Scrapbook, 14:141; *Kansas City Times,* May 11, 1915, p. 3.

58. *Kansas City Daily Journal of Commerce,* January 25, 1865, p. 1.

59. Civil Works Administration Interviews, Pam. 348/21, pp. 1-2.

60. *Kansas City Daily Journal of Commerce,* July 9, 1864, p. 2; September 14, 1864, p. 3; Francis B. Heitman, *Historical Register and Dictionary of the United States Army from its Organization, September 29, 1789, to March 2, 1903* (Washington, D.C.: Government Printing Office, 1903), 1:859.

CHAPTER 11

1. *Weekly Rocky Mountain News* (Denver), January 15, 1863, p. 3.

2. U.S., Department of the Interior, *Register of Officers and Agents, Civil, Military, and Naval, in the Service of the United States on the Thirtieth September, 1867* (Washington, D.C.: Government Printing Office, 1868), p. 842; Letter from Barlow, Sanderson and Company to Postmaster General J. A. J. Cresswell, May 1869, State Historical Society of Colorado Library, Denver.

3. W. Turrentine Jackson, "A New Look at Wells Fargo, Stagecoaches and the Pony

Express," *California Historical Quarterly* (December 1966), p. 295, a reprint by the Wells Fargo Bank, San Francisco.

4. Raymond W. and Mary Lund Settle, *War Drums and Wagon Wheels: The Story of Russell, Majors and Waddell* (Lincoln: University of Nebraska Press, 1966), pp. 101-02.

5. Ibid., pp. 203-06; Jackson, p. 303.

6. Settle and Settle, p, 167; Jackson, p. 306.

7. Settle and Settle, p. 167.

8. Ralph Moody, *Stagecoach West* (New York: Thomas Y. Crowell Company, 1967), pp. 282-87.

9. *Daily Rocky Mountain News*, April 4, 1866, p. 3.

10. Jackson, pp. 307-08.

11. *Register of Officers, 1867*, p. 842; Letter from Barlow, Sanderson and Company to Postmaster General J. A. J. Cresswell, May 1869.

12. U.S., Congress, Senate, *Annual Report of the Postmaster General of the United States*, 40th Cong., 2d sess., Ex. Doc. no. 1, p. 6.

13. Ibid.; *Register of Officers, 1867*, p. 842.

14. *Weekly New Mexican* (Santa Fe), December 7, 1869, p. 1; *Daily Rocky Mountain News*, February 28, 1868, p. 1; February 29, 1868, p. 3; *Daily New Mexican*, October 21, 1870, p. 1.

15. Letter from Barlow, Sanderson and Company to Postmaster General J. A. J. Cresswell, May 1869. The contemporary figures contrast interestingly with those given in a Sanderson obituary—5000 horses and 1100 men. *Kansas City* (Mo.) *Times*, May 11, 1915, p. 3.

16. Letter from Barlow, Sanderson and Company to Postmaster General J. A. J. Cresswell, May 1869.

17. *Daily Rocky Mountain News*, February 11, 1868, p. 4.

18. Robert M. Wright, *Dodge City, the Cowboy Capital, and the Great Southwest in the Days of the Wild Indian, the Buffalo, the Cowboy, Dance Halls, Gambling Halls, and Bad Men* (n.p., n.n., n.d.), p. 31.

19. Ibid.; *New Mexican*, January 28, 1868, p. 3; Nick Eggenhofer, *Wagons, Mules and Men: How the Frontier Moved West* (New York: Hasting House Publishers, 1961), pp. 172, 175; William H. Ryus, *The Second William Penn: A True Account of Incidents that Happened Along the Santa Fe Trail in the Sixties* (Kansas City, Mo.: Frank T. Riley Publishing Co., 1913), p. 13.

20. Ramon F. Adams, *Western Words: A Dictionary of the American West* (Norman: University of Oklahoma Press, 1968), p. 164.

21. *Daily Chieftain* (Pueblo, Colo.), May 11, 1876, p. 4.

22 Robert W. Baughman, *Kansas Post Offices, May 29, 1828-August 3, 1961* (Topeka: Kansas Postal History Society, 1961), pp. 247-48; William Frank Zornow, *Kansas, A History of the Jayhawk State* (Norman: University of Oklahoma Press, 1957), pp. 161-62.

23. Leola Howard Blanchard, *Conquest of Southwest Kansas: A History and Thrilling Stories of Frontier Life in the State of Kansas* (Wichita: Wichita Eagle Press, 1931), pp. 218-19; Zornow, pp. 161-62.

24. Thomas later became associate editor and married Flora, the sister of Mrs. William N. Byers, wife of the editor and publisher. He remained with the *News* until 1904, when he became a professor of history at Colorado A&M College at Fort Collins. He died in 1914. Robert L. Perkin, *The First Hundred Years: An Informal History of Denver and the Rocky Mountain News* (Garden City, N.Y.: Doubleday & Company, 1959), pp. 294, 395. Thomas was fond of southern Colorado and northern New Mexico, and his descriptive articles about stagecoach journeys there are invaluable sources. He signed his articles simply W. R. T., and some of his longer pieces were called "On the Wing." Other shorter, unsigned dispatches are probably his.

25. For the so-called Trinidad War, see Morris F. Taylor, *Trinidad, Colorado Territory* (Trinidad: Trinidad State Junior College, 1966), pp. 60-76.

26. Ibid., p. 69.

27. Robert W. Frazer, *Forts of the West: Military Forts and Presidios and Posts Commonly Called Forts West of the Mississippi River to 1898* (Norman: University of Oklahoma Press, 1965), p. 41.

28. Taylor, p. 71.

29. *Daily Rocky Mountain News*, February 11, 1868, p. 2; Frazer, pp. 39-40, 42.

30. *Daily Rocky Mountain News*, February 11, 1868, p. 2; LeRoy Boyd, *Fort Lyon, Colorado: One Hundred Years of Service* (Colorado Springs, Colo.: H & H Printing Company, n.d.), p. 21.

31. A very ill Kit Carson, who made his home at nearby Boggsville, had gone to Washington in January with the Ute delegation. He had left Fort Lyon in a Southern Overland Mail coach just a few days before the arrival of Thomas and the acting governor. Morris F. Taylor, "Ka-ni-ache," Part 2, *Colorado Magazine*, 44 (spring 1967): 140. Carson died at Fort Lyon on May 29, 1868. His obituary appeared in the first issue of the *Colorado Chieftain* (Pueblo), June 1, 1868, p. 1.

32. *Daily Rocky Mountain News*, February 11, 1868, p. 1; *Colorado Chieftain*, July 16, 1868, p. 3.

33. *Daily Rocky Mountain News*, February 11, 1868, p. 4; Route No. 14020, Star Route Register, Kansas Section, p. 68, Record Group 28, National Archives, Washington, D.C. Hereafter all mail routes will be cited by number, section, and page. Ocate obtained a post office in 1866. Sheldon H. Dike, *The Territorial Post Offices of New Mexico* (Albuquerque: By the Author, 1958), alphabetical listing.

34. *Daily Rocky Mountain News*, April 7, 1868, p. 4.

35. Cahill was discharged in 1869 and took a job with Barlow, Sanderson and Company as a stock tender and weigh master. Luke Cahill, "Recollections of a Plainsman," MSS 13-5a, pp. 12-14, State Historical Society of Colorado Library, Denver.

36. Zornow, p. 137; Margaret Long, *The Smoky Hill Trail* (Denver: W. H. Kistler Stationery Company, 1954), p. 70; Frazer, pp. 56-57.

37. *Colorado Chieftain*, June 25, 1868, p. 2.

38. Frazer, pp. 58-59.

39. *Colorado Chieftain*, June 26, 1868, p. 2; June 18, 1868, p. 3.

40. Route No. 14020, Kansas Section, p. 72.

41. Baughman, pp. 46, 103.

42. *Colorado Chieftain*, June 25, 1868, p. 2.

43. Route No. 14020, Kansas Section, p. 68.

44. Cahill, p. 8.

45. Route No. 14020, Kansas Section, p. 72; *Colorado Chieftain*, June 25, 1868, p. 2.

46. Letter from Barlow, Sanderson and Company to Postmaster General J. A. J. Cresswell, May 1869.

47. Route No. 14020, Kansas Section, p. 72.

48. Jim Berry Pearson, *The Maxwell Grant*, (Norman: University of Oklahoma Press, 1961), p. 26.

49. Route No. 14020, Kansas Section, pp. 70, 72; *Register of Officers, 1869*, p. 813. There was later official recognition of Barlow, Sanderson and Company's transportation of mail over the five-and-one-fourth-mile extension from Virginia City to Elizabethtown and back six times a week at $750 per annum from July 1, 1868 to June 30, 1870. Route No. 14020, Kansas Section, p. 520.

50. Route No. 14020, Kansas Section, pp. 68, 519; Dike, alphabetical listing.

51. *Colorado Chieftain*, August 6, 1868, p. 1. This is interesting because William A. Bell (one of the surveyors) in his *New Tracks in North America: A Journal of Travel and Adventure Whilst Engaged in the Survey for a Southern Railroad to the Pacific Ocean during 1867-8* (London: Chapman & Hall, 1870), pp. 539-41, indicates that Trinidad was bypassed to the northeast.

52. *Colorado Chieftain*, August 6, 1868, p. 1.

53. *The Rocky Mountain Directory and Colorado Gazetteer for 1871* (Denver: S. S. Wallihan & Company, n.d.), p. 128.

54. *New Mexican*, May 12, 1868, p. 2; *Daily Rocky Mountain News*, May 28, 1868, p. 2; Cahill, pp. 10-11; Frank Hall, *History of the State of Colorado* (Chicago: The Blakely Printing Company, 1889), 1:305. By mid-July there were six telegraph stations south of Pueblo: Doyle's Ranch and Trinidad in Colorado, and Maxwell's Ranch, Fort Union, Las Vegas, and Santa Fe in New Mexico. *Colorado Chieftain*, July 23, 1868, p. 3.

55. Named for Major General Philip H. Sheridan, famous Civil War cavalry leader and currently commander of the Military Department of Missouri.

56. Route No. 14020, Kansas Section, p. 72.

57. He was honorably mustered out of military service on January 8, 1866. Francis B. Heitman *Historical Register and Dictionary of the United States Army from its Organization, September 29, 1789, to March 2, 1903* (Washington, D.C.: Government Printing Office, 1903), 1:825.

58. *New Mexican*, June 9, 1868, p. 2; July 21, 1868, p. 1.

59. *Colorado Chieftain*, September 10, 1868, p. 1; September 17, 1868, p. 1; U.S., War Department, *Records of Engagements with Hostile Indians within the Military Division of the Missouri from 1868 to 1882, Lieutenant-General P. H. Sheridan Commanding* (Washington, D.C.: Government Printing Office, 1882), pp. 7-13.

60. Cahill, p. 8.

61. *Records of Engagements*, p. 9.

62. *Colorado Chieftain*, September 3, 1868, p. 1; September 24, 1868, p. 1; October 8, 1868, p. 3; Cahill, p. 5, Post Return from Fort Lyon, September 1868, microcopy no. 617, roll no. 659, National Archives Microfilm Publications, Washington, D.C.

63. Letter from General Penrose to the Assistant Adjutant General, September 19, 1868, Selected Letters Sent by Captain and Brevet Brigadier General Penrose, Records of United States Army Commands, 1784-1871, Record Group 98, National Archives, Washington, D.C. Hereafter cited as Selected Letters.

64. James Brice, *Reminiscences of Ten Years Experience on the Western Plains: How the United States Mails Were Carried Before the Railroads Reached the Santa Fe Trail* (Kansas City, Mo.: n.n., n.d.), pp. 20, 22.

65. *Colorado Chieftain*, September 17, 1868, p. 1.

66. *Records of Engagements*, pp. 11-12, 14-17; George E. Hyde, *Life of George Bent, Written from His Letters*, ed. Savoie Lottinville (Norman: University of Oklahoma Press, 1968), pp. 297-306, 313-22.

67. Drivers and conductors also regularly received $45 per month for their board. Letter from Barlow, Sanderson and Company to Postmaster General J. A. J. Cresswell, May 1869.

68. *New Mexican*, August 4, 1868, p. 1; August 11, 1868, p. 2; August 18, 1868, p. 2.

69. Ibid., September 15, 1868, p. 2.

70. As late as December, however, W. S. Burnett, Southern Overland Mail agent, was unsuccessfully trying to get more and better military escorts from Fort Lyon. Letter from Brevet Lieutenant Colonel R. G. Lay to W. S. Burnett, December 6, 1868, Selected Letters.

71. *New Mexican*, September 29, 1868, p. 2; November 3, 1868, p. 1.

72. A post office was reestablished at Ocate on January 10, 1870, and Ames was the postmaster. Dike, alphabetical listing; Route No. 14020, Kansas Section, p. 519.

73. *Daily Rocky Mountain News*, March 16, 1869, p. 1.

74. Route No. 14020, Kansas Section, pp. 519-20.

75. Letter from Barlow, Sanderson and Company to Postmaster General J. A. J. Cresswell, May 1869.

76. Ibid.

77. Mary Wilhelmine Williams, "John Angel James Cresswell," *Dictionary of American Biography*, ed. Allen Johnson and Dumas Malone (New York: Charles Scribner's Sons, 1930), 4:541-42. Cresswell also greatly improved the transportation of letters by steamship to foreign countries and introduced the penny postcard.

78. Mitford M. Mathews, ed., *A Dictionary of Americanisms on Historical Principles*

(Chicago: University of Chicago Press, 1951), p. 1662.

79. In 1876, Bradley Barlow and Jared Sanderson were called to testify before the House Committee on Post Offices and Post Roads about their alleged use of straw bidding for securing mail contracts during Postmaster General Cresswell's administration. Some of the testimony against Sanderson involved bribery, burned books, and threats. A. Jay Hertz, "Barlow, Sanderson and Company: Corruption Enters the Express," *Western Express* (July 1963), pp. 29-30.

80. *Colorado Chieftain,* July 22, 1869, p. 4.

81. Ibid., June 17, 1869, p. 3. Indians were active on the plains again in the summer of 1869. In late May they carried out a spectacular raid at Sheridan, running off several hundred mules in the sight of the town's population. In June 150 Cheyenne held up a wagon train carrying hides (from Cimarron, New Mexico, to Sheridan) near Fort Lyon, but they took only flour, bacon, sugar, and coffee. Later, bands of Indians were seen along the stage line from Fort Lyon to Sheridan. Ibid., June 3, 1869, p. 3; June 17, 1869, p. 3; *Daily Rocky Mountain News,* June 9, 1869, p. 4.

82. Jerome C. Smiley, *Semi-Centennial History of the State of Colorado* (Chicago: Lewis Publishing Company, 1913), 1:511-12.

83. Members of the congressional party were Senator John Scott of Pennsylvania, Senator Benjamin F. Rice of Arkansas, Representative Daniel J. Morrell of Pennsylvania, and Representative Logan H. Roots of Arkansas. *Colorado Chieftain,* July 15, 1869, p. 3.

84. Ibid., December 9, 1869, p. 3; December 16, 1869, p. 2.

CHAPTER 12

1. *Daily Rocky Mountain News* (Denver), September 1, 1865, p. 4; September 4, 1865, p. 4. The store came to be known popularly as the "76" Store. Ibid., January 30, 1868, p. 4. Jacobs was born in Bavaria in 1834 and came to Denver in 1859; he opened his first mercantile house on Ferry (Eleventh) Street. *Denver Post,* April 30, 1913, p. 14; Frank Hall, *History of the State of Colorado* (Chicago: The Blakely Printing Company, 1890), 2:558.

2. *Daily Rocky Mountain News,* April 3, 1867, p. 1.

3. Ibid., April 12, 1867, p. 2; April 18, 1867, p. 3.

4. Oliver La Farge, *The Autobiography of a Southwestern Town* (Norman: University of Oklahoma Press, 1959), p. 64.

5. "Diary of the Late Joseph Davis—1867," *Chronicle-News* (Trinidad, Colo.), November 30, 1930, p. 4; "At Trinidad—Joseph Davis," Mss P-L354, Bancroft Library, University of California, Berkeley; Lease to Davis and Barraclough, June 23, 1868, Las Animas County (Colo.) Deed Record, 1:210.

6. *Daily Rocky Mountain News,* February 28, 1867, p. 4; *Colorado Chieftain* (Pueblo), October 1, 1868, p. 3.

7. *Denver Daily,* March 23, 1867, p. 4.

8. *Daily Rocky Mountain News,* March 6, 1867, p. 4.

9. Ibid., April 12, 1867, p. 2.

10. *Colorado Chieftain,* July 16, 1868, pp. 2, 3. The first issue of the *Chieftain* was published June 1, 1868.

11. *Daily Colorado Tribune* (Denver), July 10, 1867, p. 2; *Denver Daily,* July 10, 1867, p. 2.

12. Morris F. Taylor, *Trinidad, Colorado Territory* (Trinidad: Trinidad State Junior College, 1966), pp. 60-76.

13. Ibid., pp. 69-70.

14. *Daily Rocky Mountain News,* February 5, 1868, p. 1.

15. Ibid., February 11, 1868, p. 4.

16. Ibid.; Notes on E. J. Hubbard, Samuel W. DeBusk Papers, Trinidad State Junior College, Trinidad, Colo.

17. *Daily Rocky Mountain News,* February 5, 1868, p. 1; Hicklin held a postmaster-

ship at Greenhorn since late 1866. Article by Mrs. T. R. Malone, McClelland Public Library Historical Collection, Pueblo, Colo.

18. *Daily Rocky Mountain News*, May 19, 1868, p. 4.

19. *Morning Light* (Trinidad, Colo.), August 18, 1949, p. 8; Declaration of claim of John M. Odenheimer, Las Animas County Deed Record, 1:50. The cabin is still standing.

20. *Morning Light*, August 18, 1949, p. 8.

21. *Daily Rocky Mountain News*, February 11, 1868, p. 1.

22. Ibid., February 8, 1868, p. 4.

23. Ibid., January 27, 1868, p. 1; January 28, 1868, p. 4; January 30, 1868, p. 4.

24. Mitford M. Mathews, ed., *A Dictionary of Americanisms on Historical Principles* (Chicago: University of Chicago Press, 1951), p. 1772.

25. Nick Eggenhofer, *Wagons, Mules and Men: How the Frontier Moved West* (New York: Hastings House Publishers, 1961), p. 151.

26. *Daily Rocky Mountain News*, February 5, 1868, p. 1.

27. Ibid., May 1, 1868, p. 4.

28. Ibid., February 26, 1868, p. 4; *Colorado Chieftain*, June 1, 1868, p. 3; Las Animas County Deed Record, 1:105-06; Jim Berry Pearson, *The Maxwell Grant* (Norman: University of Oklahoma Press, 1961), pp. 24-25.

29. Six mules were run off from the Santa Clara Station. *Daily Rocky Mountain News*, April 3, 1868, p. 4.

30. Ibid., April 6, 1868, p. 4.

31. Ibid., May 4, 1868, p. 4.

32. An anecdote says that Lieutenant General William Tecumseh Sherman once wrote for a pass over the Denver and Santa Fe line. He was told by Jacobs that if it was worth asking for, it was worth coming for. Amused and intrigued, Sherman called in person while in Denver, and a friendship began between the two men. *Denver Post*, April 30, 1913, p. 14. If there is any substance to the story, it probably happened in September 1868 when Sherman was in Denver. Hall, 1:464. It could have occurred in June, when Sherman was inspecting military posts in Colorado. *Colorado Chieftain*, June 18, 1868, p. 2.

33. *Colorado Chieftain*, June 1 and June 18, 1868, p. 3.

34. U.S., Congress, *Statutes at Large*, 12:158.

35. At this time Jacobs held two contracts northward out of Pueblo. U.S., Congress, House, *Letter from the Postmaster General*, 41st Cong., 2d sess., Ex. Doc. no. 314, serial no. 1427, p. 269; U.S., Department of the Interior, *Register of Officers and Agents, Civil, Military, and Naval, in the Service of the United States on the Thirtieth September, 1869* (Washington, D.C.: Government Printing Office, 1870), p. 876.

36. Original Record 1, Huerfano County, pp. 200-01, County Clerk's Office, Walsenburg, Colo.

37. *Colorado Chieftain*, October 1, 1868, p. 3.

38. *Daily Rocky Mountain News*, February 3, 1868, p. 1.

39. *Colorado Chieftain*, October 1, 1868, p. 3; December 3, 1868, p. 2.

40. Ibid., December 31, 1868, p. 2.

41. Ibid., January 14, 1869, p. 3; *Letter from the Postmaster General*, p. 420; *Register of Officers, 1869*, p. 876.

42. *Colorado Chieftain*, February 4, 1869, p. 3.

43. *Daily Rocky Mountain News*, February 11, 1869, p. 1.

44. Ibid.

45. Ibid.

46. Ibid., February 13, 1869, p. 1.

47. Ibid., February 11, 1869, p. 1.

48. John Bigelow kept the Santa Clara stage station. *Colorado Chieftain*, November 5, 1868, p. 1.

49. *Daily Rocky Mountain News*, February 11, 1868, p. 1.

50. *Colorado Chieftain*, January 7, 1869, p. 3.

51. Ibid., February 18, 1869, p. 3.

52. *Daily Rocky Mountain News,* April 13, 1869, p. 4.

53. Ibid., April 10, 1869, p. 4; *Colorado Chieftain,* April 15, 1869, p. 3.

54. *Daily Rocky Mountain News,* April 10, 1869, p. 4.

55. Ibid.; *Letter from the Postmaster General,* p. 269.

56. *Daily Rocky Mountain News,* May 12, 1869, p. 4.

57. *Colorado Chieftain,* June 10, 1869, p. 3.

58. Ibid., June 17, 1869, p. 3.

59. Ibid., July 8, 1869, p. 3. The *Daily Rocky Mountain News,* July 21, 1869, p. 4, said that the fare for the 105 miles went as low as 50 cents—an implausible figure. A story was told later that several young men from Pueblo, during the last ruthless competition, rode the stage to Trinidad for 25 cents each, while they were in Trinidad, Jacobs went out of business, and it cost them $25 apiece to get back to Pueblo. *Daily Chieftain,* May 11, 1876, p. 4.

60. *Daily Rocky Mountain News,* July 21, 1869, p. 4; August 13, 1869, p. 4. It appears that Abraham Jacobs was thwarted from even a trial transportation of mail over the local Trinidad-Virginia City route, then designated as No. 17022. Thomas J. Barnum was paid $37.50 for recognized service on the route in 1869, out of $150 bid. *Register of Officers, 1869,* p. 876.

61. *Daily Rocky Mountain News,* August 13, 1869, p. 4.

62. Ibid., August 18, 1869, p. 4.

63. Ibid., May 17, 1870, p. 1.

64. Thomas made no complaint about bean soup or dirty towels; perhaps it was a different stopping place, or the cuisine had improved.

65. *Daily Rocky Mountain News,* March 14, 1870, p. 1.

66. Ibid.; *Colorado Chieftain,* April 4, 1870, p. 3.

67. *Daily Rocky Mountain News,* February 10, 1870, p. 4.

68. Ibid., June 22, 1870, p. 4; June 24, 1870, p. 4.

69. Ibid., October 11, 1869, p. 4; July 3, 1870, p. 4.

CHAPTER 13

1. *Colorado Chieftain* (Pueblo), February 24, 1870, p. 3; March 24, 1870, p. 3.

2. Colfax County was created in January, 1869. Ralph Emerson Twitchell, *The Leading Facts of New Mexican History* (Albuquerque: Horn & Wallace Publishers, 1963), 2:415 n. 340.

3. *Daily Rocky Mountain News* (Denver), March 14, 1870, p. 1.

4. The fort was abandoned and auctioned to Lucien B. Maxwell in 1868. Robert W. Frazer, *Forts of the West: Military Forts and Presidios and Posts Commonly Called Forts West of the Mississippi River to 1898* (Norman: University of Oklahoma Press, 1965), p. 104.

5. *Daily Rocky Mountain News,* March 22, 1870, p. 2.

6. Robert M. Utley, *Fort Union National Monument, New Mexico* (Washington, D.C.: Government Printing Office, 1962), pp. 34-37, 64.

7. *Daily Rocky Mountain News,* April 7, 1870, p. 1.

8. Bill Stockton, "Frontier Stage Stop," *New Mexico Magazine* (February 1963), pp. 8-10; Kenyon Riddle, *Records and Maps of the Old Santa Fe Trail* (Raton, N.M.: The Raton Daily Range, 1949), pp. 61-65.

9. *Daily Rocky Mountain News,* April 7, 1870, p. 1; April 12, 1870, p. 1.

10. The surname is given in Notes from Duane D. Finch, Samuel W. DeBusk Papers, Trinidad State Junior College Library, Trinidad, Colo.

11. *Daily Rocky Mountain News,* April 7, 1870, p. 1.

12. John P. Clum, "Santa Fe in the '70s," *New Mexico Historical Review,* 2 (October 1927) : 382.

13. *Daily Rocky Mountain News,* April 7, 1870, p. 1.

NOTES

14. Ibid., April 12, 1870, p. 1; U.S., Bureau of the Census, *Ninth Census of the United States, 1870: Population*, 1:95, 206.
15. Elsewhere, another driver named Frank Drake was put in the same category. *Daily Rocky Mountain News*, April 4, 1870, p. 1.
16. *Daily Rocky Mountain News*, April 12, 1870, p. 1; *Colorado Chieftain*, March 10, 1870, p. 3; Record Book No. 1, Las Animas (Colo.) County Commissioners, pp. 67-68.
17. *Daily Rocky Mountain News*, April 12, 1870, p. 1.
18. Ibid., May 17, 1870, p. 1.
19. *Colorado Chieftain*, June 2, 1870, p. 3; October 13, 1870, p. 3.
20. Ibid., July 14, 1870, p. 3.
21. Ibid., August 11, 1870, p. 3.
22. *Daily Rocky Mountain News*, July 14, 1870, p. 4.
23. U.S., Department of the Interior, *Register of Officers and Agents, Civil, Military, and Naval, in the Service of the United States on the Thirtieth September, 1871* (Washington, D.C.: Government Printing Office, 1872), p. 493.
24. *Daily Rocky Mountain News*, July 9, 1870, p. 4; John and Lillian Theobald, *Arizona Territory Post Offices and Postmasters*, (Phoenix: Arizona Historical Foundation, 1966), p. 39.
25. *The Rocky Mountain Directory and Colorado Gazetteer for 1871* (Denver: S. S. Wallihan & Company, n.d.), p. 125. Kansas City was still a terminus in a sense, because the Kansas Pacific Railroad in and out of Kansas City was a major connection for the stage line, and Barlow, Sanderson and Company still held mail contracts out of Kansas City. The source cited above gives Griffin's name as Griffith—an error. Griffin had been associated with Barlow and Sanderson since 1862. *New Mexican*, August 13, 1872, p. 1. Stone's first association was with the old Santa Fe Stage Company at Junction City, Kansas, in 1866 (*Junction City Weekly Union*, December 1, 1866, p. 3). He had succeeded Captain Charles H. Reynolds as paymaster.
26. A native of New York State, Lewis Barnum went to work for the stage line to Santa Fe in 1862, the same year that his brother Thomas did. Mrs. Fred Bullen, comp., "Early History of Pueblo" Scrapbook, 1:9, McClelland Public Library, Pueblo, Colo. *Daily Chieftain*, January 15, 1876, p. 4; *Register of Officers, 1867*, p. 708.
27. *Colorado Chieftain*, November 17, 1870, p. 2; *Daily Rocky Mountain News*, May 7, 1870, p. 1; Frost had previously been a driver. T. F. Dawson Scrapbooks, 6 part 3: p. 33, State Historical Society of Colorado Library, Denver.
28. *Rocky Mountain Directory*, p. 125.
29. *Colorado Chieftain*, October 20, 1870, p. 3.
30. *Daily Rocky Mountain News*, October 15, 1870, p. 4.
31. The lease was for four years at $4 per year. J. L. Sanderson's name was erroneously recorded as Jubal G. Sanderson. Miscellaneous Record Book A, Colfax County, New Mexico, pp. 148-51.
32. Jim Berry Pearson, *The Maxwell Grant* (Norman: University of Oklahoma Press, 1961), p. 56.
33. *Daily Rocky Mountain News*, October 19, 1870, p. 4; Notes from Duane D. Finch, DeBusk Papers.
34. *Daily Rocky Mountain News*, November 8, 1870, p. 4.
35. Ibid., December 11, 1870, p. 4.
36. Ibid., October 19, 1870, p. 4.
37. Ibid., February 28, 1871, p. 4.
38. Finch, who became the Southern Overland Mail agent at Trinidad, went to work for J. L. Sanderson in Kansas City in 1866. Barlow and Sanderson used him on their mail stage lines in Missouri and Fort Scott, Kansas. Because Finch wanted to move west, out of earshot of a locomotive's whistle, he was sent to Colorado to lay out the new portion of the line. He reached Trinidad on April 5. Notes from Duane D. Finch, DeBusk Papers.

39. Ibid.; Margaret Long, *The Santa Fe Trail* (Denver: W. H. Kistler Stationery Company, 1954), pp. 192, 199-200.

40. Herbert O. Brayer, *William Blackmore: Early Financing of the Denver & Rio Grande Railway and Ancillary Land Companies, 1871-1878* (Denver: Bradford-Robinson, 1949), p. 25.

41. Henry Pickering Walker, *The Wagonmasters: High Plains Freighting From the Earliest Days of the Santa Fe Trail to 1880* (Norman: University of Oklahoma Press, 1966), p. 283.

42. *Daily Rocky Mountain News,* February 28, 1871, p. 4; Las Animas County Deed Record, Vol. 1, *passim.*

43. *Weekly New Mexican,* April 11, 1871, p. 1; April 18, 1871, p. 1. Barlow, Sanderson and Company still had mail contracts on Routes No. 10688 and 10689 in Missouri. *Register of Officers, 1871,* p. 443; *Colorado Chieftain,* April 20, 1871, p. 3; Notes from Duane D. Finch, DeBusk Papers.

44. *Daily Rocky Mountain News,* April 29, 1871, p. 1. The Santa Fe *New Mexican,* April 11, 1871, p. 1, said the branch line was reduced to weekly service, which appears to be an error.

45. Notes from Duane D. Finch, DeBusk Papers; *Chronicle-News* (Trinidad, Colo.), August 25, 1929, p. 4.

46. Notes from Duane D. Finch, DeBusk Papers.

47. *Daily Rocky Mountain News,* December 20, 1870, p. 2. The piece was signed Jay G. Kay.

48. S. W. DeBusk, *Some Items of Early History* (Trinidad, Colo.: Monitor Art Printery, 1901), p. 3.

49. Notes from Duane D. Finch, DeBusk Papers.

50. He was commandant from 1871 to 1873. Twitchell, 2:428 n. 353.

51. Notes from Duane D. Finch, DeBusk Papers.

52. *Weekly New Mexican,* September 19, 1871, p. 1.

53. Ibid., October 10, 1871, p. 1.

54. *Daily Rocky Mountain News,* October 20, 1871, p. 4; October 27, 1871, p. 1; November 8, 1871, p. 1; Oliver La Farge, *The Autobiography of a Southwestern Town* (Norman: University of Oklahoma Press, 1959), p. 73, quoting the *Weekly New Mexican,* October 16, 1871.

55. *Daily Rocky Mountain News,* October 21, 1871, p. 4; La Farge, p. 73, quoting the *Weekly New Mexican,* October 16, 1871.

56. *Daily Rocky Mountain News,* October 31, 1871, p. 1.

57. Ibid., September 30, 1871, p. 1; Jerome C. Smiley, *Semi-Centennial History of the State of Colorado* (Chicago: Lewis Publishing Company, 1913), 1:447.

58. *Colorado Chieftain,* November 2, 1871, p. 1.

59. Frances M. A. Roe, *Army Letters from an Officer's Wife, 1871-1888* (New York: D. Appleton & Co., 1909), p. 2.

60. See Nick Eggenhofer, *Wagons, Mules and Men: How the Frontier Moved West* (New York: Hastings House Publishers, 1961), p. 162.

61. Clum, p. 381.

62. *Weekly New Mexican,* August 13, 1872, p. 1.

63. Notes by Arthur Milliken, Carnegie Public Library Historical Collection, Trinidad, Colo. Milliken also recorded that Stokes, a thrifty man, loaned money at 2 percent through Duane Finch, the Barlow, Sanderson agent at Trinidad. One time Stokes called in his money (about $1300) to take a trip to his native England, but in Denver he went on a three-day drunk and lost his bank roll.

64. Hugh and Evelyn Burnett, "Foster's Place," *The Brand Book of the Denver Westerners (1964),* ed. Francis B. Rizzari (Boulder, Colo.: Johnson Publishing Company, 1965), pp. 171-72.

65. *Daily Rocky Mountain News,* November 23, 1871, p. 1.

66. William Frank Zornow, *Kansas: A History of the Jayhawk State,* (Norman: Uni-

versity of Oklahoma Press, 1957), pp. 162-63; U.S., War Department, *Records of Engagements with Hostile Indians within the Military Department of the Missouri from 1868 to 1882, Lieutenant-General P. H. Sheridan Commanding* (Washington, D.C.: Government Printing Office, 1882), p. 34.

67. LeRoy R. Hafen, ed., *Colorado and its People: A Narrative and Topical History of the Centennial State* (New York: Lewis Historical Publishing Company, 1948), 1:325-28.

68. *Daily Rocky Mountain News*, January 13, 1871, p. 1.

69. LeRoy R. Hafen and Carl Coke Rister, *Western America: The Exploration, Settlement, and Development of the Region Beyond the Mississippi* (Englewood Cliffs, N.J.: Prentice-Hall, Inc., 1950), pp. 544-45.

70. *Records of Engagements*, p. 34.

71. The agency for the Mohuache Ute and Jicarilla Apache was moved from Taos to Cimarron in 1861. Morris F. Taylor, "Fort Wise, *Colorado Magazine*, 43 (fall 1966): 286-87.

72. *Weekly New Mexican*, June 4, 1872, p. 2.

73. *Daily Rocky Mountain News*, May 28, 1872, p. 4; May 29, 1872, p. 4.

74. *Colorado Chieftain*, September 19, 1872, p. 3. The Sioux Chief Red Cloud and his band had been given permission to hunt buffalo as far south as Fort Zarah on the Arkansas. Ibid., April 13, 1871, p. 2.

75. *Daily Rocky Mountain News*, September 18, 1872, p. 1.

76. Ibid., September 18, 1872, p. 1.

77. *Daily Chieftain*, September 21, 1872, p. 4; October 1, 1872, p. 2.

78. *Weekly New Mexican*, May 21, 1872, p. 2; Hafen, 1:327.

79. *Weekly New Mexican*, August 20, 1872, p. 1.

80. Ibid., September 3, 1872, p. 2.

81. Ibid.

82. *Daily Rocky Mountain News*, September 3, 1872, p. 4.

CHAPTER 14

1. *Colorado Chieftain* (Pueblo), January 3, 1873, p. 3.

2. *Weekly New Mexican* (Santa Fe), January 7, 1873, p. 2; January 14, 1873, p. 1.

3. Ibid.

4. Ibid., February 4, 1873, p. 1.

5. Ibid., January 14, 1873, p. 2; January 21, 1873, p. 2; January 28, 1873, p. 1.

6. Ibid.

7. Ibid., April 1, 1873, p. 2.

8. *Colorado Chieftain*, January 3, 1873, p. 3.

9. *Weekly New Mexican*, January 14, 1873, p. 2; January 28, 1873, p. 2.

10. *Colorado Chieftain*, January 30, 1873, p. 2.

11. John and Lillian Theobald, *Arizona Territory Post Offices & Postmasters* (Phoenix: Arizona Historical Foundation, 1961), p. 69.

12. James Marshall, *Santa Fe: The Railroad That Built an Empire* (New York: Random House, 1945), p. 61; *Trinidad* (Colo.) *Enterprise*, July 25, 1873, p. 4.

13. *Las Animas* (Colo.), *Leader*, May 23, 1873, p. 3.

14. Ibid., July 12, 1873, p. 3.

15. *Las Animas Leader*, September 13, 1873, p. 3.

16. Ibid., September 27, 1873, p. 2; October 4, 1873, p. 3; October 18, 1873, pp. 2, 3; *Weekly New Mexican*, October 1, 1873, p. 2. The Plains tribes and the Ute were very active all over southern Colorado that summer. *Daily Chieftain* (Pueblo, Colo.), July 27, 1873, p. 4; September 27, 1873, p. 1; October 8, 1873, p. 1; October 10, 1873, p. 2.

17. *Las Animas Leader*, November 1, 1873, p. 2, and in subsequent weekly issues into February 1874. See also Herbert O. Brayer, *William Blackmore* (Denver: Bradford-Robinson, 1949), pp. 142-44.

18. Sometime in 1872 Barlow, Sanderson and Company ceased to exist, and the firm became Barlow and Sanderson Company after the withdrawal of Thomas and Lewis Barnum. *Daily Chieftain*, May 11, 1876, p. 4. The above may be slightly in error; at least, Lewis Barnum remained in the employ of the company until his death in 1876.

19. *Las Animas Leader*, July 12, 1873, p. 3. This probably was the same A. L. Carpenter, who was a driver for Barlow and Sanderson as early as 1862. T. F. Dawson Scrapbooks, 14:141, a clipping from the *Kansas City* (Mo.) *Star*, September 23, 1906, Historical Society of Colorado Library, Denver.

20. *Daily Chieftain*, November 13, 1873, p. 2, observed that the Cheyenne claimed the site of West Las Animas under the Treaty of Fort Wise, 1861. The Arapaho shared the claim.

21. *Las Animas Leader*, October 18, 1873, p. 3; October 26, 1873, p. 3; November 1, 1873, p. 2.

22. *Weekly New Mexican*, October 21, 1873, p. 2.

23. *Trinidad Enterprise*, January 9, 1874, p. 3.

24. LeRoy R. Hafen and Carl Coke Rister, *Western America: The Exploration, Settlement, and Development of the Region Beyond the Mississippi* (Englewood Cliffs, N.J.: Prentice-Hall, Inc., 1950), p. 526; L. L. Waters, *Steel Trails to Santa Fe* (Lawrence: University of Kansas Press, 1950), p. 48; Marshall, p. 64.

25. Brayer, 2:164.

26. *Las Animas Leader*, June 5, 1874, p. 3; December 19, 1873, p. 2; LeRoy R. Hafen, ed., *Colorado and its People: A Narrative and Topical History of the Centennial State* (New York: Lewis Historical Publishing Company, 1948), 1:337.

27. *Trinidad Enterprise*, May 21, 1874, p. 2; July 23, 1874, p. 3.

28. Ibid., May 21, 1874, p. 2.

29. Ibid., July 16, 1874, p. 3; September 4, 1874, p. 3.

30. Ibid., May 21, 1874, p. 3; October 17, 1874, p. 3.

31. Ibid., May 21, 1874, p. 3.

32. Ibid., July 25, 1873, p. 2; *Las Animas Leader*, August 16, 1873, p. 4.

33. Ibid., July 16, 1874, pp. 2, 3; all weekly issues of the *Leader*, July 10 through August 14, 1874.

34. Robert M. Utley, *Fort Union National Monument, New Mexico* (Washington, D.C.: Government Printing Office, 1962), pp. 46-49; U. S., War Department, *Record of Engagements, with Hostile Indians within the Military Department of the Missouri from 1868 to 1882, Lieutenant-General P. H. Sheridan Commanding* (Washington, D.C.: Government Printing Office, 1882), pp. 41-44.

35. *Trinidad Enterprise*, January 9, 1874, p. 3; Morris F. Taylor, *Trinidad, Colorado Territory* (Trinidad: Trinidad State Junior College, 1966), p. 138.

36. *Daily Chieftain*, February 14, 1874, p. 4.

37. Ibid., June 7, 1874, pp. 3-4.

38. *Trinidad Enterprise*, September 5, 1874, p. 3.

39. *Daily Chieftain*, October 6, 1874, p. 4.

40. *Las Animas Leader*, December 18, 1874, p. 3.

41. *Trinidad Enterprise*, January 14, 1875, p. 2; Frank Hall, *History of the State of Colorado* (Chicago: The Blakely Printing Company, 1895), 4:49.

42. *Las Animas Leader*, December 18, 1874, p. 3.

43. Ibid., October 30, 1874, p. 3.

44. Ibid., February 5, 1875, p. 2.

45. Ibid.

46. Ibid., August 20, 1875, p. 2; Ernst Kohlberg's letter to his mother, December 1875, Ernst Kohlberg Papers, American Jewish Archives, Hebrew Union College, Cincinnati, Ohio.

47. *Las Animas Leader*, March 26, 1875, p. 3; April 9, 1875, p. 3; May 14, 1875, p. 3; November 5, 1875, p. 3.

48. *Colorado Chronicle* (Trinidad), February 18, 1875, p. 2; January 7, 1875, p. 3.

49. Brayer, 2:173-80.

50. *Las Animas Leader*, June 12, 1875, p. 2.

51. About a month later a flood demolished the Alkali station and half of its stone corral. Ibid., September 14, 1875, p. 2.

52. James Benson was the first postmaster at the station.

53. *Las Animas Leader*, August 20, 1875, p. 2.

54. South Pueblo was one of the major promotional developments of the Central Colorado Improvement Company in association with the Denver and Rio Grande Railway. See Brayer, 2:219-30.

55. In Howard Louis Conard, *"Uncle Dick" Wootton, The Pioneer Frontiersman of the Rocky Mountain Region: An Account of the Adventures and Thrilling Experiences of the Most Noted American Hunter, Trapper, Guide, Scout, and Indian Fighter Now Living* (Chicago: W. E. Dibble and Company, 1890), pp. 433-36, there is some information about Wootton's station and a description of a stage robbery by "knights of the road" having the interesting aliases of "Chuckle Luck" and "Magpie." There is no indication of when the incident happened.

56. This was evidently part of the campaign to reelect Stephen Benton Elkins as New Mexico delegate to Congress. He did not seek the honor and was traveling in Europe at the time, but was chosen anyway. He accepted the verdict of the voters. Ralph Emerson Twitchell, *The Leading Facts of New Mexican History* (Albuquerque: Horn & Wallace, Publishers, 1963), 2:402, n. 237.

57. *Las Animas Leader*, August 27, 1875, p. 2.

58. Letter from Ernst Kohlberg to his mother, December 1875, Kohlberg Papers.

59. William H. Rideing, *A-Saddle in the Wild West: A Glimpse of Travel among the Mountains, Lava Beds, Sand Deserts, Adobe Towns, Indian Reservations, and Ancient Pueblos of Southern Colorado, New Mexico, and Arizona* (New York: D. Appleton and Co., 1879), pp. 156-65.

60. Rideing, pp. 158-63.

61. Ibid., p. 158.

62. U.S., Department of the Interior, *Register of Officers and Agents, Civil, Military, and Naval in the Service of the United States on the Thirtieth September, 1875* (Washington, D.C.: Government Printing Office, 1876), p. 620.

63. Ibid., *1873*, pp. 460, 501, 508.

64. Hall, 4:243; *Daily Chieftain*, December 28, 1875, p. 4. Construction was actually carried on by the subsidiary Pueblo and Arkansas Valley Railroad Company.

65. *Daily Chieftain*, December 18, 1875, p. 4.

66. Ibid., December 21, 1875, p. 4.

CHAPTER 15

1. *Las Animas* (Colo.) *Leader*, January 28, 1876, p. 3.

2. *Daily Chieftain* (Pueblo, Colo.), December 28, 1875, p. 4.

3. Ibid., February 24, 1876, p. 4; February 27, 1876, p. 4.

4. Herbert O. Brayer, *William Blackmore: Early Financing of the Denver & Rio Grande Railway and Ancillary Land Companies, 1871-1878*, 2 vols. (Denver: Bradford-Robinson, 1949), 2:188; *Daily Chieftain*, December 28, 1875, p. 4; February 9, 1876, p. 4; March 18, 1876, p. 3.

5. Ibid., January 15, 1876, p. 4; LeRoy R. Hafen, ed., *Colorado and its People: A Narrative Topical History of the Centennial State* (New York: Lewis Historical Publishing Company, 1948), 1:338.

6. *Western Express*, 5 (October 1955): illustration following p. 11.

7. *Daily Chieftain*, January 15, 1876, p. 4.

8. *Las Animas Leader*, March 24, 1876, p. 3. "Colonel" Sanderson went to West Las Animas shortly after hearings of the House Committee on Post Offices and Post Roads in Washington, in which strong allegations of bribery were leveled against Barlow and

Sanderson in obtaining western mail contracts during the administration of Postmaster General Cresswell (who had resigned in 1874). Bradley Barlow was called to testify particularly about a contract for the mail line between Reading, California, and Roseburg, Oregon, but it appears that questions were raised about other contracts as well. One witness stated that there were three cases of bribery—giving details—and he said that Sanderson told him the company's books had been burned. A. Jay Hertz, "Barlow, Sanderson and Company: Corruption Enters the Express," *Western Express* (July 1963), pp. 29-30, quoting the *Yreka* (California) *Union* of March 25, 1876. Colonel Sanderson's son, J. L. Sanderson, Jr., who had been agent at West Las Animas, was no longer there because of illness. He was succeeded by Ed Place, and John King became messenger. *Las Animas Leader*, November 5, 1875, p. 3.

9. Ibid., March 24, 1876, p. 3; *Daily Chieftain*, March 19, 1876, p. 4.

10. *Daily Chieftain*, April 12, 1876, p. 4.

11. *Las Animas Leader*, April 28, 1876, p. 2.

12. Brayer, 2:236.

13. *Daily Chieftain*, May 11, 1876, p. 4; July 6, 1876, p. 1; Brayer, 2:189-90, 197-200.

14. Percy Stanley Fritz, *Colorado, the Centennial State*, (New York: Prentice-Hall, Inc., 1941), pp. 236-37.

15. *Las Animas Leader*, May 19, 1876, p. 2.

16. *Daily Chieftain*, May 11, 1876, p. 4; May 13, 1876, p. 4; "The Abbotts—Early Day Recollections," *Chronicle-News* (Trinidad, Colo.), December 29, 1929, p. 4.

17. *Weekly New Mexican* (Santa Fe), August 1, 1876, p. 1.

18. *Daily Chieftain*, August 30, 1876, p. 3; September 6, 1876, p. 4.

19. *Weekly New Mexican*, September 5, 1876, p. 1. Transportation of mail by buckboard south of Santa Fe had been going on for over a year. Oliver La Farge, *The Autobiography of a Southwestern Town* (Norman: University of Oklahoma Press, 1959), pp. 90-91, quoting the *Weekly New Mexican*, July 12, 1875.

20. *Weekly New Mexican*, September 5, 1876, p. 1.

21. Ibid., February 15, 1876, p. 1; May 1, 1877, p. 2.

22. Ibid., June 13, 1876, p. 1.

23. Ibid., August 22, 1876, p. 1; November 21, 1876, p. 1; February 13, 1877, p. 1.

24. Ibid., August 22, 1876, p. 1; John and Lillian Theobald, *Arizona Territory Post Offices & Postmasters* (Phoenix: Arizona Historical Foundation, 1961), p. 40.

25. *Weekly New Mexican*, June 26, 1877, p. 2; Brayer, 2:201-08.

26. *Weekly New Mexican*, September 27, 1877, p. 1; *Daily Chieftain*, December 8, 1877, p. 2.

27. *Weekly New Mexican*, January 1, 1878, p. 2; May 1, 1877, p. 2; May 8, 1877, p. 2; Luther E. Bean, *Land of the Blue Sky People: A Story of the San Luis Valley* (Monte Vista, Colo.: *Monte Vista Journal*, 1964), p. 66; William A. Keleher, *Violence in Lincoln County, 1869-1881* (Albuquerque: University of New Mexico Press, 1957), p. 303.

28. *Daily Chieftain*, September 19, 1877, p. 2; October 14, 1877, p. 2; October 16, 1877, p. 2; Bean, p. 66; Ellen F. Walrath, "Stagecoach Holdups in the San Luis Valley," *Colorado Magazine*, 14 (January 1937): 27-28.

29. *Weekly New Mexican*, April 6, 1878, p. 2.

30. Ibid., February 23, 1878, p. 2. There are numerous references in the *New Mexican* to SOM employees booked at the Exchange.

31. For a biographical sketch of Dodge, see Jerome C. Smiley, *Semi-Centennial History of the State of Colorado* (Chicago: Lewis Publishing Company, 1913), 2:51.

32. *Weekly New Mexican*, April 6, 1878, p. 2; April 13, 1878, p. 2; May 18, 1878, p. 2.

33. A well-known conductor at this time was James Olney, *Daily Advertiser* (Trinidad, Colo.), March 5, 1905, p. 1. And also there was H. C. Carson, inevitably known as "Kit." *Weekly New Mexican*, October 22, 1872, p. 1.

34. *Weekly New Mexican*, April 4, 1878, p. 2.

35. Ibid., May 18, 1878, p. 2.

36. Ibid., September 7, 1878, p. 2; August 23, 1879, p. 2; *Daily Chieftain*, November 8, 1877, p. 2.

38. *Trinidad* (Colo.) *Enterprise*, October 11, 1878, p. 4.

39. James Marshall, *Santa Fe: The Railroad that Built an Empire* (New York: Random House, 1945), p. 141; Notes from Duane D. Finch, Samuel W. DeBusk Papers, Trinidad State Junior College Library, Trinidad, Colo.

40. *Weekly New Mexican*, February 15, 1879, p. 2; March 1, 1879, p. 2; March 15, 1879, p. 2.

41. Keleher, p. 167. For a description and pictures of the buckboard see Nick Eggenhofer, *Wagons, Mules and Men: How the Frontier Moved West* (New York: Hastings House Publishers, 1961), pp. 131-33, 136, 166-67.

42. *Daily Chieftain*, October 19, 1877, p. 2; September 22, 1878, p. 2; Frank Hall, *History of the State of Colorado* (Chicago: The Blakely Printing Company, 1895), 4:83.

43. *Daily Chieftain*, September 20, 1880, p. 4; Hafen, 1:444.

44. *Weekly New Mexican*, August 16, 1879, p. 2.

45. Ibid., August 23, 1879, p. 2.

46. Ibid.; Notes from Duane D. Finch, DeBusk Papers. Finch said he drove the last stagecoach from Otero on July 28, an obvious error of recollection. According to Marshall, p. 398, the railroad into Las Vegas became operational on July 4, and Ralph Emerson Twitchell, *The Leading Facts of New Mexican History* (Albuquerque: Horn & Wallace, Publishers, 1963), 2:426, says the first passenger service opened to Las Vegas on July 7.

47. Howard Roberts Lamar, *The Far Southwest, 1846-1912: A Territorial History* (New Haven: Yale University Press, 1966), pp. 463-64; Odie B. Faulk, *Land of Many Frontiers: A History of the American Southwest* (New York: Oxford University Press, 1968), pp. 221-22.

48. *Weekly New Mexican*, February 22, 1879, p. 3.

49. Calvin Horn, *New Mexico's Troubled Years: The Story of the Early Territorial Governors* (Albuquerque: Horn & Wallace, Publishers, 1963), pp. 109, 118; Twitchell, 2:392, 410.

50. *Weekly New Mexican*, August 23, 1879, p. 2.

51. Ibid., January 31, 1880, p. 2.

52. Horn, p. 217.

EPILOGUE

1. William H. Ryus, *The Second William Penn: A True Account of Incidents that Happened Along the Old Santa Fe Trail in the Sixties* (Kansas City, Mo.: Frank T. Riley Publishing Company, 1913), p. 89.

2. *Biographical Directory of the American Congress, 1774-1961* (Washington, D.C.: Government Printing Office, 1961), pp. 219, 516; *St. Albans* (Vt.) *Daily Messenger and Advertiser*, November 4, 1889.

Bibliography

MANUSCRIPTS

National Archives, Washington, D.C.
Record Group 28, "Records of the Post Office Department"
Record of Appointment of Postmasters
Star Route Registers, 1850-68
Record Group 29, "Records of the Bureau of Census"
Ninth Census of the United States, 1870
Record Group 75, "Records of the Bureau of Indian Affairs"
Office of Indian Affairs, Letters Received, 1824-81, Microcopy 234, Roll 878, National Archives Microfilm Publications
Record Group 94, "Army-Navy Branch"
Office of the Adjutant General, Selected Letters Received, 1853-55
Record Group 98, "Records of U.S. Army Commands"
Selected Letters Sent by Brevet Brigadier General Penrose, 1868-69
Record Group 393, "Records of United States Continental Commands"
Department of the Missouri, Letters Sent, 1859-60
Returns from United States Military Posts, 1800-1916
Post Returns of Fort Wise, Microcopy 617, Roll 659, National Archives Microfilm Publications

Other Depositories
Barlow, Sanderson and Company, MS letter, State Historical Society of Colorado Library, Denver.
Brief for Complainants, Hall vs. Huffaker, Circuit Court of the United States for the District of Kansas. Kansas State Historical Society, Topeka.
Cahill, Luke, "Recollections of a Plainsman," MS, State Historical Society of Colorado Library, Denver.
Civil Works Administration Interviews Collection, State Historical Society of Colorado Library, Denver.
Cragin Collection, Pioneers' Museum, Colorado Springs, Colo.
T. S. Dawson Collection, State Historical Society of Colorado Library, Denver.
Samuel W. DeBusk Papers, Trinidad State Junior College Library, Trinidad, Colo.
"Early History of Pueblo" Collection, McClelland Public Library, Pueblo, Colo.

cini-BIBLIOGRAPHY

Ernst Kohlberg Papers, American Jewish Archives, Hebrew Union College, Cincinnati.
Local History Collection, Carnegie Public Library, Trinidad, Colo.
Way Bill for Star Route No. 12851, New Mexico State Records and Archives Center, Santa Fe.

DOCUMENTS

U.S. Congressional Documents

Report of the Secretary of War, 31st Cong., 1st sess., Senate Ex. Doc. No. 26 (Serial 554).

Letter from the Postmaster General, 32nd Cong., 1st sess., House Ex. Doc. No. 101 (Serial 644).

Memorial of the New Mexico Legislature, 33rd Cong., 1st sess., House Miscellaneous Doc. No. 47 (Serial 741).

Letter from the Postmaster General, 33rd Cong., 2d sess., House Ex. Doc. No. 86 (Serial 789).

House Report No. 299, 34th Cong., 1st sess. Reprinted as Pamphlet V. Topeka: Kansas State Historical Society Library.

Letter from the Postmaster General, 35th Cong., 2d sess., House Ex. Doc. No. 109 (Serial 1013).

Letter from the Postmaster General, 37th Cong., 2d sess., House Ex. Doc. No. 37 (Serial 1139).

Message of the President of the United States, 40th Cong., 2d sess., Senate Ex. Doc. No. 1.

Letter from the Postmaster General, 41st Cong., 2d sess., House Ex. Doc. No. 314 (Serial 1427).

Other U.S. Government Documents

Abel, Annie Heloise. *The Official Correspondence of James S. Calhoun while Indian Agent at Santa Fe and Superintendent of Indian Affairs in New Mexico*. Washington: Government Printing Office, 1915.

Biographical Directory of the American Congress, 1774-1961. Washington: Government Printing Office, 1961.

Heitman, Francis B. *Historical Register and Dictionary of the United States Army, From Its Organization September 29, 1789, to March 2, 1903*. 2 vols. Washington: Government Printing Office, 1903.

Kappler, Charles J. *Indian Affairs: Laws and Treaties*. 2 vols. Washington: Government Printing Office, 1904.

Miller, Hunter, ed. *Treaties and Other International Acts of the United States of America*. 20 vols. Washington: Government Printing Office, 1933.

Records of Engagements with Hostile Indians within the Military Division of the Missouri from 1868 to 1882, Lieutenant-General P. H. Sheridan, Commanding. Washington: Government Printing Office, 1882.

Register of Officers and Agents, Civil, Military, and Naval, in the Service of the United States. Washington: Government Printing Office, 1868, 1870, 1872.

Report of the Commissioner of Indian Affairs, 1859. Washington: George W. Bowman, Printer, 1860.

Report of the Commissioner of Indian Affairs, 1861. Washington: George W. Bowman, Printer, 1861.

229

Report of the Commissioner of Indian Affairs, 1864. Washington: George W. Bowman, Printer, 1865.

Report of the Postmaster General, 1865. Washington: Government Printing Office, 1865.

Report of the Postmaster General, 1867. Washington: Government Printing Office, 1867.

United States Statutes at Large, vols. 5, 9, 10, 11, 12.

State Documents

Colorado, *Session Laws,* 1865

Colorado, *Session Laws,* 1866

Local Government Records

Colfax County (New Mexico) Deed Record, Raton, N.M.

Las Animas County (Colorado) Deed Record, Trinidad, Colo.

Record Book, Las Animas County Commissioners, Trinidad, Colo.

NEWSPAPERS

Advertiser, Trinidad, Colorado

Border Star, Westport, Missouri

Canon City Times, Colorado Territory

Canon Times, Canon City, Jefferson Territory

Chronicle-News, Trinidad, Colorado

Colorado Chieftain, Pueblo, Colorado

Colorado Chronicle, Trinidad, Colorado Territory

Colorado Tribune, Denver, Colorado Territory

Council Grove Press, Kansas

Denver Daily, Colorado Territory

Denver Gazette, Colorado Territory

Junction City Union, Kansas

Kansas City Daily Journal of Commerce, Missouri

Kansas City Daily Western Journal of Commerce, Missouri

Kansas City Enquirer and Star, Missouri

Kansas City Enterprise, Missouri

Kansas City Times, Missouri

Kansas Press, Council Grove, Kansas Territory

Las Animas Leader, Colorado Territory

Missouri Republican, St. Louis, Missouri

Morning Light, Trinidad, Colorado

New Mexican, Santa Fe, New Mexico Territory

New York Daily Times, New York

Rocky Mountain News, Denver, Colorado Territory

St. Albans Daily Messenger and Advertiser, St. Albans, Vermont

Santa Fe Gazette, New Mexico Territory

Santa Fe Republican, New Mexico Territory

Trinidad Enterprise, Colorado Territory

BOOKS AND PAMPHLETS

Adams, Ramon F. *Western Words: A Dictionary of the American West.* 2d ed., rev. Norman: University of Oklahoma Press, 1968.

Bandel, Eugene. *Frontier Life in the Army, 1854-1861.* Southwest Historical Series, vol. 2. Edited by Ralph P. Bieber. Glendale, Calif.: Arthur H. Clark Co., 1932.

Banning, William and George Hugh. *Six Horses.* The Century Company, 1930.

Baughman, Robert W. *Kansas Post Offices, May 29, 1828—August 3, 1961.* Topeka: Kansas Postal History Society, 1961.

Bean, Luther E. *Land of the Blue Sky People: A Story of the San Luis Valley.* Monte Vista, Colo.: Monte Vista Journal, 1964.

Bearss, Ed and Arrell, M. Gibson. *Fort Smith: Little Gibraltar on the Arkansas.* Norman: University of Oklahoma Press, 1969.

Bell, William A. *New Tracks in North America: A Journal of Travel and Adventure Whilst Engaged in the Survey for a Southern Railroad to the Pacific Ocean during 1867-8.* London: Chapman and Hall, 1870; reprinted, Albuquerque: Horn and Wallace, 1965.

Berthrong, Donald, J. *The Southern Cheyennes.* Norman: University of Oklahoma Press, 1963.

Billington, Ray Allen. *The Far Western Frontier, 1830-1860.* New York: Harper and Row, 1956.

Biographical Sketch of Col. J. L. Sanderson of St. Louis, Mo. Kansas City: Ramsey, Millett and Hudson, 1880.

Blanchard, Leola Howard. *Conquest of Southwest Kansas: A History and Thrilling Stories of Frontier Life in the State of Kansas.* Wichita: Wichita Eagle Press, 1931.

Bonner, T. D. *The Life and Adventures of James P. Beckwourth, Mountaineer, Scout, and Pioneer, and Chief of the Crow Nation of Indians.* First published in 1856. Minneapolis: Ross and Haines, Inc., 1965.

Boyd, LeRoy. *Fort Lyon, Colorado: One Hundred Years of Service.* Colorado Springs: H. & H. Printing Co., n.d.

Brayer, Herbert O. *William Blackmore: The Spanish-Mexican Land Grants of New Mexico and Colorado.* Denver: Bradford-Robinson, 1949.

———. *William Blackmore: Early Financing of the Denver & Rio Grande Railway and Ancillary Land Companies, 1871-1878.* Denver: Bradford-Robinson, 1949.

Brice, James. *Reminiscences of Ten Years Experience on the Western Plains: How the United States Mails Were Carried before the Railroads Reached the Santa Fe Trail.* Kansas City, Mo.: n.p., n.d.

Calvin, Ross, ed. *Lieutenant Emory Reports: A Reprint of Lieutenant W. H. Emory's "Notes on a Military Reconnoissance."* Albuquerque: University of New Mexico Press, 1951.

Carter, Harvey Lewis. *"Dear Old Kit," The Historical Kit Carson.* Norman: University of Oklahoma Press, 1968.

Child, Hamilton. *Gazetteer and Business Directory of Franklin and Grand Isle Counties, Vermont, 1882-1883.* Syracuse: Journal Office Printers, 1883.

Conard, Howard Louis. *Encyclopedia of the History of Missouri: A Compendium of History and Biography for Ready Reference.* New York: The Southern History Co., 1901.

———. *"Uncle Dick" Wootton, The Pioneer Frontiersman of the Rocky Mountain Region: An Account of the Adventures and Thrilling Experiences of the Most Noted American Hunter, Trapper, Guide, Scout, and Indian Fighter Now Living.* Chicago: W. E. Dibble and Company, 1890.

Davis, William W. H. *El Gringo; or, New Mexico and Her People.* New York: Harper and Brothers, 1857.

DeBusk, S. W. *Some Items of Early History*. Trinidad, Colo.: Monitor Art Printery, 1901.

Dick, Everett. *The Sod-House Frontier, 1854-1890*. Lincoln, Neb.: Johnsen Publishing Co., 1954.

Dike, Sheldon H. *The Territorial Post Offices of New Mexico*. Albuquerque: by the author, 1958.

Duffus, R. L. *The Santa Fe Trail*. New York: Longmans, Green and Company, 1930.

Eblen, Jack Ericson. *The First and Second United States Empires: Governors and Territorial Government, 1784-1912*. Pittsburgh: University of Pittsburgh Press, 1968.

Eggenhofer, Nick. *Wagons, Mules and Men: How the Frontier Moved West*. New York: Hastings House Publishers, 1961.

Faulk, Odie B. *Land of Many Frontiers: A History of the American Southwest*. New York: Oxford University Press, 1968.

Foreman, Grant. *Marcy and the Gold Seekers: The Journal of Captain R. B. Marcy, with an Account of the Gold Rush over the Southern Route*. Norman: University of Oklahoma Press, 1939.

Frazer, Robert W. *Forts of the West: Military Forts and Presidios and Posts Commonly Called Forts West of the Mississippi to 1898*. Norman: University of Oklahoma Press, 1965.

Fritz, Percy Stanley. *Colorado, The Centennial State*. New York: Prentice-Hall, Inc., 1941.

Garrard, Lewis H. *Wah-To-Yah and the Taos Trail*. Introduction by Carl I. Wheat. First published in 1850. Palo Alto, Calif.: American West Publishing Co., 1968.

Garwood, Darrell. *Crossroads of America: The Story of Kansas City*. New York: W. W. Norton and Co., 1948.

Glaab, Charles N. *Kansas City and the Railroads: Community Policy in the Growth of a Regional Metropolis*. Madison: The State Historical Society of Wisconsin, 1962.

Grant, Blanche C. *One Hundred Years Ago in Old Taos*. Taos, N.M. 1925.

Gregg, Josiah. *Commerce of the Prairies*. Edited by Max L. Moorhead. Norman: University of Oklahoma Press, 1954.

Hafen, LeRoy R., ed. *Colorado and Its People: A Narrative and Topical History of the Centennial State*. 2 vols. New York: Lewis Historical Publishing Co., 1948.

————. *The Overland Mail, 1849-1869: Promoter of Settlement, Precursor of Railroads*. Cleveland: Arthur H. Clarke Co., 1926.

Hafen, LeRoy R. and Ann W. Hafen, eds. *Relations with the Plains Indians, 1857-1861*. Far West and the Rockies Historical Series, vol. 9. Glendale, Calif.: Arthur H. Clark, Co., 1959.

Hafen, Le Roy R. and Carl Coke Rister. *Western America: The Exploration, Settlement, and Development of the Region beyond the Mississippi*. Englewood Cliffs, N.J.: Prentice-Hall Inc., 1950.

Hall, Frank. *History of the State of Colorado*. 4 vols. Chicago: Blakely Printing Co., 1889-95.

Hall, Martin Hardwick. *Sibley's New Mexico Campaign*. Austin: University of Texas Press, 1960.

Harlow, Alvin F. *Old Waybills*. New York: D. Appleton-Century Co. 1934.

Hart, Herbert M. *Old Forts of the Southwest*. Seattle, Wash.: Superior Publishing Co., 1964.

Heap, Gwinn Harris. *Central Route to the Pacific*. Far West and Rockies Historical Series, vol. 7. Edited by LeRoy and Ann W. Hafen. Glendale, Calif.: Arthur H. Clark Co., 1957.

Hemenway, Abby Maria, ed. *Vermont Historical Gazetteer*. Montpelier: Vermont Watchman and State Journal Press, 1882.

Hoig, Stan. *The Sand Creek Massacre*. Norman: University of Oklahoma Press, 1961.

Hollon, W. Eugene. *The Great American Desert*. New York: Oxford University Press, 1966.

Horn, Calvin. *New Mexico's Troubled Years: The Story of the Early Territorial Governors*. Albuquerque: Horn and Wallace, 1963.

Hyde, George E. *Life of George Bent, Written from His Letters*. Edited by Savoie Lottinville. Norman: University of Oklahoma Press, 1968.

Inman, Colonel Henry. *The Old Santa Fe Trail: The Story of a Great Highway*. Topeka: Crane and Co., 1916.

Jackson, W. Turrentine. *Wagon Roads West: A Study of Federal Road Surveys and Construction in the Trans-Mississippi West, 1846-1869*. Berkeley: University of California Press, 1952.

Keleher, William A. *Turmoil in New Mexico, 1846-1868*. Santa Fe: Rydal Press, 1962.

―――. *Violence in Lincoln County, 1869-1881*. Albuquerque: University of New Mexico Press, 1957.

Kelly, Clyde. *United States Postal Policy*. New York: D. Appleton and Co., 1932.

Kenner, Charles L. *A History of New Mexico-Plains Indian Relations*. Norman: University of Oklahoma Press, 1969.

Klose, Nelson. *A Concise Study Guide to the American Frontier*. Lincoln: University of Nebraska Press, 1964.

La Farge, Oliver. *The Autobiography of a Southwestern Town*. Norman: University of Oklahoma Press, 1959.

Lamar, Howard Roberts. *The Far Southwest, 1846-1912: A Territorial History*. New Haven: Yale University Press, 1966.

Lavender, David. *Bent's Fort*. Garden City, N.Y.: Doubleday and Co., 1954.

Letters from Old Friends and Members of the Wyoming Stock Growers Association. Cheyenne, Wyo.: S. A. Bristol Co., 1923.

Long, Margaret, *The Santa Fe Trail*. Denver: W. H. Kistler Stationery Co., 1954.

―――. *The Smoky Hill Trail*. Denver: W. H. Kistler Stationery Co., 1943.

McKee, Major James Cooper. *Narrative of the Surrender of a Command of U.S. Forces at Fort Fillmore, New Mexico, in July, A.D. 1861*. Houston: Stagecoach Press, 1960.

McMaster, John Bach. *A History of the People of the United States from the Revolution to the Civil War*. 8 vols. New York: D. Appleton and Co., 1884-1921.

Magoffin, Susan Shelby. *Down the Santa Fe Trail and into New Mexico*. Edited by Stella M. Drumm. Foreword by Howard W. Lamar. New Haven: Yale University Press, 1962.

Marcy, Randolph B. *The Prairie Traveler: A Hand-book for Overland Expeditions*. New York: Harper and Brothers, 1859.

Marshall, James L. *Santa Fe: The Railroad That Built an Empire*. New York: Random House, 1945.

Mathews, Mitford M., ed. *A Dictionary of Americanisms on Historical Principles*. Chicago: University of Chicago Press, 1951.

Meriwether, David. *My Life in the Mountains and on the Plains*. Edited and with an introduction by Robert A. Griffen. Norman: University of Oklahoma Press, 1965.

Moody, Ralph. *Stagecoach West*. New York: Thomas Y. Crowell Co., 1967.

Oliva, Leo E. *Soldiers on the Santa Fe Trail*. Norman: University of Oklahoma Press, 1967.

Pearson, Jim Berry. *The Maxwell Land Grant*. Norman: University of Oklahoma Press, 1961.

Perkin, Robert L. *The First Hundred Years: An Informal History of Denver and the Rocky Mountain News*. Garden City, N.Y.: Doubleday and Co., 1959.

Pike, Albert. *Prose Sketches and Poems Written in the Western Country*. Edited by David J. Weber. Albuquerque: Calvin Horn, Publisher, 1967.

Riddle, Kenyon. *Records and Maps of the Old Santa Fe Trail*. Raton, N.M.: *Raton Daily Range*, 1949.

Rideing, William H. *A-Saddle in the Wild West: A Glimpse of Travel among the Mountains, Lava Beds, Sand Deserts, Adobe Towns, Indian Reservations, and Ancient Pueblos of Southern Colorado, New Mexico, and Arizona*. New York: D. Appleton and Co., 1879.

Rittenhouse, Jack D. *American Horse-drawn Vehicles*. Los Angeles: by the author, 1948.

Rocky Mountain Directory and Colorado Gazetteer for 1871. Denver: S. S. Wallihan and Co., n.d.

Roe, Frances M. A. *Army Letters from an Officer's Wife, 1871-1888*. New York: D. Appleton and Co., 1909.

Root, Frank A. and William E. Connelley. *The Overland Stage to California*. Topeka: by the authors, 1901.

Ryus, W. T. *The Second William Penn: A True Account of Incidents That Happened Along the Old Santa Fe Trail in the Sixties*. Kansas City, Mo.: Frank T. Riley Publishing Co., 1913; reprinted, Fort Davis, Tex.: Frontier Book Co., 1969.

Salpointe, Most Rev. J. B. *Soldiers of the Cross: Notes on the Ecclesiastical History of New Mexico, Arizona and Colorado*. First published in 1898. Albuquerque: Calvin Horn, Publisher, 1967.

Settle, Raymond W. and Mary Lund Settle. *War Drums and Wagon Wheels: The Story of Russell, Majors and Waddell*. Lincoln: University of Nebraska Press, 1966.

Smiley, Jerome C. *Semi-Centennial History of the State of Colorado*. 2 vols. Chicago: Lewis Publishing Co., 1913.

Taylor, Morris F. *Trinidad, Colorado Territory*. Trinidad: Trinidad State Junior College, 1966.

Taylor, Ralph C. *Colorado, South of the Border*. Denver: Sage Books, 1963.

Theobald, John and Lillian. *Arizona Territory Post Offices and Postmasters*. Phoenix: Arizona Historical Foundation, 1961.

Thomas, Joseph. *Universal Pronouncing Dictionary of Biography and Mythology*. Philadelphia: J. B. Lippincott Co., 1930.

Twitchell, Ralph Emerson. *The Leading Facts of New Mexican History*. First published in 1912. Albuquerque: Horn and Wallace, 1963.

———. *Old Santa Fe: The Story of New Mexico's Ancient Capital*. First published in 1925. Chicago: Rio Grande Press, 1963.

Utley, Robert M. *Fort Union National Monument, New Mexico*. Washington: Government Printing Office, 1962.

Walker, Henry Pickering. *The Wagonmasters: High Plains Freighting from the Earliest Days of the Santa Fe Trail to 1880*. Norman: University of Oklahoma Press, 1966.

Wallace, Ernest, and E. Adamson Hoebel. *The Comanches: Lords of the South Plains*. Norman: University of Oklahoma Press, 1952.

Ware, Captain Eugene F. *The Indian War of 1864*. Introduction and notes by Clyde C. Walton. First published in 1911. Lincoln: University of Nebraska Press, 1960.

Waters, L. L. *Steel Trails to Santa Fe*. Lawrence: University of Kansas Press, 1950.

Whitford, William Clarke. *Colorado Volunteers in the Civil War: The New Mexico Campaign in 1862*. Denver: State Historical and Natural History Society, 1906.

Whitney, Carrie Westlake. *Kansas City, Missouri: Its History and Its People, 1808-1898*. Chicago: S. J. Clarke Publishing Co., 1908.

Winther, Oscar Osburn. *Via Western Express & Stagecoach*. Stanford: Stanford University Press, 1945.

Wright, Robert M. *Dodge City, the Cowboy Capital, and the Great Southwest in the Days of the Wild Indian, the Buffalo, the Cowboy, Dance Halls, Gambling Halls, and Bad Men*. n.p., n.d.

Young, Otis E. *The West of Philip St. George Cooke, 1809-1895*. Glendale, Calif.: Arthur H. Clark Co., 1955.

Zornow, William Frank. *Kansas: A History of the Jayhawk State*. Norman: University of Oklahoma Press, 1957.

ARTICLES

Barry, Louise. "Kansas before 1854: A Revised Annals," *Kansas Historical Quarterly*, vol. 30 (autumn 1964), pp. 339-412.

———. "Kansas before 1854: A Revised Annals," *Kansas Historical Quarterly*, vol. 30 (winter 1964), pp. 492-559.

———. "Kansas before 1854: A Revised Annals," *Kansas Historical Quarterly*, vol. 31 (autumn 1965), pp. 256-339.

———. "Kansas before 1854: A Revised Annals," *Kansas Historical Quarterly*, vol. 32 (spring 1966), pp. 33-112.

———. "Kansas before 1854: A Revised Annals," *Kansas Historical Quarterly*, vol. 32 (summer 1966), pp. 210-82.

———. "Kansas before 1854: A Revised Annals," *Kansas Historical Quarterly*, vol. 32 (winter 1966), pp. 426-503.

———. "Kansas before 1854: A Revised Annals," *Kansas Historical Quarterly*, vol. 33 (spring 1967), pp. 13-64.

———. "Kansas before 1854: A Revised Annals," *Kansas Historical Quarterly*, vol. 33 (summer 1967), pp. 172-213.

Bieber, Ralph P. "Some Aspects of the Santa Fe Trail," *Chronicles of Oklahoma*, vol. 2 (March 1924), pp. 1-8.

Bloom, Lansing B., ed. "From Lewisburg (Pa.) to California in 1849: Notes from the Diary of William H. Chamberlin," *New Mexico Historical Review*, vol. 20 (January 1945), pp. 14-57.

Burnett, Hugh and Evelyn. "Foster's Place," *The Brand Book of the Denver Westerners* [1964], edited by Francis B. Rizzari. Boulder, Colo.: Johnson Publishing Co., 1965, pp. 163-79.

Callon, Milton W. "The Merchant-Colonists of New Mexico," *The Brand Book of the Denver Westerners* [1965], edited by Arthur L. Campa. Boulder, Colo.: Johnson Publishing Co., 1966, pp. 3-26.

Clum, John P. "Santa Fe in the '70s," *New Mexico Historical Review*, vol. 2 (October 1927), pp. 380-86.

Dallas, E. J. "Kansas Postal History," *Transactions of the Kansas State Historical Society*, vol. 2 (1879-80), pp. 255-60.

Dike, Sheldon H. "Early Mail Contracts on the Santa Fe Trail," *American Philatelist*, vol. 72 (August 1959), pp. 809-13.

———. "The Postal History of New Mexico Territory," *Western Express*, vol. 8 (April 1958).

235

———. "The Postal History of New Mexico Territory," *Western Express*, vol. 9 (January 1959), appended alphabetical list of territorial post offices.

Drumm, Stella M. "David Waldo," *Dictionary of American Biography*, vol. 19, edited by Dumas Malone. New York: Charles Scribner's Sons, 1936, pp. 332-33.

"Early Military Posts, Missions and Camps," *Transactions of the Kansas State Historical Society*, vol. 2 (1879-80), pp. 263-70.

Foreman, Grant. "Early Trails through Oklahoma," *Chronicles of Oklahoma*, vol. 3 (June 1925), pp. 99-119.

Ghent, W. J. "Edward Fitzgerald Beale," *Dictionary of American Biography*, vol. 2, edited by Allen Johnson. New York: Charles Scribner's Sons, 1957, p. 89.

Hardeman, Nicholas P., ed. "Camp Sites on the Santa Fe Trail in 1848 as Reported by John A. Bingham, *"Arizona and the West*, vol. 6 (winter 1964), pp. 313-19.

Hertz, A. Jay. "Barlow, Sanderson & Company: Corruption Enters the Express," *Western Express*, vol. 13 (July 1963), pp. 29-31.

Hurd, Charles W. "A History of Southeastern Colorado," No. 77 of a series published in the *Arkansas Valley Journal*. Copy in the Local History Collection, Carnegie Public Library, Trinidad, Colorado.

Jackson, W. Turrentine. "A New Look at Wells Fargo, Stagecoaches and the Pony Express," *California Historical Quarterly* (December 1966), pp. 291-324. Reprinted by the Wells Fargo Bank, San Francisco.

Lambert, Julia S. "Plain Tales of the Plains," *The Trail*, vol. 8 (April 1916), pp. 5-11.

McDonald, William. "Schuyler Colfax," *Dictionary of American Biography*. vol. 4, edited by Allen Johnson and Dumas Malone. New York: Charles Scribner's Sons, 1930, pp. 297-98.

McKennan, Bess. "The Toll Road over Raton Pass," *New Mexico Historical Review*, vol. 2 (January 1927), pp. 83-89.

Miller, Nyle H., ed. "Surveying the Southern Boundary Line of Kansas: From the Private Journal of Colonel Joseph E. Johnston," *Kansas Historical Quarterly*, vol. 1 (1931-32), pp. 104-39.

Minor, Eleanor and Grace. "William McCoy," *Journal of the Jackson County* (Mo.) *Historical Society*, vol. 7 (March 1964), p. 10.

Missouri Historical Review, vol. 23 (October 1928-July 1929), pp. 335-36.

Möllhausen, H. B. "Over the Santa Fe Trail through Kansas in 1858," edited by Robert Taft, translated by John A. Burzle, *Kansas Historical Quarterly*, vol. 16 (November 1948), pp. 337-80.

Moorehouse, George P. "Diamond Springs, 'The Diamond of the Plains,'" *Collections of the Kansas State Historical Society*, vol. 14 (1915-18), pp. 794-804.

Myers, Lee. "Military Establishments in Southwestern New Mexico: Stepping Stones to Settlement," *New Mexico Historical Review*, vol. 43 (January 1968), pp. 5-48.

Oliva, Leo E. "Fortification on the Plains, Fort Dodge, Kansas, 1864-1882," *The 1960 Brand Book of the Denver Posse of the Westerners*, edited by Guy M. Herstrom. Boulder, Colo.: Johnson Publishing Co., pp. 136-79.

Owsley, Frank L. "Aaron V. Brown," *Dictionary of American Biography*, vol. 3, edited by Allen Johnson. New York: Charles Scribner's Sons, 1957, pp. 98-99.

Parish, William J. "The German Jew and the Commercial Revolution in Territorial New Mexico, 1850-1900," *New Mexico Historical Review*, vol. 35 (January 1960), pp. 1-29.

"Place Names in Colorado," *Colorado Magazine*, vol. 19 (September 1942), pp. 175-84.

Schnell, J. Christopher. "William Gilpin and the Destruction of the Desert Myth," *Colorado Magazine*, vol. 46 (Spring 1969), pp. 131-44.

Shaw, Dorothy Price. "Jimmy's Camp on the Cherokee Trail," *Colorado Magazine*, vol. 27 (January 1950), pp. 63-72.

Shields, Clara M. Fengel. "The Lyon Creek Settlement," edited by William E. Connelley, *Collections of the Kansas State Historical Society*, vol. 14 (1915-18), pp. 143-70.

Sloan, Waldo Douglas. "Dr. David Waldo," *Journal of the Jackson County* (Mo.) *Historical Society*, vol. 11 (spring 1968), p. 6.

Smith, Eudochia Bell. "Women," *Colorado and Its People: A Narrative and Topical History of the Centennial State*, vol. 2, edited by LeRoy R. Hafen. New York: Lewis Historical Publishing Company, 1948, pp. 557-70.

Stephens, F. F. "Missouri and the Santa Fe Trade," *Missouri Historical Review*, vol. 11 (July 1917), pp. 289-312.

Stockton, Bill. "Frontier Stage Stop," *New Mexico Magazine* (February 1963), pp. 8-10.

Taylor, Morris F. "Fort Wise," *Colorado Magazine*, vol. 46 (spring 1969), pp. 93-119.

———. "Ka-ni-ache," part 1, *Colorado Magazine*, vol. 43 (fall 1966), pp. 275-302.

———. "Ka-ni-ache," part 2, *Colorado Magazine*, vol. 44 (spring 1967), pp. 139-61.

Tisdale, Henry. "Travel by Stage in the Early Days," *Transactions of the Kansas State Historical Society*, vol. 7 (1901-02), pp. 459-64.

Utley, Robert M. "Fort Union and the Santa Fe Trail," *New Mexico Historical Review*, vol. 36 (January 1961), pp. 36-48.

Wallace, William S. "Stagecoaching in Territorial New Mexico," *New Mexico Historical Review*, vol. 32 (April 1957), pp. 204-20.

Walrath, Ellen F. "Stagecoach Holdups in the San Luis Valley," *Colorado Magazine*, vol. 14 (January 1937), pp. 27-31.

Willard, James F. "A Raton Pass Mountain Toll Road Book," *Colorado Magazine*, vol. 7 (March 1930), pp. 77-83.

Williams, Mary Wilhelmine. "John Angel James Cresswell," *Dictionary of American Biography*, vol. 4, edited by Allen Johnson and Dumas Malone. New York: Charles Scribner's Sons, 1930, pp. 541-42.

Woodward, Arthur. "Sidelights on Bent's Old Fort," *Colorado Magazine*, vol. 33 (October 1956), pp. 277-82.

Wright, Arthur M. "Colonel John P. Slough and the New Mexico Campaign, 1862," *Colorado Magazine*, vol. 39 (April 1962), pp. 89-105.

Index